STATE OF THE UNION, 1994 : THE

DE 23 '94		
AP 12 97		
AP 3 98		
JE 18 98		
MY 18 '99		
JE 1 0 00		
NO 2 7 00		
AP 2 3 '01		
JY 3 0 01		
DE 15 01		
AP 15 '02		
FE 11 '03		

ideology
4 inferiority

pg 253

STATE
of the
UNION
1994

A Project of the Institute for Policy Studies

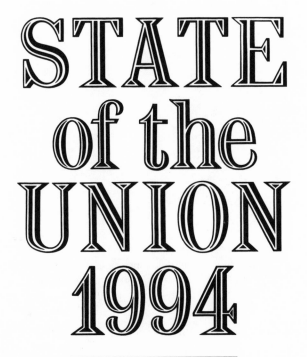

STATE
of the
UNION
1994

The Clinton Administration
and the
Nation in Profile

edited by
Richard Caplan and John Feffer

Foreword by Barbara Ehrenreich

Westview Press

Boulder • San Francisco • Oxford

Copyright © 1994 by Westview Press, Inc., except Chapter 14 (© by the Institute for Local Self-Reliance)

Published in 1994 in the United States of America by Westview Press, Inc., 5500 Central Avenue, Boulder, Colorado 80301-2877, and in the United Kingdom by Westview Press, 36 Lonsdale Road, Summertown, Oxford OX2 7EW

Library of Congress Cataloging-in-Publication Data
State of the union 1994 : the Clinton administration and the nation in
    profile / edited by Richard Caplan and John Feffer ; foreword by
    Barbara Ehrenreich.
      p.   cm.
    Includes bibliographical references (p.) and index.
    ISBN 0-8133-2022-4 — ISBN 0-8133-2023-2 (pbk.)
    1. United States—Politics and government—1993–   . 2. United
States—Foreign relations—1993–   . 3. Clinton, Bill, 1946–   .
I. Caplan, Richard.   II. Feffer, John.
E885.S73   1994
973.929'092—dc20   93-41134
                                                                                  CIP

Printed and bound in the United States of America

The paper used in this publication meets the requirements
of the American National Standard for Permanence of Paper
for Printed Library Materials Z39.48-1984.

10   9   8   7   6   5   4   3   2   1

Contents

Foreword

BARBARA EHRENREICH

Clinton rode into office on the promise of "change." It was a safe, content-free slogan. After all, in recent years, the most radical proposals for change have come not from the Democrats but from the Republican right. "Change" could mean the further downsizing of government and neglect of social problems, or, of course, the reversal of these trends. When they went to the polls in 1992, however, most Americans had a good idea of what kind of change they wanted.

The prevailing sentiment was that the United States had been so busy rushing around the world "doing good"—defeating Communism, freeing Kuwait, delivering aid to Africa—that it had neglected to take care of its needs at home. We began to see ourselves as a militarily overdeveloped superpower in an advanced stage of domestic decline—a heavily armed warrior living, Mad Max–style, in a dilapidated hovel. We could accomplish almost anything abroad, it seemed, but at home the young were undereducated, the infrastructure rusted and rotted, jobs were scarce, crime worsened, and beggars multiplied in the streets.

There had been, in the last year of the Bush administration, an almost palpable sense of foreboding. The Republicans offered either the comfort of denial or the excitement of televised wars; it was always either "morning in America" or another "great test of our nation's will." But the frightening truth kept resurfacing in ways that were hard to ignore or repress: We were no longer "number one"—and often more like tenth—in measures of public health and standard of living. The Los Angeles riots in April 1991 showed what the price could be for the neglect of the urban poor. Even Hurricane Andrew joined a growing list of "wake-up calls": The United States could mobilize a mighty military presence to beat back Iraqi forces in Kuwait, but it could respond only falteringly to a natural disaster on its own shores. We could house hundreds of thousands of American men and women in the Arabian desert but not in our own ruined cities.

Hopelessness added to the sense of decline. For more than a decade the Republicans had argued, first of all, that nothing was wrong and, second, that nothing could be done about it anyway. This was their oft-stated "law of unintended consequences": Try to assist the poor, and you will only make them more "dependent" and demoralized. Try to regulate the economy, and you will only squelch the productive energies of free enterprise. Attempt to use the government for any purpose—other than law enforcement or military actions—and you will merely swell the deficit and the already bloated federal bureaucracy.

All problems should be left to Adam Smith's "invisible hand," according to Republican reasoning. If private business is not interested in cleaning up the environment or providing affordable housing or offering health insurance to the poor, too bad. An op-ed article by an anonymous federal employee, published in the *New York Times* in March 1991, acknowledged chillingly that the government "is no longer responsible for anything. The unequivocal message throughout the Federal bureaucracy is that nothing is to be accomplished by this Government except the creation of good feelings and the illusion of action."

What had to change, then, was something that went far beyond the realm of politics. At some deep, subconscious level, we had ceased to believe that purposeful change was even possible. We no longer seemed to have any faith in our own capabilities—that we could size up a problem, decide what to do, and then proceed to get it done.

The great hope aroused by Clinton's victory was that we might regain this fundamental sense of competence. No one could mistake Clinton himself for a liberal; he in fact came out of the most illiberal faction of the Democratic party. Yet everyone knew that he represented the long-lost idea of an "activist government." Here was the chance, even many erstwhile Republican voters realized, to apply the same "can-do" spirit that characterized our many military interventions to the mounting social and economic problems at home. Clinton was young, smart, and, in marked contrast to his immediate predecessors, clearly engaged by the challenges of governing.

Now, almost a year into Clinton's presidency, most of the optimism and good will that accompanied the inauguration has dissipated. For better or worse, Clinton's precipitous slide in the polls has had little to do with any substantive programmatic issues. He underestimated the opposition he would encounter from the right on what should have been an almost cosmetic matter—the lifting of the military's ban on gays. And he let support dribble away by waffling on dozens of issues large and small. Free vaccines for all children? A meaningfully sized National Service Program? Comprehensive health insurance for all? Maybe … maybe not.

By mid-year it was clear that even "change" would be too strong a word for what was afoot in Democratic Washington. The economic plan that finally squeaked through Congress could have been written by the bondholders on Wall Street: The campaign theme of investing in America's people and resources had been dropped for a Scrooge-like fixation on the deficit. Instead of an activist government earning its tax revenues through improvements brought about in people's lives, we returned to the notion that government cannot be a means to a solution; it can only be another problem.

In foreign and military policy, the changes were even harder to discern. Military spending remained at Cold War levels, although there was no longer a Cold War going on. No moral principle guided the decision to re-bomb Iraq while ignoring the slaughter in Bosnia. If anything, we were back to the Reagan-Bush policy of using military actions, like hits of cocaine, to lift the national mood and boost the president in the polls.

The danger is that we will descend into even greater cynicism and hopelessness than marked the end of the Reagan-Bush era. If in three years, people can sigh and say, "We tried change, but it turned out to be exactly like no change at all," and if "plus ça change" begins to sound more and more like "déjà vu," then our national decline will only accelerate until there is nothing left to do but hang on for the ride.

This book was written by people who do not give up so easily. They are men and women who hold to the old-fashioned, quintessentially human idea that, given enough imagination and effort, any problem is potentially soluble. In the chapters that follow they take on all the issues that have so baffled and benumbed our elected leaders in the areas of foreign policy, the environment, poverty, gender and racial justice, taxes, and political reform. They offer hard-headed analysis and genuine, achievable solutions. This book, in other words, is about real change.

One hope in offering a volume like this is that it will fall into the hands of our political leaders, who will read it and cry out, "Aha! So that's how you do it." This is not a completely quixotic expectation, for what follows goes well beyond the usual liberal wish-list and familiar boilerplate. There are new and innovative ideas assembled here as well as vintage ones that have grown out of years of activism and discussion. Readers should feel free to take these ideas as their own.

But any canny political leader will quickly realize that the proposals outlined here cannot simply be willed into action. In every problem area under discussion, the solution will require a political confrontation with the interests that profit from the status quo—big business; corrupt politicians; defenders of racial, class, and gender inequality. There can be no real change, then, without the political mobilization of the people whose futures depend on it.

Whether or not this book rouses the Democratic administration to a new burst of legislative activism, it has a key role to play. The ideas presented here reflect decades of experience on the part of community organizers, labor advocates, grassroots environmentalists, and civil rights and feminist activists. If we are going to mobilize people for genuine, progressive change, there can be no better inspiration and guide than *State of the Union 1994.*

Introduction

MICHAEL H. SHUMAN

The United States is on the wrong track. That's what three out of four Americans told pollsters before the November 1992 election. Despite political rhetoric from both Republicans and Democrats about the nation being "number one" and "the sole superpower," more and more Americans expressed concern that their quality of life was deteriorating.

In fact, the signs of political, economic, and social decay are everywhere:

- Wages of production workers in America have declined 20 percent since 1973, as corporations have shifted millions of jobs overseas.[1]
- The cost of health care has exploded, and a record number of Americans—37 million—are now without health insurance.[2]
- The ranks of the poor have officially swelled to 36 million, including 14 million children.[3] Unofficially there are probably 60 million poor.[4]
- Crime in America is at an all-time high, even though our prison population is proportionally larger than that of any other country in the world.[5]
- Nineteen countries have infant mortality rates lower than that of the United States.[6]
- The United Nations calculates that if African-Americans comprised a single country, their level of development would rank thirty-one globally—at about the level of Trinidad.[7]
- Among the twenty most developed nations, the United States is first in divorce and teen pregnancy.[8]

1

■ Despite a massive backlog of neglected domestic ills, the Pentagon continues to absorb 20 percent of the federal budget—over a third of it devoted to protecting Europe against an enemy that no longer exists.[9]

It's no wonder that 62 percent voted for "change" and swept the Republicans out of the White House. But thus far, the change brought about by President Bill Clinton has been underwhelming. As a result, a majority of Americans once again believe the country is heading in the wrong direction.[10]

Is this judgment of the American people premature and overly harsh? Just how healthy is the nation? What have been the accomplishments and the failures of the Clinton administration in its first year? What new policies should be emphasized in 1994? What kind of change does the country really need?

State of the Union is an effort by the Institute for Policy Studies (IPS) and its network of public scholars to answer these questions. The volume begins with an assessment of the opportunities and challenges the Clinton administration faced coming into office—the vast possibilities opened up by the end of both the Cold War and the Reagan-Bush era, and the manifold social, economic, and political difficulties it had to confront. Seventeen contributors then examine fourteen key problems and evaluate the progress made by the administration toward solving them. Finally, five leading political thinkers explore, in a roundtable discussion, the issue of translating progressive ideals into political reality. Spread throughout the book are graphs, diagrams, and various other indicators that depict the health of the country.

State of the Union is one of many projects that IPS has been working on since its inception in 1963 to define and promote progressive change in both foreign and domestic policy. IPS has occasionally produced volumes like this one mapping out where the country should go, but with *State of the Union* we hope to do this on a more regular basis.

Because we expect to produce other *State of the Union* volumes in coming years, we have not attempted to make this book comprehensive. Instead, we have concentrated on those issues that the Clinton administration has highlighted or that, in our view, deserve urgent attention. Important issues that are not directly discussed in this volume, such as education and crime, will be covered in future editions.

Progressive Change

The emphasis of this book and its contributors is on progressive change. Because the term "progressive" is used these days by everyone from open-minded Republicans to Democratic Socialists, it warrants clarification.

In 1911, Sen. Robert M. La Follette of Wisconsin formed an insurgency within the Republican Party called the Progressive Republican League. La Follette's platform was to avoid war, strengthen unions, break up corporate trusts, tax income, lower trade tariffs, conserve natural resources, and open up the political system. These positions had deep roots in American history: in the anti-federalists who sought to decentralize political power at the birth of the nation, in the abolitionists like Frederick Douglass who risked their lives to end slavery, in the farmers revolts of the late nineteenth century that challenged the robber barons and usurious lending practices, in the tax resistance and civil disobedience of Henry David Thoreau, in the anti-imperialist writings of Mark Twain and W.E.B. Du Bois, and in the organizing efforts of Harriet Tubman, Emma Goldman, Eugene Debs, Mother Jones, and John Dewey.

Since La Follette's time, progressives have all but abandoned the Republican Party; instead they can be found almost entirely within the Democratic Party (though their loyalty there is waning). The key groups that made up the Progressive Party of 1912—conservationists, pacifists, labor organizers, suffragettes—remain the essential participants of the progressive movement of 1994, only now they call themselves greens, peace activists, trade unionists, and feminists. Joining their ranks are blue-collar workers, family farmers, minorities, and consumer groups.

Beginning in the late 1980s, the Democratic Leadership Council (DLC), under the guidance of its chair, Gov. Bill Clinton, attempted to blunt the influence of these "special interests" within the Democratic Party. It is more than a little ironic, therefore, and a testament to the absence of truth in advertising, that the think tank for the DLC should call itself the *Progressive* Policy Institute (PPI).

PPI was built on winning elections, not on promoting progressive change. Its seminal paper, "The Politics of Evasion," published in 1988 and written by William Galston and Elaine Ciulla Kamarck, analyzed why the Democrats lost presidential elections in 1980, 1984, and 1988, and why they were doomed to lose the next election unless they changed course. PPI's thesis was that "upscale liberals" and Jesse Jackson supporters were leading the Democratic Party astray and driving white conservative voters into the hands of Republicans. Winning back the presidency required packaging a Democrat to appeal to these swing voters.

State of the Union, though written with the obstacles to political change in mind, is not a primer on electoral expediency. It grows instead out of the century-old tradition of progressive political thinking and activism. The aim of this book is to clarify, unify, and amplify progressive ideas and to present a set of coherent proposals derived from them. It is our belief that the most promising basis for a successful electoral strategy is a clear, compelling political program that truly addresses the dire problems Americans face.

What exactly *are* progressive goals? Progressives can distinguish themselves today from most Republicans and Democrats on nine key issues:

- *Economic Security.* Republicans and Democrats believe in the free market as the most efficient allocator of resources and differ largely over how much of a social safety net to provide against the "creative destruction" of capitalism. Progressives, while not opposed to the free market and supportive of a safety net, believe that every American has the right to a basic level of food, clothing, housing, education, health care, and child care. This requires an active, effective government and the development of major social-welfare programs. Whatever the costs of these programs, they pale in comparison to the known costs of poverty—crime, drug abuse, family violence, malnutrition, suicide, ignorance, and political apathy.
- *Full Employment.* Both mainstream parties are satisfied with a "natural rate of unemployment" hovering between 5 and 10 percent. Progressives start with the assumption that no level of unemployment is acceptable. Every American has a right to a decent job, and the government has a responsibility to serve as the employer of last resort. There is no shortage of essential public needs—pollution clean-up, environmental restoration, housing rehabilitation, rural health care, highway construction—that today's unemployed could be hired to address.
- *Economic Justice.* Progressives also are committed to reducing the extremes of rich and poor within countries and between the developed nations of the North and the developing nations of the South and East. Unlike Republicans and Democrats, they favor steep income taxes and wealth taxes on those who can pay. Progressives are not afraid to use the dreaded "R" word—redistribution.
- *Social Equality.* Everyone believes in equality of opportunity, but progressives also believe in creating special opportunities for victims of discrimination—women, ethnic and racial minorities, gays and lesbians, the handicapped. While money cannot just be thrown at inequality, it's clear that serious government programs are needed to combat discrimination in schools, communities, and workplaces.
- *Sustainable Development.* Progressives are much more willing than Republicans and Democrats to enact tough regulations and reorient incentives toward industry to ensure greater use of renewable resources and lower levels of pollution. Progressives are prepared, if

necessary, to curb economic, scientific, or technological "progress" to protect species and ecosystems. Republicans and Democrats emphasize ever increasing personal consumption and economic growth while progressives emphasize sustainability. Progressives are also more open to changing their lifestyles to reduce their burden on the earth's ecosystems.

- *Democratic Participation.* Republicans and Democrats are reluctant to support electoral reform, for fear of destroying their existing power base. Both parties have become institutionalized rackets for raising money and selling political influence. Progressives, in contrast, support dramatic changes in the political system, including proportional representation, participatory citizen boards, government financing of elections, and the elimination of barriers to the entry of third parties.

- *Demilitarization.* Unlike Republicans and Democrats, who together supported the development of a gigantic military-industrial complex and who now are content with only minor budget reductions, progressives would slash military spending, dismantle much of the Central Intelligence Agency, and remove other vestiges of the Cold War. One reason progressives feel comfortable shrinking the Pentagon is that they reject unilateralism, particularly the unilateral use of force. They believe instead in the virtues of multilateral cooperation. They would take some of the money now being squandered on aircraft carriers and B-2 bombers and invest it instead in international institutions like the United Nations and World Court that can often prevent and resolve conflicts with less violence.

- *Global Fair Play.* Republicans and many Democrats wish for a laissez-faire world order, in which corporations and goods—but not labor—can move more freely from country to country. Progressives favor a Global New Deal, with enforceable international rules of fair play to ensure that no corporation or country can profit by abusing human rights, workers, or the environment.

- *Community Empowerment.* Conservative Republicans are distrustful of all government, while liberal Democrats place their faith in the federal government. Progressives steer a middle course by emphasizing the role of communities, where citizens are most likely to achieve the ideals of self-governance.

To say that progressives support these goals is not to sweep spirited disagreements under the carpet. There's plenty of debate over policies, strategies, and tactics, much of which can be found in this volume. Nevertheless, the convergence of thought not only among today's progressives but also with numerous citizens movements throughout U.S. history suggests that progressive thinking and activism are likely to remain permanent, powerful features of the American political landscape—and possibly may become the basis for the nation's next major political party. The Democrats therefore would be wise to take notice that the consensus of the writers in this volume, who well represent today's progressive movement, is that the first year of the Clinton administration has been a profound disappointment.

A Gentleman's "C"

Washington began the year by embracing the self-proclaimed "New Democrat" from Arkansas with open arms. Clinton's inauguration was marked by two dozen spectacular balls (including one broadcast on MTV), concerts and parades featuring American icons from Michael Jackson to Cookie Monster, and handshaking that began with the president's early-morning jog and ended in the White House corridors in the wee hours of the morning. By June, however, pundits across the political spectrum had all but written off Clinton, and the public largely agreed. Rarely in modern times had pollsters registered such a precipitous drop in a president's popularity during his first 100 days in office.[11]

To be sure, many of the carps against Clinton were nit-picking and the result of poor public relations. The media, incensed at Clinton's reluctance to hold press conferences and at his visible disdain for reporters, went into paroxysms over a $200 haircut and the firing of the White House travel staff. But the president's problems went much deeper, as the reports by our contributors underscore.

Despite some inspired appointments, noble symbolic gestures, and moving speeches, the administration has done surprisingly little to alleviate the principal ailments afflicting America. This becomes clear as one reviews the record in each of the nine areas of critical importance to progressives.

Economic security? Clinton's first proposed budget had several constructive components: expansion of Head Start and the WIC (Women, Infants, and Children) program to include all eligible poor people; a $21 billion increase in the Earned Income Tax Credit (over four years), to help bring working families above the poverty line; and modest increases for other entitlement programs, such as housing subsidies, Job Corps, and Legal Services.[12] But because Clinton placed these proposals in a larger package of deficit reduction and did not fight for other sources of funding (such as income-tax hikes or serious defense cuts), many were butchered by Republicans and conservative Democrats.

Full employment? Joblessness has dropped a few tenths of a percent since Clinton took office.[13] Yet 8 million people remain officially unemployed, and another 4 million either hold part-time jobs while looking for full-time employment or have given up seeking jobs altogether.[14] The meager stimulus package Clinton proposed might have created half a million jobs, but Republicans and conservative Democrats rallied against the plan, in part because it would not have significantly changed the unemployment picture.[15] Unfortunately, they were right, though the package at least affirmed the government's role as a job provider. If Clinton's proposals for throwing people off the welfare rolls after two years are enacted, another 1 to 2 million people will enter the labor market with no prospects for work.[16]

Economic justice? The poor in America have more hope, but that's all they have to show for voting Democratic. Clinton introduced several changes into the tax system. Some, like the special tax on millionaires and the elimination of write-offs for business entertainment, were progressive. Others, like the gasoline tax, were regressive. Overall the president increased the tax burden slightly for rich individuals, but they are still paying only a fraction of the income taxes they did in the late 1970s. A wealth tax isn't even on the table.

Social equality? Never has there been such diversity in a president's political appointments (except for the fact that so many of them were also corporate lawyers). And Clinton deserves credit for a good choice for Supreme Court Justice, Ruth Bader Ginsburg. But he seriously strained his relations with minority and women's groups when he abandoned Lani Guinier, his nominee for assistant attorney general, before she could defend her writings on Capitol Hill.

Sustainability? Here Clinton has taken several useful steps. Despite the disappointing choice of Hazel O'Leary as energy secretary, he has supported energy conservation and renewables like solar and wind, and he's beginning to wind down federal subsidies to the Jurassic nuclear-power industry.[17] He finally signed the agreement on biodiversity concluded at the Rio Earth Summit that President Bush had opposed. And the gasoline tax will put a modest damper on carbon-dioxide emissions that cause global warming. But Clinton's support for several incinerator projects conspicuously opposed by environmentalists and his commitment to push ahead with the North American Free Trade Agreement (NAFTA) without adequate environmental safeguards reinforces the overall message that development trumps ecology.

Democratic participation? Citizen groups have more access practically everywhere in the government, but they are gradually learning that access does not necessarily mean power. The president signed into law a campaign reform bill that puts some limits on money in politics but falls well short of full federal financing of elections.

Demilitarization? Give Clinton credit for extending the U.S. moratorium on nuclear testing for eighteen months, but not much else. His five-year military budget is just 8 percent lower than Bush's.[18] Even though the next three largest military budgets in the world are $42 billion (United Kingdom), $40 billion (Germany), and $37 billion (Japan), he argues with a straight face that the Pentagon, spending $277 billion in 1994, has been cut to the bone.[19] He continues to fire cruise missiles periodically at Saddam Hussein and to show no interest in reaching a political settlement with Iraq. And his Bosnia policy has been a wash. He avoided the temptation of trying to end the fighting there through a unilateral use of force that almost certainly would have become his Vietnam, but he never seized the chance to help bring peace to the region by organizing a stronger UN peacekeeping operation on the scale of Desert Shield.

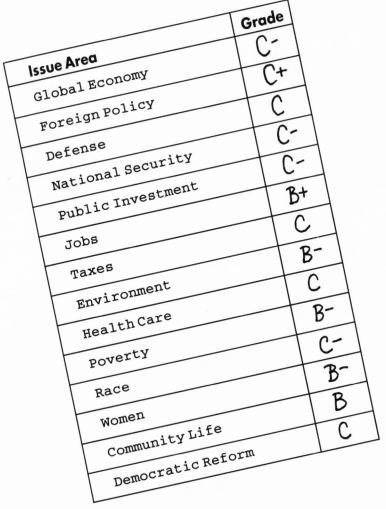

Issue Area	Grade
Global Economy	C-
Foreign Policy	C+
Defense	C
National Security	C-
Public Investment	C-
Jobs	B+
Taxes	C
Environment	B-
Health Care	C
Poverty	B-
Race	C-
Women	B-
Community Life	B
Democratic Reform	C

Global Fair Play? Supporting Bush's NAFTA may prove to be Clinton's biggest mistake. By transforming Mexico into an enormous low-wage zone, NAFTA will accelerate the ruin of that country's ecosystems, the drain of manufacturing jobs from the United States, and the undercutting of state and local health and safety standards throughout North America. Consumers may have access to modestly cheaper products, but the problem is that fewer Americans will be employed and have the income to enjoy the cornucopia of new gadgets.

Community empowerment? With a former governor now in the Oval Office, Washington's twelve-year war against states and cities appears to be over. Clinton is to be congratulated for giving communities greater flexibility in handling various problems. The president also has shown commendable support for community policing, community banking and reinvestment, and lump-sum community development block grants. But across the country the number one problem afflicting state and local governments is budget fatigue, and Clinton's first budget provides them with trivial financial relief.[20]

It's no wonder that our contributors have judged the Clinton administration so critically. Even though they acknowledge the serious political obstacles the president faces, nearly everyone considers his performance average or below average. Based on the evaluations of our analysts, we have prepared the grade card opposite. Clinton's marks range from B+ on creating employment opportunities to C− on dismantling the Cold War–era national security state, with a grade-point average of C+. The key question is this: Why has a president who clearly has enormous intelligence and good political instincts fumbled so badly?

The Jello Presidency

Deep down, President Clinton probably has some progressive beliefs. His much publicized opposition to the Vietnam War reflected a laudable aversion to military adventurism. His long-standing circle of black friends and advisers has underscored his commitment to racial harmony. His wife's active work as chair of the board of the Children's Defense Fund, an endeavor he fully supported, suggests a heartfelt desire to end poverty.

Whatever Bill Clinton's real feelings, however, the disturbing fact is that his positions have been driven more by polls than by conviction. His entire presidential campaign, incubated at the DLC and hatched in PPI policy papers, was based on capturing swing voters. He won back the support of "Reagan Democrats" through conservative proposals like giving businesses more capital-gains tax breaks, removing the poor from welfare rolls after two years, and slashing federal spending. He appealed to "hawks" by reminding voters of his support for President Bush's military actions in Panama and the Persian Gulf and by suggesting that he'd be more likely than Bush to use force everywhere from Cuba to Bosnia. He shamelessly played the "race card" by snubbing Jesse Jackson over a rapper named Sister Souljah and by flying back to Arkansas before a critical primary to electrocute a retarded black man on death row.

To be sure, Clinton's campaign was not entirely antagonistic to progressive values. He advocated health-care reform and tax relief for the middle class. He endorsed modest cuts in military spending and economic conversion. He supported the right of women to choose and the right of gays to serve. He selected a strong environmentalist, Sen. Al Gore, as his vice-presidential candidate.

What seemed to drive most of Clinton's progressive choices, however, was political calculation. He knew he could not abandon progressives and win the election. From the ranks of progressives would come key funders, organizers, thinkers, and strategists essential for victory in November. He reckoned, no doubt, that to turn out the crucial women's vote, he would have to abandon his prior position against federal funding of abortion and embrace a strong pro-choice position.

The very factors that made Clinton a brilliant candidate have rendered him a weak president. Switching positions on issues during the campaign was smart, though cynical, politics; doing so as president has undercut his credibility as a leader. Before assuming office, Clinton announced his commitment to end the military's discrimination against gays and lesbians, only to back off at the first signs of opposition and to delay the decision with six months of "consultations." The end result was a policy of "don't ask, don't tell" that all but wrote anti-gay witch hunts into federal law. He proposed charging cattlemen market-cost fees for grazing on federal lands, then dropped the proposal as soon as a handful of western senators complained, and six months later raised the fees to a third of market cost. He campaigned on a $60 billion annual investment package, promised $30 billion in his February budget address, submitted a request to Congress for $16 billion, and settled for virtually nothing.[21] All these incidents, and many others like them, wound up rewarding opponents and punishing those who went out on a limb to offer him early support, only to have the limb sawed off later.

Try to imagine President Ronald Reagan engaging in this kind of backpedaling. Reagan would have issued an executive order on gays and lesbians and vetoed any legislation attempt to reverse it. He would have confronted the western senators on the hypocrisy of their position vis-à-vis their free-market principles. He would have taken the case for a $60 billion stimulus package to the American people and submitted a bill for not a penny less. Reagan might have wound up ultimately compromising on each issue, but he would have fought for basic principles until the bitter end. No one is sure what Bill Clinton's basic principles are.

How can Clinton help the poor and the middle class without putting substantial new burdens on the rich? How can he put people first without seriously cutting the Pentagon's lavish Cold War budgets? How does he make the trade-off between free trade and protection for workers and the environment? Give Clinton a tough question, and he'll deliver a lawyerly, two-sided answer. Clinton wants to help the poor *and* the rich; he believes in spending money on guns *and* butter; he supports free trade *and* labor *and* the environment.

A real leader must define what's worth fighting for—exactly what Clinton refuses to do. Indeed, despite all the talk about "change," Clinton has proven to be largely a custodial president, more in the tradition of tepid Republicans like Eisenhower and Bush than bold Democrats like Roosevelt or Johnson. His presidency is becoming more and more like that awful grape jello our mothers used to feed us when we were sick: formless, artificial, and cold. It tastes okay going down, but has zero nutritional value.

A Way Forward

It's far too early to write off the Clinton presidency, as many pundits have done. Three long years remain, and there's much Clinton still can accomplish, if he wants to.

The view of the contributors to *State of the Union* is that the president *can* alleviate many of the nation's key problems, if he's willing to move from political expediency back to progressive principles. If he cuts defense spending significantly and raises taxes on the very wealthy, the budget deficit can be shrunk to manageable levels and a variety of new programs can be introduced. If he promotes a Global New Deal, Americans can enjoy the benefits of trade without a loss of jobs and devastation of the global environment. If he makes guaranteed employment a priority, he can end much of the insecurity, poverty, homelessness, and crime that plague the country.

A coherent political program would ensure Clinton a second term and provide the country with a brighter future. Tough political battles will be necessary to implement this program. But if the president supports an agenda that is worth fighting for, tens of millions of workers, women, minorities, and environmentalists stand ready to help him. That, we hope, is the ultimate message of this book.

Challenges of a
New Era

RICHARD CAPLAN AND JOHN FEFFER

"The great thing about the dead," John Updike once wrote, is that "they make space." The collapse of the Cold War order and the end of the Reagan-Bush era have indeed opened up enormous opportunities at the international and national levels. The Berlin Wall, symbolic of the world's partition into two hostile camps, is no more. The Doomsday Clock, which once ticked but three minutes from nuclear midnight in the *Bulletin of the Atomic Scientists*, has been turned back to a more reassuring 11:43 P.M. The vast sums of money devoted to keeping the blocs armed to the teeth can now be reinvested into improving the lives of people, nations, and the planet itself.

Meanwhile, the end of twelve years of Republican presidential rule, which greatly encouraged divisions of wealth and power both at home and abroad, has elevated hopes for a sweeping domestic renewal. Reaganomics, with its Laffer curves, trickle-down rhetoric, and Dickensian miseries, has been publicly repudiated. A national health-care system is in the offing. Campaign-finance reform, designed to inject a dose of democracy into the political system, is finally on the table.

Of course, the obstacles to renewal are both many and great. The Cold War and the Reagan-Bush presidencies may be dead, but their legacies are not easily overcome. Into the space created by their official demise has rushed all manner of ills. Madness is raging across the former Yugoslavia. Wars are burning throughout the former Soviet Union. India seems on the verge of anarchy. Latin America and Africa are struggling with the debt and economic misery of the "lost decade" of the 1980s. The global economy is stagnant. Threats to the ecosystem have grown ever more menacing.

Here in the United States, economic decline and social discord have taken their toll on the nation's health. An enormous federal debt and a deteriorating public infrastructure are the results of astronomical military expenditures and imprudent taxation policies. U.S. citizens have lost faith in a political system characterized by a surfeit of corruption and a dearth of accountability. Society at large struggles with persistent homelessness, crumbling cities, and a woefully inadequate educational system.

The world and the nation are thus caught between singular opportunity and the stale residue of the past. It is a time of seismic shifts in international and domestic events that permits a rethinking of policy in both the grandest sweep and the most stubborn of details. With so much at stake—for the globe and for our country—the Democratic administration of Bill Clinton has taken office. It is a presidency that has promised change, and the American people in turn now expect a great deal of the new president.

How well the president has delivered after one year in office—not just on his promises but on the promise inherent in the moment—is the subject of the essays that comprise this book. To gauge the administration's performance, however, one must first understand the international and domestic context of its actions. What are the dimensions of this space that has opened up before us at the end of the Cold War and the Reagan-Bush era?

The End of the Cold War

Rare are the moments in world history when events allow a virtual remaking of global policy. The failure of the Napoleonic campaigns pre-

"The end of the Cold War and the Reagan-Bush era has opened up enormous opportunities at the international and national levels."

sented the European powers in 1815 with an opportunity to construct a reactionary political order of such durability that their Concert of Europe lasted nearly 100 years. World War I's devastation inspired a much shorter-lived attempt at global order epitomized by the League of Nations. And from the wreckage of World War II emerged a commitment to collective security and global Keynesianism in an era defined, no less, by the decades-long Cold War.[1]

The end of that conflict represents another historic opportunity both to revamp the global order and to redefine America's national strategy within it. The dissolution of the Soviet empire, the eclipse of national economic sovereignty, the emergence of an environmental crisis of staggering proportions—these developments bespeak the end of an era and the increasing obsolescence of the post–World War II verities. It is against this broad international backdrop that Bill Clinton assumed the U.S. presidency—the first president since Harry Truman to face truly fundamental choices concerning America's role in the world.[2]

For nearly fifty years, U.S. foreign policy has been governed by two overriding and largely unquestioned objectives: the containment of Communism and the promotion of a liberal economic order. Both goals required that the United States play a leadership or, more accurately, a hegemonic role—to bear the costs of an enormously expensive military alliance and to provide the resources needed to fuel worldwide economic development.

The price America has paid for its anti-Communist crusade cannot be measured solely by the trillions of dollars it has spent. We must also count among the costs the legacies of that crusade—among them an entrenched national security state, a triumphalist faith in the virtue of military solutions, the nuclear contamination of the environment, and an international arms trade that eludes regulation.

U.S. underwriting of the postwar liberal economic order has meanwhile yielded certain advantages. For one thing, the dominance of the dollar has allowed the United States to finance enormous budget deficits by simply going into debt to foreign creditors, much to the resentment of every Third World country forced to atone for its "profligacy." Yet those deficits have also had negative economic and political effects. And a dollar-denominated world economy has at times brought U.S. economic requirements into conflict with the needs of the international economy.[3]

Despite the end of the Cold War, George Bush chose to navigate by the same compass that has guided the United States for nearly half a century. He spent massively on military preparedness even after the Soviet Union had collapsed. He supported repressive governments around the world (Zaire, Haiti, China, Mexico) in the belief that U.S. security and economic needs dictated such a policy. He touted the virtues of collective security yet viewed the United States as the self-appointed guardian of global stability. And while stubbornly insisting on the prerogatives of a world hegemon, he relied increasingly on other countries such as Japan and Germany to bail out the international economy.

"Bush studiously avoided
the many difficult adjustments
the new era requires.
Clinton has no such luxury."

George Bush, the last World War II–era president, used his tenure to buy time. He studiously avoided the many difficult adjustments the new era would require. His successor has no such luxury. The global order is under strains too serious to continue to ignore for very long. This is evident if one considers the specific international challenges Clinton faced in each of three areas—security, the world economy, and the global environment—on the eve of his first year in office.

International Insecurity

In a speech at Georgetown University in 1989, then Deputy Secretary of State Lawrence Eagleburger expressed some unease about the end of the Cold War. "For all its risks and uncertainties, the Cold War was characterized by a remarkably stable and predictable set of relations among the great powers," he observed.[4] Conveniently ignoring the price paid for that "stability"—nuclear terror, proxy wars, exorbitant military budgets—Eagleburger nevertheless anticipated correctly the turbulent period that lay ahead.

With the end of the Cold War, the old bipolar world has given way to a brave new world fraught with conflicts once considered unthinkable. In the past, one could scarcely have imagined violent conflict between "fraternal republics" within the Soviet Union, as was now occurring between the newly independent states of Armenia and Azerbaijan and between Georgia and Russia. Just as implausible had been the possibility of conflict in Yugoslavia, a traditional buffer zone between the East-West blocs. Indeed conflict appeared to be erupting across the globe. Early in 1993 the *New York Times* published a listing of violent conflict in forty-eight countries, and that was just a partial count.[5] Conditions, of course, had been ripe for conflict in many of these areas for quite some time, but the superpower standoff—Eagleburger's stability—had frequently exerted a strong restraining effect.

These violent impulses had not resulted simply from the collapse of the bipolar order. In many cases violence had sprung from aggressive forms of nationalism, which, with worsening economic conditions, fragmenting political institutions, and the weakening of secular authorities, offered an attractive ideology for dispirited populations. Aggressive nationalism, and the demagogues that frequently exploited it, thus represented a serious security challenge in the post–Cold War world—with the former Yugoslavia the most pressing case. As pundits and editorial writers insistently reminded their audiences, much was at stake in the Balkan crisis: the danger of a wider war in a notoriously volatile region, the future of the Atlantic Alliance, and, not least of all, operative norms and values in the fabled "new world order."

Other security challenges confronting Clinton more accurately reflected the stubborn persistence of practices and ways of thinking commonly associated with the old world order. A corrupt military continued to threaten democratic rule in Haiti, where a popularly elected government led by the Rev. Jean-Bertrand Aristide had been toppled by a coup a year and a half earlier. The dangers of nuclear proliferation were heightened by the emergence of new nuclear states in the wake of the Soviet collapse. The unrestrained traffic in conventional arms and military technology that played such a central role in major conflicts—Somalia, Cambodia, and Angola—continued to bedevil the international community. Peace talks between Israel and its Arab neighbors in the wake of the war against Iraq were at a standstill. And the deterioration of relations between the two Koreas—where the United States maintains its second-largest assembly of forces—was a growing concern.

These threats, old and new, all increased the strain on U.S. and multilateral capacities. With the end of the Cold War came stepped-up demands and higher expectations—for peacekeeping (with as many new UN operations in the past five years as in the previous four decades), for peacemaking (in strife-torn El Salvador, Angola, and Haiti), and even for military intervention (in Iraq and then Somalia). But these developments also revealed the deficiencies of the global security order: its seeming arbitrariness (why Somalia and not Bosnia?), its contradictions (selling arms to belligerent nations), its improvisational basis (funding peacekeeping operations on the fly), and its failure to emphasize early, preventive diplomacy.

Geoeconomic Rut

Clinton assumed the presidency at a time when traditional conceptions of security had been shattered by the growing importance of economic factors. It was, after all, the Soviet Union's inability to compete economically, not militarily, that led to its demise. While the world's largest and most dynamic economy is unlikely to share the fate of its erstwhile opponent, the erosion of U.S. economic strength is a clear and unmistakable trend. From the height of U.S. dominance in the early 1950s until the early 1990s, the U.S. share of global output has declined by 50 percent. U.S. productivity growth, once the envy of the world, has fallen behind that of Japan and Germany. And the dollar, the cornerstone of the world economy, has been weakened by hegemonic overstretch, to paraphrase historian Paul Kennedy.[6]

Of course, these shifts have been taking place gradually over the course of decades, and the United States could never have expected to maintain its post–World War II economic dominance indefinitely. Still, to be a lesser giant, as Clinton was no doubt aware, meant that the United States was now more vulnerable to outside pressures, and therefore less secure, than at any other time in its recent history.

Reprinted by permission of TOM and the Cartoonists & Writers Syndicate

Clinton the candidate emphasized the economic underpinnings of U.S. security. "Economic strength," he wrote in his campaign manifesto *Putting People First*, "is a central element of our national security policy."[7] The challenge Clinton faced, however, was made more difficult by the very nature of a changing international order. It is no longer possible to devise a national economic policy, strictly speaking, when trade constitutes 20 percent of the nation's gross domestic product, when U.S. firms rely increasingly on overseas workers, when foreigners hold nearly one-fifth of all U.S. government debt, and when the United States no longer controls the flow of capital in and out of its borders. The U.S. economy, in short, is intricately bound up with the international economy. It is still true that if the United States sneezes, the rest of the world catches cold. But it is now no less true that if Japan or Germany applies the economic brakes, the United States is likely to get whiplash.

And apply the brakes they did. When Clinton entered office, the continuing strain of German unification and the collapse of the East European economies were seriously hampering economic growth in Europe and, therefore, in the rest of the world as well. Also contributing to this global economic slowdown was Japan's descent into the worst economic and political crisis of its postwar history. And much of the Third World either remained mired in debt—conveniently forgotten now that the big commercial banks had reduced their exposure—or, at the urging of the World Bank and the International Monetary Fund, had oriented their economies toward the export, not the consumption, of goods. All of this translated into stagnant or declining living standards at home and abroad.

In the past, under these circumstances, the United States might have been expected to prime the global economy. But precisely because the U.S. economy had taken such a battering—the consequence both of "natural causes" and several decades of misguided policies—the political climate on the eve of the Clinton presidency did not permit anything but a nod in this Keynesian direction. The federal debt already stood at more than $4 trillion; the trade deficit was at $84 billion; and the dollar—at an all-time low against the yen—could not sustain any further loss in confidence. As *The Economist*, speaking for many, would intone later in 1993, "Past profligacy has left [the United States] with little or no scope to use borrowed money to support demand."[8]

As with the global security order, then, so too with the global economic order: the strains were outstripping the capacity of any single nation or multilateral institution to cope effectively. Bush sought a way out by loosening restrictions on regional and international trade, bequeathing to his successor the chronically stalled world trade talks under the auspices of the General Agreement on Tariffs and Trade (GATT) and a framework treaty for a North American Free Trade Agreement (NAFTA).

Freer trade, the argument went, would open markets and thus stimulate growth. Moreover, it would strengthen U.S. competitiveness, granting U.S. firms greater access to sources of cheaper labor and to production sites free of onerous regulations.

But this approach was deeply flawed. In an age of increased capital mobility, it threatened to pit nation against nation in a race to attract capital on the basis of lower wages and lax health, safety, and environmental standards. Unregulated free trade was a prescription not for enhanced competitiveness but for global decline.

The Fragile Environment

Properly speaking, the challenge the Clinton administration faced coming into office was not to promote global economic growth but to encourage efforts to manage the world economy in an environmentally sustainable manner. Since 1950, the world's population has grown from 2.6 billion to 5.5 billion, and the world economy has expanded fivefold. This increased economic activity has placed enormous demands on the biosphere—so much so that in the estimate of Worldwatch Institute president Lester R. Brown, "we have begun to outstrip the carrying capacity of biological support systems."[9]

With the threat of nuclear extinction significantly diminished, environmental degradation arguably poses the greatest threat to humanity today. Since World War II, industrial activity has increased the concentration of carbon dioxide in the atmosphere by almost 25 percent—contributing to a global warming trend that could disrupt agricultural patterns and displace millions of people worldwide. The disappearance of rainforests and other natural habitats has led to the loss of species of animals and plants around the world at a rate 1,000 times faster than at any time in the past 65 million years.[10] And land degradation in the Third World threatens to turn vast stretches of vital cropland and rangeland into desert as a result of overexploitation.

Awareness of the urgency of these and other environmental problems has grown steadily since the first UN environmental summit in Stockholm twenty years ago. So, too, has the recognition that these problems concern everyone and consequently require shared responsibility. Yet under Reagan and Bush the environment took a back seat to industry concerns, thus alienating large segments of the world community and damaging the prospects for international cooperation. Reagan set the tone when just days after his inauguration he repealed U.S. controls over international trade in toxic substances. And Bush completed the circle when at the end of his tenure he refused to accept an agreement that would have required industrial nations to reduce their carbon dioxide

---

"Under Reagan and Bush
the environment took a back seat
to industry concerns."

---

emissions to 1990 levels. This move prompted the developing countries, invoking the principle of burden-sharing, to renege on their offer to negotiate a treaty protecting endangered rainforests.

Despite these obstructionist policies, a common environmental agenda has gradually emerged over the past two decades, as the various international covenants to protect the ozone layer, reduce greenhouse emissions, and retard deforestation would suggest. Yet these efforts, while laudable, are piecemeal. They fall short of fundamentally redirecting the global economy and putting it on a sound and sustainable footing.

The United States is in a position to provide leadership on this critical question. No other nation commands the same authority if only because no other nation's economy has as much impact on the global environment (the United States, for instance, is the largest producer of carbon dioxide emissions). Such leadership will mean entertaining some unpopular notions—unpopular in certain circles, at least—such as forgiving debts so that developing countries no longer need to ravage their natural resource base to service their loans, or transferring technology to China and Poland so that they are not forced to use "dirty" coal reserves as an energy source. And it will mean recognizing the importance of democracy, human rights, and equitable patterns of land ownership so that all who depend on the proper stewardship of the environment are empowered to protect the ultimate source of their livelihood.

Domestic Troubles

At home, America was likewise caught between grand opportunities and perennial problems on the eve of the Clinton presidency. The administration, eager to hit the ground running, took office with an almost revolutionary charge: to transform the U.S. economy, polity, and society simultaneously. Echoing his equally youthful predecessor John F.

Kennedy, Clinton called for "a new beginning," a reorienting of American society toward contemporary realities and fresh possibilities.

This transformation, so easy in words, has not been so easy in deeds. For America of late has been wrestling with the twin demons of decline and division. The two maladies are unfortunately related. As we become more ensconced in our national malaise, we seem able to muster energy only for mutual acrimony—blame, destructive criticism, episodic violence. The country is like a leaking lifeboat, in which a harried group of survivors trade epithets at one another even as the water creeps slowly up their legs.

This "sinking lifeboat" syndrome is not a historical accident or simply a result of the vagaries of international fortunes. Nor have our national "disagreements" been the sign of a healthy democracy. Rather, our current decline and discord have proceeded from undemocratic policies, deliberately undertaken by leaders in government and business to benefit the special interests of a few.

Consider decline. It is important to recognize that America's current economic difficulties do not derive simply from the latest downturn in our sinusoidal business cycles. Instead, as we approach the millennium, our economy has fallen into severe structural disequilibrium. Each recovery now peaks a little lower than the last, each recession places us a little further from a just prosperity.

To get a better fix on the angle of our decline, take 1974 as a reference point, a year that found America in particularly dire straits. In 1974 unemployment hovered around 7 percent and inflation stood in the double digits. Mass layoffs were a daily staple of newspaper headlines. "For the current generation of working people," *Newsweek* reported in its year-end analysis, "times have never been so hard."[11] The political realm was in no better shape. In August of that year, Richard Nixon had resigned the presidency, leaving Gerald Ford to repair the public's loss of confidence in American statecraft. During that post-Watergate season of discontent the country seemed to be unraveling—economically, politically, and socially.

In 1974 the United States was in its worst recession and greatest political crisis since World War II. Yet, by a variety of indicators, we were better off then than we are today. In 1974 for instance, the U.S. government was frustrated that it could not erase a $20 billion budget deficit. Today the government struggles with an annual deficit of roughly $350 billion. In 1974 America was fighting both the Cold War and the Vietnam War, yet our military expenditures as a percentage of gross national product (GNP) were roughly the same as they are today when we have no such perceived threats. In 1974 the government declared a health-care crisis

> ## *"In 1974 the United States was in its worst recession and greatest political crisis since World War II. Yet, by a variety of indicators, we were better off then than we are today."*

because the percentage of GNP spent on medical costs was 7.5 percent. Today we spend 14 percent and the number of uninsured has ballooned to 37 million. The United States was a creditor nation in the 1970s. In the 1980s, for the first time in the century, it became the world's largest debtor nation.

In 1974 we worked shorter hours for more money. Real wages peaked in 1973 and have been declining every since, yet we work on average one month more per year now than we did two decades ago.[12] The picture is even more dismal for those out of work. In 1974 a 6 percent unemployment rate was considered both economically and politically unacceptable. Today it is the target figure for the current administration. Moreover, income distribution was more equitable in 1974, when the top tax bracket stood at 70 percent. It subsequently declined to 28 percent during the Reagan era, allowing wealth to concentrate further among the elite. For the poor, the past two decades have been especially cruel. The poverty rate among children, for instance, has risen dramatically, striking one in five today compared with only one in seven in 1974. Homelessness barely existed as a category in the 1970s. Today more than 1.2 million people live on the streets and in temporary shelters.[13]

Although Gerald Ford was presiding over the most dismal moment in post–World War II politics, there was still reason to be optimistic. A new wave of politicians—young and outspoken—was sent to Washington in 1974 to "clean house." Today, although a passel of new faces likewise populate the House and Senate, public disenchantment with the political process is profound. In the early 1970s, reforms within the Democratic Party were opening up the patronage system to greater participation. Today the party is ever more beholden to vested interests. In 1974 investigations into FBI and CIA abuses were just beginning. Today these organs have strayed even farther from democratic control.

In society at large, the women's movement was winning victories in the 1970s on issues of both pay equity and sexual freedom. Today we are firmly in the grips of a "backlash," with more female-headed families in poverty, a doubling of reported rapes, and a stubbornly persistent pay gap.[14] Affirmative-action programs were beginning to have their first positive effects, as a historic number of blacks were going on to college and, upon graduation, earning as much as their white counterparts.[15] But the subsequent economic downturn has penalized African-Americans disproportionately, as the widening gap between black and white unemployment rates indicates.[16] Today riots and rage convulse our inner cities, endemic racism still holds our minority communities in thrall, and a spirit of nihilism and despair has infected our young people.

What Went Wrong?

We were told in the 1980s that it was morning in America, that the country was enjoying its greatest economic expansion since World War II. But that rhetoric merely masked the nightmarish processes that took a society clearly in trouble in the early 1970s and pushed it to new levels of instability. It is no wonder, then, that at the beginning of the 1990s, Americans began to ask themselves: What went wrong? How did the United States, once the envy of the industrialized world, become so mired in its own problems? On so many indicators—from per capita wealth to literacy to health care—the United States could no longer claim to be number one. True, we still boasted the most billionaires in the world and the largest salaries for corporate executives. But in terms of overall quality of life, we had slipped noticeably with respect to our global peers. Worse, we had become dangerously accustomed to this erosion of our national health.

These trends are not simply impersonal or politically neutral. Successive political administrations must shoulder the responsibility for the deteriorating state of the nation. A special burden, however, rests with the Reagan-Bush team. From 1981 on, the Reagan "revolution" severely weakened the U.S. economy by undercutting the manufacturing base, slashing funding for critical public programs such as education and job retraining, effectively ignoring civilian research and development, and engaging in deficit spending to promote the largest peacetime increase in military expenditures. Because of the laissez-faire thinking of the Reagan years, the United States has lost its competitive edge. Productive investment has declined steadily, mirroring a drop in real economic growth and a levelling off of productivity. Where growth has taken place—in the service sector—it has provided low wages, tenuous job security, and minimal benefits.[17]

The Reagan-Bush solution to economic stagnation was to sweep away government regulations and unleash the corporate sector. This remedy proved more harmful than the disease. Responding to the new business-friendly climate, U.S. corporate investment either went overseas for cheap labor and tax shelters or sought high-risk and short-term financial speculation at home. While U.S. corporations were studiously avoiding investment in America's future, other corporations were less reticent. In the 1980s foreign companies swooped in to snatch up undervalued U.S. investments in what two leading analysts have called "the biggest firesale held by any advanced industrialized country in history."[18] Thrown on the defensive, organized labor has been incapable of counterbalancing the increasingly unregulated power of corporate multinationals.

Adding insult to injury, the U.S. economy has not only stagnated, it has become increasingly polarized. To return to the sinking lifeboat metaphor, some of the shipwreck's survivors have profited handsomely from the disaster. They have collected large insurance dividends on the destruction of the U.S.S. America and have escaped harm in their own private leak-proof vessels. "Between 1977 and 1990 the average income of the poorest fifth of Americans declined by about 5 percent, while the richest fifth became about 9 percent wealthier," writes Robert Reich, now secretary of labor.[19]

The savings-and-loan crisis, which broke into the media in the late 1980s, not only exposed the fatal fragility of our financial system. It also revealed one of the hitherto hidden mechanisms of redistributing wealth upward, through real estate scams and the finagling of accountants. The bill for this decade-long exercise in corporate indulgence was, in the end, presented to the American people: $325 billion at the very minimum. As analyst David Calleo writes, "The price for this 'economic Vietnam' will very probably exceed, in real terms, all the aid given to Europe under the Marshall Plan, plus the subsequent bailouts of Lockheed, Chrysler, Penn Central, and New York City combined."[20]

Political Decline

The political system should have functioned as the nervous system that informed the body politic of these economic illnesses. But our political system has not served that function. Neither the existing political parties nor the nonpartisan political structures adequately informed the majority of Americans that their economic well-being was eroding. Why? The influence of money on the political process—including increasing corporate control of the media—is one reason. The situation has become so absurd that members of Congress who want to work on the public's behalf must revise legislation furtively in order not to alert corporate interests. Taking a cue from citizens' groups, corporate lobbyists have resorted to stage-managing grass-roots reaction (known in the P.R. business as "astroturf") to convince politicians that the public holds a particular position on an issue.

"The Democratic Party, which has traditionally cast itself as the people's party, is having ever greater difficulty living up to its name."

The Democratic Party, which has traditionally cast itself as the people's party, is having ever greater difficulty living up to its name. Instead of representing the majority of Americans by supporting egalitarian economic policies and significant campaign-finance reform, the Democratic Party has simply kowtowed to its wealthiest contributors, a powerful phalanx of individuals, corporations, and interest groups. Then, at the tail end of the 1984 and 1988 Democratic presidential campaigns, the party got religion: A populist "soak-the-rich" rhetoric allowed both Mondale and Dukakis to close the gap with their Republican opponents. But the gap, it turned out, could not be closed so late in the game. Reagan and then Bush coasted to relatively easy victories. In 1992, the Democratic Party finally adopted a more populist message and succeeded at the polls. The degree to which this tactically adopted rhetoric of redistribution and reform translates into actual policies will no doubt determine the longevity of the current administration.

It is a constant source of embarrassment that the American political system, which served as the inspiration for thousands of activists from Warsaw and Timisoara to Beijing and Rangoon, suffers from a growing democratic deficit. The governed are increasingly isolated from the governors. This isolation can be discerned in low voter turnouts, marked enthusiasm for autocratic political candidates such as Ross Perot, concerns over congressional gridlock, and distrust of career politicians. A declining faith in democracy—America's civil religion—is not as easily quantified as our economic deterioration. But its effects are no less real or disturbing.

Social Division

Three Republican administrations did more to divide Americans by class, gender, age, and race than any administration since the Civil War. It was Spiro Agnew who declared in 1971 that "dividing the American people has been my main contribution to the national political scene."[21] But the statement could easily have been made by either Ronald Reagan (whose tax policies pitted rich against poor) or George Bush (whose campaign ads featuring Willie Horton and whose Supreme Court nomination of Clarence Thomas split the American public along race and gender lines).

According to the logic of this divisive politics, social factors become more significant than economic ones. Both the Reagan and Bush administrations realized that, because their policies benefited so few, a coalition based on economic interests could unite to overturn their neoconservative agenda. Rather than create a national consensus to revive the economy and restore faith in the polity, the U.S. government pursued divide-and-conquer strategies for twelve years to distract attention from a comprehensive, oligarchical transformation of American society. Uneasy about its own relationship with powerful economic interests, the Democratic Party simply played along.

Poverty therefore became a social issue rather than an economic problem. "The problem of poverty is presumed to reside in the poor people themselves, not in the structure of wages available in the private economy," writes journalist William Greider.[22] Crime and drug use did not arise from growing economic divisions in society but grew out of the supposed cultural pathologies of particular groups in society. Blacks were stigmatized as the misfits responsible for these social ills, even though the "underclass"—judged both by economic well-being and educational attainment—was overwhelmingly white.[23]

Because they argued that poverty stemmed from behavior and not economic distress, the neoconservatives could dismiss redistributive government programs aimed at equalizing social disparities. In 1981 the Reagan administration attacked social spending, arguing that it simply poured money down the poverty drain. This broadside ignored three fundamental facts. First, only 20 percent of social welfare spending went explicitly to low-income families.[24] Second, these programs had been, in many cases, very successful. Programs directed at the elderly managed to raise them as a group out of poverty; Head Start, although it reached only a small percentage of eligible children, also registered significant successes, along with other programs such as food stamps and Medicaid. Third, compared with other industrialized countries, the United States was shirking its responsibility to its poor.

Reprinted by permission of KAL and the Cartoonists & Writers Syndicate

It has not simply been on class issues that the 1980s proved divisive. On race, gender, and generational issues, too, the United States became substantially disunited. But it was not identity politics or the imagined machinations of the multiculturalists that threatened the American mosaic. For instance, in a 1988 departmental memorandum, Attorney General for Civil Rights William Bradford Reynolds wrote that the administration "must polarize the debate" on black-white relations.[25] The bitter fruits of this strategy could thereafter be discerned in the confrontations between blacks and Orthodox Jews in the Crown Heights section of New York City, the ongoing tensions between Hispanics and whites in Miami, the eruption of skinhead violence in the Pacific Northwest, and the explosion of conflict in the south-central section of Los Angeles—the most costly riot in U.S. history.

Perhaps the greatest symbol of divisiveness was the nomination struggle in the fall of 1991 that pitted two black conservatives, Supreme Court nominee Clarence Thomas and law professor Anita Hill. The Bush administration pushed the nomination through by driving a wedge between the sympathies of African-Americans and a mostly white women's movement.[26] A wedge was also driven into the black community itself, forcing African-Americans either to adopt a "closing ranks mentality" or criticize a black nominee for his minimal credentials, appalling political beliefs, or unrepentant sexism.[27]

The phenomenon of backlash reflects the neoconservative attempt to roll back gains made by the feminist movement over the past two decades. While men and women were forced to compete for a dwindling number of high-paying jobs in the 1980s, women were also set against one another, encouraged by a neoconservative climate to choose between a series of false choices: being single and career-oriented or married and at home, having a baby or holding down a job, respecting the mother or protecting the fetus, engaging in public service or focusing on self-help. A women's movement divided between rich and poor, white and black, gay and straight has only been a boon to conservative forces.

Finally, the political economy of the 1980s drove a wedge between generations. For it was not only the poor that suffered during the decade, but the sons and daughters of the middle class as well. As anthropologist Katherine Newman points out, "Boomers assumed they would live adult lives akin to those their parents had and have been crushed to discover that this is not to be. Their dismay has been compounded by the realization that they may not be able to do as much for their own children as their parents did for them."[28] And, if trends continue, succeeding generations will be even worse off. The high hopes of earlier decades—rising waters lifting all boats, the Great Society—have been dashed against the rocks of 1990s realities.

These processes of decline and discord, together with the enormous changes taking place at the global level, ensured that the incoming administration of Bill Clinton would not have it easy. To meet the challenges of a new era, bold departures from past policies would be required. But even then Clinton would have to make fundamental choices with respect to the broad direction of national and international policy. After one year in office, has Clinton shown that he has the vision and the determination to put the country on the right track? This is the question that our contributors address in the essays that follow.

WORLD
ECONOMY

Forging a
Global New Deal

JOHN CAVANAGH, ROBIN BROAD, AND PETER WEISS

Bill Clinton won the presidency of a recession-torn United States largely because he was able to convince millions of voters that he would address the economic problems to which George Bush seemed oblivious. Within weeks of Clinton's inauguration, the new president boosted his public approval ratings by articulating an economic plan that promised jobs and stimulus and at the same time sought to contain the staggering national debt.

Yet Clinton's first year cannot be judged a success, and not simply because of his inability to steer his preferred economic program through the famed "gridlock" of a special-interest laden Congress. The bigger problem was the administration's inability to understand that the United States is part of a global economy and that most U.S. workers are part of a global labor pool. James Carville's campaign mantra—"The Economy, Stupid"—was brilliant in capturing the fears of an electorate whose living standards had ceased to rise; the Clinton administration, however, failed to define the boundaries of that economy broadly enough. This inability to appreciate the new global boundaries of U.S. policy has not only crippled domestic economic policy, but it has also led to costly missteps on trade, aid, debt, and other policies toward the rest of the world.

The most important new reality for any U.S. president to grapple with is that the United States can no longer have a domestic jobs strategy without a global jobs strategy: The United Nations conservatively estimates that each year 47 million people enter the job market around the world, 38 million of them in the poorer countries where wages remain a mere fraction of prevailing U.S. levels.[1] Thanks to technological revolutions that shrink time and space, U.S.-based firms now have access to millions of these workers and, in many sectors, are pitting them against U.S. workers for jobs. The result has been a steady erosion of U.S. manufacturing wages and benefits and, more recently, the spread of this global competition into the vast service sector on which more and more U.S. workers depend.

Clinton's articulate labor secretary, Robert Reich, appeared before countless congressional committees in 1993 arguing that the United States could outcompete other nations with aggressive worker retraining and selective government subsidies. Yet in the current deregulated world economy, firms compete by trimming workforces and slashing costs, often pitting workers, communities, and countries against one another to offer the lowest wages, shoddiest working conditions, and most lax health, safety, and environmental standards. Hence, fewer new jobs are being created in the United States for retrained workers, and many of them offer lower wages.

Administration policies also mistakenly continue to be premised on the old adage that what is good for General Motors is good for the United States. In its first year, the Clinton administration's policies on the world economy equated the "national interest" primarily with large corporate interests, while treating the majority—environmentalists, women's groups, organized labor, family-farm groups, and related citizens groups—as "special interests," instead of the other way around. As General Motors and other firms reorganized production lines globally to minimize costs, they continued to place relatively cheap products in showrooms and malls; yet the number of Americans who had the cash or credit to purchase them was no longer growing.

The lack of boldness of the administration's economic policy was due in part to the legacy of the Reagan and Bush era. The tripling of the national debt during twelve years of Republican rule helped turn the United States from the biggest creditor to the biggest debtor nation on earth. The United States, like the rest of the debtor world, had less cash and more worries about keeping its creditors happy. As Clinton began to name his cabinet in December 1992, it became clear that the government's creditors, many of them overseas, were utmost in his mind. Lloyd Bentsen in Treasury, Robert Rubin in the new National Economic Council, Mickey Kantor at the Trade Representative's Office, and Ron Brown at Commerce were all names familiar and soothing to Wall Street and in-

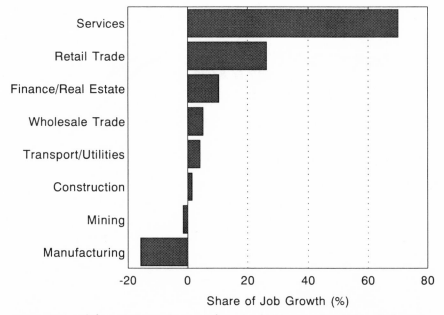

Figure 2.1   Shift in U.S. Employment from High-Wage to Low-Wage Industries, 1979–1991

Source: Cuomo Commission on Competitiveness.

ternational bond markets. Yet these were not men with much understanding of how to address social and environmental challenges in a new global economy.

This new Clinton team attempted to build bridges to a Wall Street that was busy building bridges to the rest of the world. Over the past decade, large corporations from the United States, Japan, Germany, and a few other industrialized countries have been weaving global webs of production, marketing, finance, and culture.[2] Ford creates a car on the global assembly line as Citibank expands credit card service to the wealthy of Asia. Malls from Lagos and Manila to Tokyo and Minneapolis deliver the goods whose images are projected to remote barrios in poorer countries through Western films and videos.[3]

Yet the new world order that global corporations and banks have been shaping increasingly resembles the old South African apartheid system. As many as 1 billion people (a fifth of the world's population) live today in utter, degrading poverty, barely on the edge of subsistence, if not falling off the edge. In the eyes of Philip Morris or Citibank, these people are largely outside the money economy; at best as window shoppers in the world's malls, they have no potential as credit card holders. Close to half of the world's people are only slightly better off and participate in the

_____

"The Clinton team attempted to build bridges to a Wall Street that was busy building bridges to the rest of the world."

_____

world economy as occasional buyers of Marlboro cigarettes, Coca Cola soft drinks, Nescafé coffee, and Tide detergent as they interlope into global production chains as assemblers of televisions, sewers of shirts, stuffers of toys, or punchers of data in global offices. These are the people who, effectively, have been placed in competition with U.S. workers.

The remaining third of the planet are the winners in this increasingly polarized global economy—the rich of the poor countries and the middle and upper classes of the rich countries who constitute a new "global North." Private banks along with the World Bank and the International Monetary Fund have fueled the inequalities since the early 1980s by demanding more from poorer countries in debt service than they have given in new loans; between 1985 and 1992, an astounding $280 billion more flowed out of the South than flowed in.[4]

For the past four decades, the problem of how to close the ever widening gap between the earth's rich and poor occupied an important place in the political discourse of the United States and the other industrialized nations. Yet in the turning inward that has afflicted all major economic powers since the end of the Cold War, this concern has largely disappeared. It was not a topic in the 1992 presidential campaign and, except in the discussion around the reform of bilateral aid, it has practically disappeared from the Clinton political agenda.

The retreat from the two-thirds of the world who, in Franklin Delano Roosevelt's phrase, are ill-fed, ill-clothed, and ill-housed, is bound to have consequences as grave as the failure to recognize the linked nature of ecological problems. In *The Debt Boomerang*, development specialist Susan George and her colleagues at the Transnational Institute persuasively demonstrate the effects of Third World debt and poverty on the industrial world: large debts pressure countries to cut forests for foreign exchange and for agricultural use, adding to global warming and swelling the numbers of environmental refugees; debt and poverty stimulate coca production and marketing; debt-induced austerity programs restrict countries' imports from the United States, which costs jobs; grinding poverty fuels instability in many nations, and the resulting conflict and war affect us all.[5]

The notion that no man or woman is an island, that the world cannot live half-slave, half-free, half-starving, half-overfed, is hardly a novel one. In 1977, a group of eminent scholars warned: "Unless current patterns of socio-economic growth and development are modified, the world may be heading for catastrophe. The gap between rich and poor nations will widen, the poorest will be unable to survive, and mounting pressures will erupt into acts of terrorism and ultimately war."[6] What is new is that the poor can now replace U.S. workers.

The overall failure by the Clinton administration to understand these global interconnections as it focused its energies on a domestic economic plan led it into a series of misplaced policies vis-à-vis the world economy.

Trade

Thanks in good part to initiatives of the Reagan and Bush administration, trade policy has become the main arena where North-South issues are addressed by the U.S. government. In 1986, the Reagan administration launched comprehensive negotiations to liberalize global trade rules concerning agriculture, services, and investment under the auspices of the General Agreement on Tariffs and Trade (GATT). In 1990, the Bush administration began negotiations with Canada and Mexico for a North American Free Trade Agreement (NAFTA) that would erase most trade and investment barriers among the three nations.

It is in the arena of trade that the Clinton administration's failure to grasp the challenges of an integrated world economy is most evident. The failure comes into sharpest focus in U.S. relations with two nations that have become two of our biggest trading partners: Mexico (our third largest trading partner after Canada and Japan) and China (which accounts for over a quarter of the U.S. trade deficit). Mexican wages vary widely but average near one-tenth of U.S. wages; with China the gap is even wider. In Mexico, global firms like Ford have engaged in brutal labor repression even as they have brought in some of their most advanced production technology. Indeed, productivity levels in some factories approach U.S. levels. Chinese technology by and large lags further behind, but in both countries the productivity gaps are far narrower than the wage gaps—an enormous incentive for firms to relocate production there.

In this global economic atmosphere, the Clinton administration's rallying cry to U.S. firms and workers to outcompete other nations in a "free-trade" atmosphere becomes little more than a license for U.S.-

based firms to bargain down wages and working conditions, and to "downsize" by slashing workforces. This opens a downward spiral of destructive competition for U.S. workers since foreign firms (many of them U.S.-owned) in Mexico and China are likely to continue to upgrade factories with their latest technological breakthroughs while the governments there continue to keep wages low through repression.

The key policy venue through which the Clinton administration has addressed the poorer nations of the world is NAFTA. Bill Clinton, the candidate, took a politically astute position on NAFTA in October 1992. To appease Wall Street, he said that he would not renegotiate the free-trade accord that George Bush was about to sign and, to appease citizen critics of the agreement, he promised not to send NAFTA to the U.S. Congress without negotiating tough side agreements on workers' rights and the environment. In that one speech, Clinton refuted George Bush's charge that he was against free trade while simultaneously keeping labor and environmental allies on his side.

> *"Bill Clinton, the candidate,*
> *took a politically astute position*
> *on NAFTA."*

As president, however, Clinton failed dismally to address the problems of a rich country integrating with a country where labor rights and environmental standards are routinely violated. Part of the problem lies in the inherent difficulties of making a free-trade agreement worker- and environment-friendly when you have already said that you will not touch the basic text. Even worse was the attitude that the administration brought to the task of negotiating labor and environmental agreements. The two central actors on the U.S. side, Kantor and Rubin, started the spring 1993 negotiations with a position that would have made it virtually impossible for victims of labor or environmental abuses in any of the three countries to expect enforcement of standards. As Kantor made clear in meetings with labor and environmental groups, he did not believe that trade agreements were an appropriate venue for enforcement of labor and environmental standards.

With China, Clinton missed another opportunity to make the same linkages. The U.S. trade deficit has edged upward with China over the past decade as thousands of subsidiaries of foreign firms have moved to take advantage of the extraordinarily low wages and virtually limitless supply of workers, and have used China as the new export platform to the world.[7] Again, candidate Clinton made a principled promise: he would condition China's continued access to U.S. markets on that nation's human rights and arms sales records. Worker-rights advocates then highlighted the continued use of prison labor in China and the denial of basic worker rights, and their pressure convinced Levi Strauss to announce a phase-out of its apparel subcontracting there. Yet, in May 1993, after a concerted lobby effort by Weyerhaeuser, General Electric, and other Fortune 500 firms that export to China, Clinton renewed China's most-favored nation status. In the end, Clinton caved in to a well-financed corporate lobby.[8]

The other two major trade issues of the administration's first year were the trade talks at GATT and the U.S. trade deficit with Japan. The GATT negotiations reached into almost every arena of global economic integration and, at a time when recession plagued most industrialized countries around the world, few were offering concessions on the trade liberalization agenda. As with NAFTA, the Clinton administration passed up the opportunity to insert social and environmental issues into the GATT agenda, and it let the talks slip onto the back burner. With respect to Japan, President Clinton launched a desperate attempt at bilateral negotiations during a July summit of the leading industrial nations. He trumpeted a last-minute agreement wherein the Japanese agreed to pursue a "highly significant" reduction in its trade surplus; in Japanese, the phrase was translated as *jubun iminoaru*, which means "sufficiently meaningful," and no details were agreed to on how to move toward either phrase.[9]

Aid

While the administration's approach toward trade failed to offer fresh departures from the free-trade approach of the Bush administration, in the area of aid there were some hopeful early signs. During the campaign, both Clinton and Gore latched onto a blistering September 1992 "60 Minutes" segment that exposed the U.S. Agency for International Development (AID) for encouraging U.S. businesses to take advantage of nonunion industrial zones in El Salvador. The candidates pledged to clean up the agency and to reorient bilateral aid to support development.

Early in the administration, Clinton set up a task force headed by Deputy Secretary of State Clifton Wharton that launched a fundamental rethinking of AID. By spring 1993, drafts of the "Wharton Report" demonstrated that a fairly radical rethinking of AID was under way, one that would push AID to support sustainable development where participation by community groups was central. This was noteworthy since so many U.S. aid projects have failed simply because the people they were supposed to benefit were never let into the process of design or implementation.

Early into the review process, however, the task force got embroiled in a battle with an interagency working group that Clinton had set up under the more conventional leadership of the National Security Council and the National Economic Council to assess overall U.S. security and economic interests in the rest of the world. This new working group pressed the structural adjustment, free-market model of development popular with the World Bank and International Monetary Fund (IMF) that pushes governments to spend less, privatize more, and gear their economies toward the export of everything from coffee to toys. With such contradictory visions, AID reform slowed down. While the top AID bureaucrats understand the need for fundamental change, the failure to move quickly and decisively in a new direction killed a great deal of the momentum for reform. Likewise, early Clinton pledges of major assistance for Russia got bogged down in congressional debates over pressing economic concerns at home, and the size of the package dwindled as the year progressed.

As important as shifting the direction of U.S. bilateral aid is changing course at the major multilateral economic institutions, particularly the World Bank and IMF. The Bank and Fund have been at the forefront of pushing the structural adjustment approach to development, an approach that has exacerbated poverty and accelerated environmental decline in already poor countries. (As the journalist Alexander Cockburn aptly puts it, "There is precious little meat left on the [Third World's] bones for the pinstripe SWAT squad from the IMF to get their knives into.")[10] It is still too soon to judge whether the Clinton administration will help shift the orientation of the Bank, its regional counterparts, and the Fund, but early indications are that no fundamental rethinking will take place. However, one minor but important step in the right direction is that, after a lot of prodding by the environmental and development community, the administration is backing new reforms at the World Bank to set up an appeal mechanism whereby people can complain about problem loans and to provide more access to internal information.

Debt and Democracy

In the flurry of publicity and negotiations for free trade, the fundamental imbalance between rich and poor countries that has been aggravated by

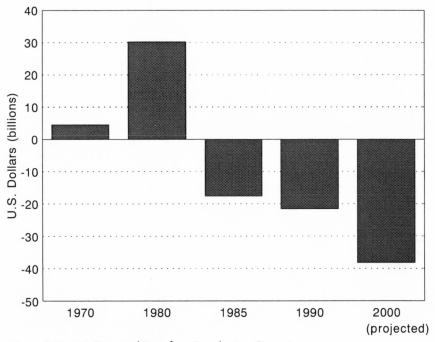

Figure 2.2   Net Financial Transfers: Developing Countries
Source: Overseas Development Council.

the debt crisis has all but disappeared from the policy agenda. The Bush administration helped kill the last serious call for a new global initiative to address the crisis—an appeal by the French government of François Mitterrand in the late 1980s to convene creditor and debtor governments to work out a coordinated debt-reduction scheme. Today, with the major private banks in a position to withstand Third World debt defaults, the Clinton administration has demonstrated no interest in taking leadership on this issue.

The administration did take a step to deal with a tiny portion of the problem by proposing that the U.S. government write off 50 percent of debts owed to it by eighteen of the world's poorest nations, mainly in Africa. However, as an indication of the reluctance of both the administration and Congress to expend much effort in this direction, these two branches of government became embroiled in a fight over the details of the scheme, with the administration offering $4 million less than Congress—a sum the *Wall Street Journal* pointed out was what "the Pentagon spends in less than a half-hour."[11]

The struggle for human rights and democracy around the world received some notable support from the Clinton administration in its first year. This struggle is relevant to U.S. interests—economic and otherwise—in at least two ways. Countries where human rights are respected and where democracy is practiced tend to be more stable. And, in countries like South Korea and South Africa, where organized labor is a pillar of the democratization struggle, enhanced worker rights lead to higher purchasing power and expanded trade.

The Clinton administration made a significant departure from the Bush administration on human rights. At the June 1993 United Nations Conference on Human Rights, the administration announced its support for a UN Declaration on the Right to Development that the Reagan administration opposed in 1986. It also declared that the United States should ratify the UN Convention on Economic, Social, and Cultural Rights, and a number of other UN agreements.

Despite these important steps toward reestablishing the United States as a law-respecting international actor, the administration failed to seize opportunities to give teeth to these concerns. By deciding not to take stronger steps after its review of trade relations with China, and by avoiding the firm linkage of worker and environmental rights to trade sanctions in NAFTA and GATT, the administration's human rights policy began to ring hollow.

Setting a New Course

If the Clinton administration is to change course in its second year in office, it must change the way it thinks about the rest of the world and about how conditions in the rest of the world increasingly influence U.S. living standards. A more realistic set of policies would begin with the understanding that the fate of our workforce is intimately tied up with the fate of 85 million Mexicans, 1.2 billion Chinese, and the rest of the world's poor. Over the next generation, corporations will drive all of our working conditions and basic standards in the same direction; the only question is whether the standards will move toward U.S. levels or the United States will continue to fall toward lower levels. The implication is that a U.S. jobs strategy must be a global jobs strategy.

At the same time, the goal cannot be to turn Mexicans and Chinese into natural resource destroyers, ozone depleters, and garbage producers on the scale of the richer three-quarters of Americans; the planet cannot sustain 6 billion overconsumers. In our country and elsewhere, incentives must be created to rebuild economies with energy conservation, alternative energy sources, and less wasteful manufacturing processes.

A bold new policy toward the rest of the world should be rooted in the principles of economic justice, democracy, and human rights.[12] The centerpiece of a new U.S. policy needs to be a fundamental shift in the kind of development that the United States and the multilateral development agencies promote in the rest of the world. The current deregulatory, free-market policies embraced by our government, these agencies, and most trade agreements offer protections for private corporations to bargain down wages, working conditions, and health and safety standards to the lowest common denominator.

Instead, we need to promote policies that enhance livelihoods in a fashion that is conscious of the ecological limits of the planet. In the words of development specialist David Korten, the goal should be people-centered development: "a process by which the members of a society increase their personal and institutional capacities to mobilize and manage resources to produce sustainable and justly distributed improvements in their quality of life consistent with their own aspirations."[13] The more governments and corporations are accountable to people and communities, the more we will have dignified jobs, healthy environments, and viable communities.

The administration is to be applauded for making the case that the promotion of democracy is crucial to U.S. interests. Yet the goal of promoting democracy needs to extend beyond support for fair elections and for democratically elected governments. Democracy also means freedom of expression, civilian control of the armed forces, a judicial system that is independent, and citizen participation in economic life and the decisions that affect their well-being. Most people in the developing world are denied this broader set of democratic norms, and the United States currently inhibits progress by promoting nondemocratic economic policies and projects through narrow trade agreements, World Bank loans, IMF programs, and arms-export policies (the United States exports more than three times the arms of its closest competitor). All of these policies must change.

The fundamental determinant of U.S. relations with any government should be that government's ability to keep its own forces from threatening, detaining arbitrarily, torturing, or murdering citizens, or from facilitating such actions by others. In addition, U.S. policy should promote economic, social, and cultural rights such as decent wages, health and education, and the political rights to assemble, speak freely, and choose one's government. Political rights and economic and social rights are equally important; the absence of one undermines the other. In order to strengthen its ability to promote human rights, the United States must welcome international scrutiny of its own performance and commit itself to specific targets in improving political and economic rights at home.

To advance democracy and human rights and to reduce global inequalities and harmonize upward without surpassing the earth's ecological limits require bold new departures in resetting the rules of the global economic game and in reversing the perverse negative flow of resources from poor to rich. A highly visible first step would be for the United States to convene a world conference to launch an integrated approach to the world economy for the elimination of mass poverty and the reduction of gross inequalities within the next generation.

Aid Reform and Debt

In the meantime, there are other steps that should be taken. Aid reform and debt reduction are central to initiatives to reduce global inequalities in a fashion that reinforces the interests of both U.S. citizens and the rest of the world. On the aid front, the Clinton administration faces two sets of institutions in need of reform: global lending institutions and the U.S. bilateral lending agency. As to the first, the economic journalist Walter Russell Mead reminds us that Keynes and Roosevelt intended the World Bank and International Monetary Fund to play key expansionary roles in the world economy.[14] Instead, during the past decade, they have become the chief enforcers of draconian austerity measures in the developing world and have overseen the yearly financial outflows from poor debtors to creditor banks and institutions.

> *"Until the World Bank shifts its approach to development, the U.S. government should make major cuts in contributions."*

The Clinton administration should take the lead to work with other donor and borrower countries to insist not only that equitable and sustainable policies be the foundations of World Bank adjustment programs but also that Bank projects incorporate significant public participation in design and implementation through regular consultation with organizations of the poor, women, peasants, workers, and others in affected areas. Many citizens groups are calling for a 1994 Bretton Woods II conference around the 50th anniversary of the Bank and Fund to address these issues and to rebuild institutions based on democratic procedures and voting rights that reflect the world of 1994, not 1944. Until the World Bank shifts its approach to development, the U.S. government should make major cuts in contributions. The same criteria should apply to our contributions to other multilateral institutions.

As to AID, the U.S. government should separate the reform agenda there from the deliberations of the National Security Council and the National Economic Council. Aid should be delinked from the vestiges of Cold War strategic alliances, and security assistance should be phased out. In addition, as we work toward more sustainable economies, one of the great new challenges of the 1990s is the overdependence of many economies, led by our own, on the manufacture of arms. We suggest serious study of a proposal by Burns Weston: the establishment of an "international weapons into plowshares agency through which the conversion of national arms industries to socially redemptive production could be facilitated."[15]

To slow environmental degradation in poorer countries, U.S. aid should also stress the need to democratize control of resources so that communities can manage them more sustainably.[16] The goal is clear: getting smaller amounts of aid—grants, not loans—to organizations that are committed to more equitable and participatory development. Viable plans already exist. The Development Group for Alternative Policies, along with fifteen other U.S. citizens groups and in consultation with organizations in the developing world, crafted a "Development Cooperation Act" three years ago.[17] The act spelled out guidelines to ensure "consultation with the poor at all stages of the development process" and new mechanisms to get aid directly to women, the landless, subsistence producers, migrants, and others who need it most and can use it best. Now is the moment to refine and implement such an act.

In addition to these plans, there have been actual experiments in getting small amounts of aid directly to citizens organizations. In the Philippines, $25 million in U.S. aid funds was approved to endow a new Foundation for the Philippine Environment through a debt-for-nature swap. Based in Manila, the foundation is run by a board composed primarily of leaders of the Philippine organizations that work on sustainable development. The board approves small grants to nongovernmental organizations, communities, and training institutions to fund new experiments in natural resource preservation, community management of natural resources, and education on the environment. Despite some tensions with the U.S. government, the foundation has begun to approve grants to worthwhile projects.

We can also learn a great deal from other nations such as the Netherlands, Canada, Australia, and Sweden that have made small amounts of aid money go a long way. The Dutch government targets its aid on poverty alleviation. It disburses up to one-tenth of these outlays through Dutch agencies that fund grassroots development initiatives directed at the poor. Part of this pays for education and training of individuals in citizens organizations to increase the participation of more of its people in the development process. Likewise, a share of Canadian and Australian aid supports sustainable development programs that are designed by Canadian and Australian citizens groups in collaboration with nongovernmental groups in the recipient countries. These programs have stressed sound ecological practices, advocacy for human rights, and the active involvement of women.

How can we pay for such aid schemes in a period of widespread economic downturn? One innovative solution comes from Jan Tinbergen, the noted economist, who calls for a large-scale global realignment of resources through an international income tax, as well as taxes on luxury durables, armaments, and natural resources, including those from the global commons.[18] Other notable ideas in the tax realm include a worldwide system of checkoffs on tax returns, by which citizens could make voluntary contributions to sustainable development funds, or an international tax of 0.5–1.0 percent a year on assets above a certain amount, say $500,000.

On the issue of debt, the administration should take the lead in an international conference that aims to reduce commercial Third World debt by at least 50 percent over the next five years and official debt by even more. Debt reduction should be delinked from World Bank and IMF conditionalities. Instead, debts should be reduced by countries repaying in local currencies into the kinds of national development endowments outlined above that have broad representation of citizen organizations. (This is the financing mechanism already used in a number of countries in debt-for-nature swaps.)

A Global New Deal

Beginning in the 1930s, as corporations extended their production and marketing networks across the continental United States, they often took advantage of the existence of poor, nonunion states to bargain down conditions in richer, more unionized states. After a long struggle between corporations and a powerful movement of organized labor, the country agreed to a new set of social standards to counteract the destructive side effects of national economic integration, including a minimum wage, maximum hours of work, and later a comprehensive set of health, safety, and environmental regulations.

In the 1990s, corporations are weaving together a global economy that in many ways resembles the United States of a half century ago. There are rich and poor countries, countries where worker rights are respected and environmental standards are high, and those where rights are abused and standards are not enforced. In short, the global economy is coming together with the absence of any coherent set of global rules to address the social and environmental disintegration that is accompanying economic integration.

While the power and mobility of large, private firms to shift jobs, capital, factories, and goods across borders has increased, the ability of our governments to ensure the basic social rights of our people has decreased. As governments find it harder to meet the employment and other needs of citizens, corporations have not been inclined to fill the vacuum. We desperately need to address this adverse shift in power and press governments to create the necessary checks and incentives to ensure that corporate activity does not undermine the common good. A new New Deal is needed, one that is global in scope.

A good place to start is North America, where a broad range of environmental, labor, family farm, religious, and consumer groups has begun to piece together a "Just and Sustainable Development Initiative for North America."[19] The initiative suggests that NAFTA be replaced by a new set of continental rules and measures, including the protection of labor rights and workplace health and safety standards. The labor-related provisions of the UN's Universal Declaration on Human Rights and conventions of the International Labor Organization (ILO) could serve as the basis for standards to be enforced by each country.

The Clinton administration would do well to study Western Europe's four-decade experience with economic integration, where development funds to poorer peripheral countries and a "social protocol" on basic worker rights have helped pull the poorer countries up toward the living standards of their richer neighbors. The key to any new North American agreement would be that violations of internationally recognized worker rights would be subject to trade sanctions. The precise composition of "internationally recognized" worker rights would be negotiated by the three countries, but they must include, at a minimum: the rights of free association and collective bargaining; the right to strike; and protections against child labor, slave labor, and all forms of discrimination. Complaints about violations of these rights could be filed by any party either to a trinational labor commission or with the administrative agencies or courts of one's own country or of the home country of the firm guilty of the infraction.[20] Penalties could be imposed on individual corporations when they use violations of labor rights to gain unfair advantage in trade.

Over time, the administration should also work with other countries to create mechanisms to raise wages worldwide as firms increase productivity. In the context of a new North America agreement, the minimum wages in the traded goods sectors of the two lower wage countries should move rapidly toward that of the highest wage country.[21] The

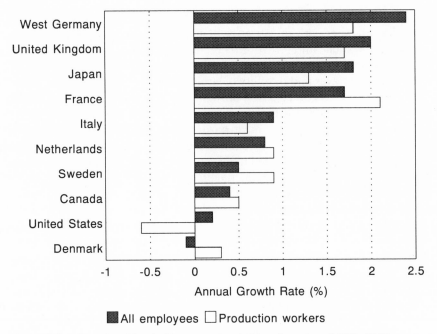

All employees □ Production workers

Figure 2.3   Growth in Hourly Compensation in Manufacturing, 1979–1989

Source: Economic Policy Institute.

United States must promote high-skill, high-wage strategies around the world if it is to help stimulate enough purchasing power among the world's hundreds of millions of workers to reinject dynamism into the world economy.

There is no international equivalent to the ILO in the field of the environment and hence no set of internationally recognized environmental standards. The trinational citizens meetings in North America have identified, as a first step in this direction, a number of basic environmental rights, such as the right-to-know and the right to a toxic-free workplace. They also propose the initiation of a process for working toward minimum regional (or international) environmental standards that would be tied to trade sanctions.

One other piece of the North American agenda that must be addressed by the Clinton administration is the movement of people across borders. Perhaps the most glaring omission in NAFTA was immigration. The rights of immigrants need to be recognized and safeguarded. As an immediate step, the administration should initiate a bilateral commission with citizen participation on violence along the U.S.-Mexican border. Such a commission could investigate the excessive use of force by border-control agents from both countries.[22] Another proposal worthy of support, advanced at a 1993 Latino Summit, is to create a trinational commission on immigration issues that could recommend policies to foster development strategies to reduce migration, protect the human and civil rights of migrants, and ensure equal treatment for Mexican and Canadian citizens in terms of entry and mobility in the United States.

Historically, most trade agreements have enhanced the capacity of corporations to shift investment and goods across borders without imposing responsibilities on firms to address the social or environmental impact of these activities. As corporations become more global, there is a need for new codes to increase the public accountability of private firms. Beginning in the mid-1970s, the United Nations began negotiating a code of conduct on transnational corporations that, among other measures, prohibited bribery of public officials, required corporate disclosure of potential dangers of products and production processes, and banned the export of goods or factories that are deemed unsafe in the home country. The Reagan administration heavily politicized the negotiations, and by the early 1990s they descended into stalemate. With the support of the Clinton administration, the process could be revived. As a first step, the administration should encourage its allies to adopt their own versions of the U.S. Foreign Corrupt Practices Act, which has been quite successful in reducing bribery by U.S. firms.

U.S. workers and consumers elected Bill Clinton a little over a year ago because he promised to focus his administration's energies on the economic woes that had become the electorate's major concern. In his first year, Clinton raised the public's hopes and then largely dashed them because he failed to create a strategy that reflected the expanding linkages that bind the U.S. economy and workforce to a shaky world economy. It has been a disappointing performance. However, there is still time for this administration to change course. Through bold initiatives on aid, debt, trade, and corporate accountability, such as those sketched above, Bill Clinton has a chance to create a global economic strategy that meets the challenges of the emerging world order.

FOREIGN
POLICY

3

Promoting
Democratic Stability

RICHARD J. BARNET

Bill Clinton was elected president on the promise to "change" the United States, but the rapid, profound, multi-directional, and often mysterious changes in the rest of the world threaten to cripple his presidency. In his first year in office the president's performance on the world stage has been wobbly, and his words and actions concerning national security, to borrow a Churchillian metaphor, so far amount to a themeless pudding.

The administration has expended little effort to assess the tectonic changes in world politics that culminated in the collapse of communism, the Soviet Union, and other multi-ethnic states, much less to develop a coherent national security strategy that takes all this into account. Although the president has continued to cut spending, the shrunken U.S. military establishment retains virtually all the missions it had during the Cold War. Yet what most of the forces will actually do in the post–Cold War world remains uncertain. There is no clear sense of American priorities, no consensus on the limits of American power, no vision of the decent world order we seek.

Yet the president seems determined to sweep away Cold War debris where it is politically feasible to do so. He extended the moratorium on nuclear testing, thanks to pressure from parts of the scientific establishment and from citizens lobbies. He recognized Angola, a former Soviet ally, and ended U.S. support for the long war to unseat the government of that country. As with Angola, there are political and economic interests to be served by the normalization of relations with Vietnam, and this too is likely to happen. In addition, Clinton played a constructive role in dissuading the Guatemalan army from openly taking power by threatening trade sanctions, and he facilitated a major breakthrough in Arab-Israeli negotiations.

The president also took leadership in mobilizing capital contributions for Russia. But whether the money will be well spent is dubious. The gifts come burdened with largely ideological "free market" ideas that produce immediate pain for most Russians, and the untested advice of foreign advisers is unlikely to produce the miraculous transformation of the shattered Communist system the experts promise. The actual flow of funds has been slow, and donor nations have not taken concerted action to discourage the rampant pirating of Russian assets by former Soviet bureaucrats and foreign entrepreneurs.

The greatest foreign policy challenge for Clinton came in Bosnia—the problem from hell, as Secretary of State Warren Christopher called it. During the campaign and in his early days in the White House, Clinton strongly hinted that he would use force in Bosnia, but he withdrew the threat in the face of European opposition. He was right to insist that any larger military intervention into Bosnia be a genuinely multilateral operation, not a U.S.-organized attack under a UN fig leaf. But the tough rhetoric that accompanied indecisive and belated action sent a disheartening message to the victims and the wrong signals to Serbia.

Other dangers that call for a strong international response are looming. More than a million Hungarians living outside Hungary are at risk—potential victims of Slovak, Serbian, and Romanian nationalism. The multiple wars on the territory of the former Soviet Union, largely driven by economic distress and ethnic politics, imperil the economic future and stability of Eastern Europe and the Middle East. And ethnic strife threatens to tear India apart. What would the United States do in these situations? Based on the experience of Clinton's first year in office, the indications are not much.

In sum, Clinton's national security policy has been mostly reactive and incoherent. The president still has time to take the lead in pushing for international strategies to prevent and resolve looming conflicts. But so far at least, the historic opportunity that George Bush missed is still being missed.

Being in Touch with the Times

By what criteria should a citizen judge the president's handling of national security? Three come to mind. How accurately does he assess the most significant trends in world affairs? How sensibly does he set the nation's priorities? How well does he understand and meet the challenges posed by political, economic, and military developments beyond our shores?

Bill Clinton has had the good luck to come to the presidency at a time of major transition. True, the dangers are less familiar, and American resources much more limited than at the last great transition in the years immediately following World War II. But Clinton has the opportunity to be an important world leader, if only because of the significant lack of leadership throughout the world. The president of the United States can no longer single-handedly design a new international system, as was virtually the case in Truman's day, but he can be the prime mover in focussing attention and energy on what is now a global crisis.

> *"Clinton has the opportunity to be an important world leader, if only because of the significant lack of leadership worldwide."*

Unfortunately, Clinton has had the bad luck to arrive at the White House when much of Europe is in recession, Japan's boom has collapsed, and the effects of a prolonged world economic slowdown are felt almost everywhere. If ever there was a time for coordinated policies to get the world economy moving and to head off trade wars, it is Clinton's time in the White House. "It's the *world* economy, stupid" would be a good slogan were the administration still in its cocky phase. But the risks of failure are awesome, and there is little in Clinton's experience to prepare him for the job. To orchestrate major policy changes requires clarity of purpose and fierce determination, and these are not exactly the character traits he has most convincingly exhibited.

The president has the exciting but hazardous responsibility of developing long-term strategies for fundamental changes at the global level needed to enable the structural changes in the United States he promised the American people. Crucial to any such strategy is a serious dialogue with the American people about how changes at the global level are needed to confront the mounting insecurity in their own lives. As at the dawn of the Cold War, when public support for a militarized, interventionist strategy was built on a shared understanding of a common peril, a new vision of the world we seek must rest on a shared understanding of what is happening around us. Such a dialogue involves risks, however. As in the Cold War, the pressures to capture subtle realities in sound bites—to make things clearer than truth, as Dean Acheson put it—can produce hysteria, despair, or other public reactions that inhibit the execution of sensible policies.

But without communicating at least the contours of a vision based on an understanding of new global realities, the president will not have the political support to do more than react to those political figures across the world whom we characterize as upstarts, troublemakers, and terrorists. (The bombing of Baghdad in June, an inhumane, futile act that advanced the national interest in no way the administration could explain, provided the president with only a momentary boost in the polls.) The increasing unease Americans feel about the chaotic new world will be exploited by the Doles, Perots, and Kemps who are waiting to wrest the banner of change from a floundering president.

In his inaugural address, the president alluded to the increasing entanglement of the U.S. economy with the world economy. He did not say clearly, however, that these changes are so pervasive that nation-states everywhere are not what they were. Leaders of nation-states are losing much of the control over their own territory they once had because more and more they must conform to the demands of the outside world. The outsiders are already inside the gates. Powerful business enterprises that routinely operate across borders are linking far-flung pieces of territory into a new world economy that bypasses all sorts of established political arrangements and conventions. Tax laws intended for another age, traditional ways to control capital flows and interest rates, full employment policies, and old approaches to resource development and environmental protection are becoming obsolete, unenforceable, or irrelevant.

Take one example: Every day an estimated $150 billion in U.S. government bonds changes hands across a global computerized trading network that virtually never stops. As of November 1993, the U.S. government owed $2.7 trillion in long-term Treasury obligations to private investors, 17 percent of whom live outside the United States.[1] Since the nongovernmental bondholders are free at any time to sell millions of dollars of U.S. securities literally in seconds, they hold enormous power over the economic decisions of any president. As early as the transition, Clinton was made acutely aware that, as Robert Hormats, vice-chairman of Goldman Sachs International puts it, "the global bond market can be a very tough disciplinarian."[2] The president was forced to give up an essential component of his job-creation program because bondholders were in a position to kill it by unloading their Treasury obligations.

For the United States, as for every other country, the price of economic integration has been a loss of political autonomy. For years managers of the U.S. economy assumed that because America was the flagship of the world economy, indeed the printer and prime manager of the world's reserve currency, the country was relatively free to tune its own economy by raising and lowering taxes and adjusting interest rates. But by the mid-1980s, crucial decisions that were traditionally the exclusive province of the president and the Federal Reserve Board were now being held hostage to international pressures. With the demise of the Soviet Union, the United States has lost much of its influence over major competitors who no longer act as if they need a protector.

It is no coincidence that the leaders of Britain, Germany, Japan, Italy, and the other major industrial countries also face severe domestic political problems. As the twentieth century draws to a close, much of the official truth that sustained and guided governments for fifty years or more has collapsed and new practical political visions are in short supply. The repudiation of socialism is of course the most spectacular ideological turnabout of the 1990s, but the inevitable intrusions of a world economy over which national governments exercise diminishing control have drained other established political orthodoxies of meaning and power. Like Leninism, Keynesianism also was premised on the idea that national economies were real. Within the borders of a nation-state, at least within militarily powerful, advanced industrial nations, the state could provide economic stability, development, and social progress.

But in the new global environment, it is as yet unknown what it takes to manage a successful national economy to achieve stability and growth without destroying people, crushing their spirit, or wrecking the ecosystem. Political programs can stimulate short-term booms, but all across the political spectrum long-term economic management has become a mystery since nothing quite works as theory suggests. Juggling interest rates, adjusting exchange rates, and raising and lowering taxes all produce unwelcome surprises. In large measure this crisis is the result of growing tension between the most powerful economic units—global corporations able to exploit their mobility and distance themselves from the problems of any given piece of real estate—and local businesses, workers, and citizens who are rooted in a particular place.

Ironically, at the very historical moment when the vulnerabilities of the nation-state as an institution have become increasingly evident, every major industrial nation is turning inward. The United States took on self-described "world responsibilities" in the Cold War years, and the simple ideological framework offered off-the-rack policies that could be applied anywhere in the world. If the Kremlin disapproved, it was almost certainly a good thing to do. Clinton is the first president in more than forty years without the ideological security blanket of the Cold War. But because of his limited experience, the pressures of domestic politics, and the crises other major powers are facing, the president, despite sweeping Wilsonian rhetoric about democratizing the world, appears committed to a Fix America First policy that cannot work.

Why the artificial separation of domestic policy (economics) and international security policy (politics) will not work can be seen by looking at the job crisis. In the election Bill Clinton zeroed in on the plight of the American "middle class" and promised that an activist president would "renew" the economy and reward the voters with good jobs. The global system for producing goods and services requires a growing population of consumers with enough money in their pockets to keep expanding a global production system that is more and more dependent on mass consumption. But job destruction and the depressing effects on wages around the world are producing exactly the opposite result. Even in the United States 18 percent of the work force works forty hours a week or more for poverty-level wages.[3]

> "Clinton is the first president in more than forty years without the ideological security blanket of the Cold War."

As the organization of the world's work shifts, more and more of us— from waste basket emptiers to chief executive officers of multinational corporations—are realizing that we are swimming in a global labor pool. What we have not faced is the reality that at least 47 million more people are jumping into that pool every year.[4] Just because we have lived and worked in Connecticut all our lives is no guarantee that our Connecticut-based employer will not hire a Malaysian or a Russian to do our job. For years people in poor countries all over the world who sew, punch data, and assemble radios for pennies an hour have been successfully competing with Americans for jobs. But now actors, cameramen, engineers, lawyers, biologists, and medical researchers too can be hired in Ireland, Russia, Singapore, Hungary, China, or India for a fraction of a U.S. salary.

The global job crisis is so profound that all currently fashionable nation-state based strategies for creating jobs seem puny, perverse, or beside the point. At the same time fear and confusion about unemployment keep governments from initiating sensible national security policies, including environmental policies that are at the heart of any search for security in the twilight of the twentieth century. The spread of

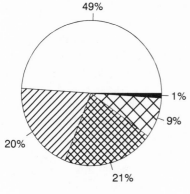
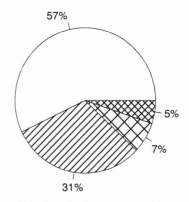

1991 (% of all agreements)   1992 (% of all agreements)

☐ United States ▨ W. Europe* ⊠ Russia ■ China ◩ All Others
*France, UK, Germany, Italy

Figure 3.1   Arms Transfers to the Third World

Source: Congressional Research Service.

weapons around the world is making the planet ungovernable because the great powers regard overarmed societies that are coming apart as too dangerous and expensive to police. Hence the impotent hand-wringing over Bosnia. Yet no government, including the "sole remaining super-power," is taking any initiative to stop the arms traffic or prohibit weapons production. Because there are no serious international efforts to promote conversion of weapons production, the Czech Republic, despite its 1990 pledge to end arms exports, has sold arms to Nigeria and Pakistan and is contemplating the shipment of advanced equipment to Iran.[5]

The dollar cost of continuing weapons traffic may not be calculable, given the secondary and tertiary effects of even small wars fought with advanced weapons, but politicians everywhere have a pretty good sense of the number of jobs lost by reining in sales. (The already projected cuts in the U.S. military budget will cause the loss of 1.9 million jobs by 1997, according to calculations by the Bureau of Labor Statistics.)[6] The fact that sensible reinvestment and industrial conversion strategies to meet a host of private and public needs could eventually create many more jobs than are lost is cold comfort for politicians facing an election this year or next. The choices are much the same with respect to the environment: water, air, trees, and fish are routinely traded for jobs—disappearing jobs in many cases.

The worldwide job crisis threatens not only global economic growth but the international system itself. President Clinton proposed a summit on the global job problem, a good idea if only to heighten public attention. Such a forum should be seen as the beginning of a long dialogue to address some very basic questions. Contemporary society is built on a social system in which the individual's livelihood, place, worth, and sense of self are increasingly defined by his or her job, but at the same time the jobs are disappearing. The anger and despair this breeds is a major spur to violence for millions of young people without prospects or hope who have nothing to lose by living dangerously and taking revenge on societies that have no place for them. Joblessness and poverty trigger hopelessness and social dissolution; all four are root causes of the violence within nations that is becoming a global epidemic. Unless these security problems we traditionally classify as "economic" issues are confronted collectively by the members of the United Nations, and with great urgency and energy, the classic security threats that now baffle and embarrass the great powers—military aggression and civil strife—will escalate and doom efforts to achieve either domestic renewal or a more peaceful world.

The Requirements of Peace

The Clinton administration proclaims democracy and human rights to be central tenets of its foreign policy. This is commendable but as the Bosnia fiasco makes clear, high-flying rhetoric about democratizing the world can backfire by raising hopes that cannot be realized. Before democracy can be promoted, much less enforced, it must be better defined and understood.

The idea that the United States is in the business of spreading democracy was a keystone of Cold War propaganda, even when Cold War policy required the unswerving support of anti-Communist dictators.[7] By and large, the official U.S. definition of democracy is limited to political participation in free elections and the absence of political prisoners. These are vitally important issues, but there are other issues that are equally decisive in shaping the character of a regime: the treatment of women, ethnic and religious minorities, and poor people; the state of public health; job opportunities and conditions of work; and income distribution. These fundamental human rights issues often spark domestic violence that spills over borders. Neither governments nor footloose corporations around the world are taking responsibility for the disastrous human rights consequences of global competition to eliminate work and shave payrolls.

Although there is an urgent need for new understandings of political and economic rights, their intimate connections, and how they can be enforced, this will be difficult to achieve, as the recent United Nations

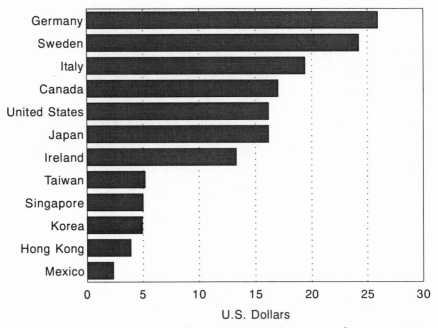

Figure 3.2 Hourly Compensation for Production Workers in Manufacturing, 1992
Source: Bureau of Labor Statistics, U.S. Department of Labor.

conference on the subject makes clear.[8] Wages in the United States will continue to be driven down by cheap labor and inhumane working conditions in other countries unless standards in those countries are raised. But poor nations that base their economic future increasingly on foreign trade, often under pressure of the industrial countries, the World Bank, and the International Monetary Fund, resist the imposition of international labor standards as a device to keep their cheaper goods out of international markets and to reinforce the inequalities between the developed and the developing nations.

To its credit, the United Nations has focused more on the rights of women and children in recent years. Yet progress toward broader and more enforceable human rights standards is unlikely without new rules of the game for world trade and investment. Large areas of the world are now being drawn into an increasingly integrated world economy on terms that are heavily stacked against them. In such a situation the only comparative advantage such nations have is their appallingly underpaid and unsupported labor force. Unless international efforts are made to boost the economies of poor countries where billions live, their governments will not cooperate in a global regime in which their selling of cheap labor in one form or another can be used to block their access to foreign markets.

The end of the Cold War removed the lid that discouraged secessionary wars. We do not know how much racial, ethnic, and religious violence was bubbling under tightly controlled Communist regimes, but there is evidence that cohabitation of Croats, Serbs, and other ethnic groups worked reasonably well. One reason is that for almost fifty years multi-ethnic states such as the former Yugoslavia, the former Czechoslovakia, and the former Soviet Union preserved the appearance at least of being viable economic and social entities. But once the system collapsed and the unifying ideology was discredited, more people began to define their relevant community by race, by religion, or by shared memories and legends of the enemies they had in common. The national capital became the symbol of discredited politics, of cultural repression and religious persecution, and of disillusionment with "scientific" secular answers to their needs.

Frightened, confused people around the planet who become accomplices of demogogic leaders in crusades against "infidels" and murderous campaigns of "ethnic cleansing" are a small minority of the world population. But in the absence of an effective international response ethnic and religious zealots are wielding great power. Not only Serbian nationalists but also Muslim extremists and Hindu fundamentalists in India (who have vowed to wipe out the more than 100 million Muslims in that country) are reviving the politics of religious and racial extermination. Concerted efforts to deal with the underlying economic and political causes cannot now save Bosnia, but they are essential to any strategy for containing the spread of violence and for creating the conditions for effective protection of vulnerable individuals.

The desperate economic plight of large areas of the world now effectively written off by the great powers requires a global response. Otherwise, the breakup of nations will accelerate and so will the violence that invariably accompanies this process. War prevention is cheaper than war-fighting. The fact that ethnic and religious violence is pronounced in countries such as India and Iran that have experienced significant economic development in the past forty years should not mislead us. It is precisely such countries where the development process dramatizes the growing gap between winners and losers in the struggle over modernization that offer fertile ground for brutal backlashes against cultural penetration of the West and humiliating memories of foreign domination.

Is self-determination a human right? Over the years there has been much confusion about this. Throughout the Cold War the issue was prominently employed as a weapon in the superpower struggle. In the early years there was strong bipartisan support for "captive nations," some of which had never been independent nations. Others, including the Baltic states, were hasty creations of the peacemakers at Versailles in 1919, small chunks of land in which the United States had no strong interest, except as an issue to exploit in propaganda leaflets. After years of nervousness that global human rights standards could be used by its enemies to whip the United States over its own vulnerabilities on matters of racial justice, the Carter administration took the initiative to make human rights a visible issue on the world agenda, but it did not support national self-determination for the Eritreans, the Kurds, or anyone else. For a few ideologues in the Reagan and Bush administrations the breakup of the Soviet empire was a passionate goal, but it was never U.S. policy to favor the multiplication of nations through division until after it began happening. The Bush administration, as the president made clear in a 1991 speech in Kiev, supported Gorbachev's efforts to hold the Soviet Union together.[9] (In the twilight days of the Soviet Union, the Bush administration showed considerable reluctance to recognize Lithuania, Latvia, and Esthonia as independent states.) As the system collapsed and the empire fell apart, self-determination became a battle cry, especially on the right, but little thought was given to where the unraveling of Soviet Europe might lead.

What does Bosnia tell us about what should be done in the future to satisfy self-determination claims? Over the past two centuries leaders of the great powers have been creating and recreating nations, drawing borders in French, German, and Austrian palaces for distant countries of which they knew little. It is not a record we should wish to continue. There are several reasons why U.S. policy should discourage, not celebrate, ethnic and religiously based states. In a globally integrated world multi-ethnic and multi-religious states are unavoidable. Our own ideology proclaims the richness of a multi-racial polyglot society, although the experience of racial minorities within our midst often mocks our beliefs. William Pfaff correctly argues that the idea of the ethnic state, a nineteenth-century Romantic extravagance, is a most reactionary notion because "it is a permanent provocation to war."[10] The Serbian leader Slobodan Milosevic, like the Austrian with pan-German dreams who started World War II, uses ethnicity as an excuse to gather into the fold blood brothers or fellow communicants who are living in other countries. Those who have chosen to live in the targeted regions or have been forced to live there as a result of wars fought long ago are turned into "spies and prospective insurgents." They then become victims of persecution by their own anxious government simply because a foreign demogogue has designated that government to be an enemy from which they must be liberated.

Multi-racial, secular communities can work, however, only if the rights of minorities are protected. There are many ways this can be done short of breaking up countries into ethnic enclaves. Indeed, many countries around the world protect their minorities tolerably well. But international law guaranteed by legitimate international authority is also needed to deter regimes that persecute minorities. There is no international authority with the legitimacy or effective power to redraw boundaries, but under its Charter the United Nations does have a credible role to play in the enforcement of the principle of peaceful change.

Wars for Peace?

The whiff of genocide is in the air, and the great military powers of the world are immobilized. But neither callousness nor cowardice is an adequate explanation. In the anarchic post–Cold War order the problems in using force in pursuit of legitimate political objectives without causing unacceptable harm are immense. The Somalia intervention is an important illustration of the difficulties. The moral case for intervening against warlords stealing food intended for a starving population was clear, provided one accepted the claim that there was no alternative. (This claim some of the relief agencies on the ground disputed.) The military terrain and the balance of forces seemed favorable to a quick and successful limited mission. But the mission could not achieve its objective of protecting the population from the warlords unless it disarmed them or paid them off on a grand scale; they were prepared to hide their weapons and bide their time until the UN forces left. After a Somali leader ambushed UN forces, Clinton was pushed into a retaliatory air attack on Somalia in the name of the United Nations. The lightly armed UN forces suddenly became belligerents, losing much of their legitimacy, which was based on neutrality. A few American casualties were announced and a debate erupted over whether the United States should stay in Somalia.

Two conclusions should be drawn from the incident. First, armed contingents flying the UN banner should not be put into such situations without sufficient means to defend themselves and the people they are sent to protect. To be forced to stand by while civilians are being raped and murdered in a territory they are supposed to be policing sends a message of impotence and hopelessness; it insures that they will not be taken seriously. Second, the idea, which some are calling the Clinton Doctrine, that U.S. airpower provide the military clout to back up a largely non-U.S. ground force under the UN flag should be reconsidered. It virtually guarantees that the United States will be blamed for the escalation of violence on the ground. Precision bombing is mostly a myth, and Americans will be killing civilians from the relative safety of high-flying planes and will also bear responsibility for the killings that local authorities order in retaliation.

Table 3.1   Current UN Peacekeeping Operations, May 1993

Name	Rough Annual Cost	Current Strength
Truce Supervision Organization (Israel)	$31 million	224
Military Observer Group in India and Pakistan	$70 million	38
Peacekeeping Force in Cyprus	$19 million	1,519
Disengagement Observer Force (Golan Heights)	$36 million	1,116
Interim Force in Lebanon	$146 million	5,227
Iraq-Kuwait Observation Mission	$65 million	3,645
Angola Verification Mission II	$36 million	103
Observer Mission in El Salvador	$34 million	380
Mission for the Referendum in Western Sahara	$35 million	1,603
Protection Force (former Yugoslavia)	$1,020 million	24,197
Transitional Authority in Cambodia	$1,002 million	19,628
Operation in Mozambique	$210 million	6,164
Operation in Somalia II	$1,550 million	16,446

Source: United Nations

Many situations that cry out for humanitarian intervention are not susceptible to policing. The restoration of order in the short term requires a willingness to fight a ground war and to take responsibility for the casualties, the destruction, the costs of reconstruction, and ultimately the remaking of the nation. In many cases such a course would be a replay of tragic history. There may be situations so compelling as to justify such radical action, despite all the warnings of history, but military force can only work in conjunction with a clear political and economic strategy that is widely understood and widely supported. Of course any police force must be prepared to take risks, but sending an ineffective force into danger to relieve a nation's sense of collective guilt is neither morally acceptable nor politically rational.

It is ironic that the United States has come much closer to accepting the military provisions of the UN Charter at the very moment in world history when the political limits on the use of force by established powers to stop military aggression are becoming more apparent. Many of the assumptions that governed the amassing of armaments, the relationship between force and diplomacy, and the domestic political support for the use of force all during more than sixty years of global hot and cold war no longer apply in the disorderly world now emerging.

The United States employed massive force in World War II to crush the Axis powers, occupy their territory, and help reconstruct their societies. In the Cold War years the preponderance of U.S. military power served two primary functions. One was to deter the use of Soviet military power and to squeeze the Soviet economy by challenging it to an arms race it could not win. The other was to assume the role of protector of the Free

World, a status that for many years carried with it great influence over the foreign and domestic policies of the other industrial nations. During the Cold War years military power was also effectively used as a psychological instrument.

The greatest victories were won in wars that were never fought, notably the vaunted Soviet *blitzkrieg* into Europe that never happened, or they were achieved by nonviolent means such as the Berlin Airlift. Failures of deterrence, such as the Soviet occupation of Eastern Europe in the face of the U.S. nuclear monopoly, were simply ignored. With a few important exceptions—Korea, Indochina, and the ill-fated dispatch of Marines to Lebanon in 1982—the United States committed its forces to limited, controllable situations favorable for declaring victory and getting out. Since the prime public issue in almost every case was the threat of a Soviet takeover, direct or indirect, the defeat of the "pro-Soviet forces" in places such as Guatemala and Iran and the low number of American casualties was enough to certify that a victory had been won.

With the Cold War framework gone there are no such easy victories. The critical difference is that the criteria of success are much clearer and less subjective. In the Cold War it was enough for a president to say that he was sending troops into battle to "signal" to another country that it should watch its step or to reassure an ally. But international police operations in the postwar world are expected to produce some visible result on the ground—an end to killing and the restoration of some sort of stable political order. In the age of CNN this is not the sort of situation where victory can be declared and the troops quickly brought home for the parades. It is dangerous, frustrating, and heart-breaking work for which conventional military forces are ill prepared. The stated war aims themselves invite political trouble, because they either involve huge, open-ended commitments for which there is little domestic political support, or else limited objectives that leave the situation messy. (After characterizing Saddam Hussein as the Hitler of the 1990s and crushing his forces, George Bush left him in power because of his fear that otherwise Iran would end up as the master of the region.)

It is hardly surprising, therefore, that the U.S. military is unenthusiastic about intervening in wars in mountainous terrain to remake the map of Europe. The domestic political hyperbole that was used to gather broad public support for two world wars and a forty-five-year-long Cold War is not available to mobilize opinion in favor of humanitarian military intervention into Bosnia and Georgia, much less Cambodia and Liberia. From Woodrow Wilson to George Bush the case for intervention depended on painting the target leader as some sort of physical threat to the people and territory of the United States. The Kaiser would be marching down Main Street, Woodrow Wilson's propagandists insisted, if Americans did not buy Liberty Bonds. Hitler would be in Kansas,

Franklin Roosevelt hinted darkly to an audience in Topeka in 1940, if the United States did not move toward war. Do we want to fight the Communists in Indochina or San Francisco, Lyndon Johnson asked in many different ways. Nicaragua is only a day and a half journey from Texas, Ronald Reagan continually reminded us as he sought support for the Contras. But now for the first time in this century neither the threat of World War III nor a full-scale military attack on the United States is convincing. This political reality helps to explain why the top military brass exhibit all the symptoms of the Vietnam Syndrome, while many liberal politicians and columnists without the same responsibilities offer armchair battle plans on where and how to bomb.

But while the perception of danger is lower, the physical threat to the territory of the United States could actually turn out to be greater than it was in the Cold War. The danger of nuclear armageddon has receded, but most of the bombs remain. In an increasingly anarchic world the possibility that someone somewhere will explode a nuclear bomb in anger is increasing. Control over the nuclear warheads on the territory of the former Soviet Union is less secure. Political leaders in Ukraine, Belarus, Kazakhstan, and Russia face economic pressures to aid other countries to develop or acquire such weapons in return for desperately needed cash. Individual nuclear scientists face some of the same temptations. Indeed, there are a number of indications that since the end of the Cold War nuclear technology is spreading to Iran and other countries with which the United States has poor relations. The breakup of Cold War alliances, the inward-looking postures adopted by the major powers, and the anarchy and confusion that characterize contemporary international politics are creating fertile ground for adventurous leaders and political terrorists. It is a time when small nations or breakaway groups with little to lose are becoming more audacious in challenging a global status quo they believe to be stacked against them. But neither amassing nor distributing arms nor demonstrations of military might are likely to have much deterrent effect in such situations.

Toward Real Security

Although he gave hints during the campaign that he was engaged in trying to understand the new world he wished to help lead, President Clinton's performance as educator and mind-changer has been underwhelming. Seizing the bully pulpit to enlist public support for new ways of looking at politics was the only way to build presidential power, especially for a largely unknown politician elected with 43 percent of the vote, and it remains the only way he can make the enormous changes that are needed to move the nation toward real security in the twenty-first century.

It is obvious that nothing could enhance the security of the American people more than a strong national policy aimed at controlling weapons proliferation. A world awash in arms is not policeable by anyone, whatever color helmet the force wears. Tens of thousands of nuclear weapons are still spread around the world, any one of which could cause unprecedented catastrophe if exploded. Since nuclear technology is already widely shared, the greatest hope for controlling the nuclear danger is that political leaders, would-be political leaders, and criminals become convinced that the advantages of nuclear weapons are illusory and the disadvantages are real.

> *"Nothing could enhance the security of the American people more than a strong national policy aimed at controlling weapons proliferation."*

This requires changing the political culture, and it can be done only if the present nuclear powers take major steps to reject nuclear weapons as instruments of diplomacy and to change military doctrine and deployment to make it clear that these are not militarily useful or legitimate weapons. It was the devaluing of nuclear weapons in the Reagan administration—the presidential mantra "Nuclear war cannot be won and must never be fought"—that opened the way to the first nuclear arms reductions. The United States and the lesser nuclear powers can further devalue nuclear weapons only if they substantially reduce nuclear stockpiles and denuclearize their forces, military doctrine, deployment, and rhetoric. Clinton's extension of the moratorium on nuclear testing was a good step but hardly enough.

President Clinton can craft an appropriate new role for the United States by taking leadership in a concerted effort to stimulate the world economy and to reverse growing economic disparities that breed disorder and violence. He should propose an agenda for new policies to promote global growth that would close the widening gaps in labor standards and minimize the adverse environmental impacts.

A new Bretton Woods agreement to provide new rules of the game for the international economy is urgently needed to head off trade wars within the industrial world, to control unregulated capital flows that exceed $1 trillion a day,[11] and to address the mounting economic distress in Africa and much of Latin America and Asia, all of which pose a serious obstacle to economic growth and threaten political stability.

An international agency to offer technical advice and to help finance and monitor the conversion of armaments is needed to break the dangerous and expensive addiction of so many countries, including our own, to weapons production and arms sales. The operation could be financed by diverting a percentage of current military budgets, which now support forces and missions that no longer make sense.

The International Atomic Energy Agency should be given adequate powers to police nuclear proliferation and clandestine traffic in nuclear arms and technology. A parallel agency should be given jurisdiction over the enforcement of conventional arms control agreements.

A permanent UN military force as contemplated by the UN Charter should be established, but it should be deployed only in situations where its symbolic authority and its use of primarily nonviolent means are likely to be effective. The United Nations should not be a belligerent.

The legitimacy of the United Nations can be strengthened by directing greater resources into the development of peace-building functions such as health, education, water management, and environmental protection. Permanent membership on the Security Council should be opened up to include Germany, Japan, and other nations so that the body can reflect the real world. The veto—an undemocratic mechanism—should be ended after a trial period under the new arrangements.

Any large-scale war for peace will, in any event, be conducted by an ad-hoc coalition of forces with or without UN blessing. However, the overwhelming lesson of the twentieth century is that wars to restore peace are likely to breed new wars. The religious faith in war as the ultimate source of security runs deep. The perception that nuclear deterrence worked for almost fifty years has surrounded faith in war preparation with the aura of science. But the bipolar world that made nuclear deterrence plausible no longer exists.

No political leader can produce the cultural shift we need for the survival of the human race. But if Bill Clinton were willing to talk honestly about the bankruptcy of the war system in the twenty-first century and put the prestige of his office behind economic and political strategies for a legitimate world order, he could make an historic contribution.

NATIONAL DEFENSE

Meeting Real Security Needs

ROBERT L. BOROSAGE

As a candidate for president, Bill Clinton called upon the nation to seize the possibilities posed by the end of the Cold War. "We have a historic opportunity," he proclaimed in his campaign manifesto, *Putting People First.* "The human and physical resources we once dedicated to winning the Cold War can now be rededicated to fulfilling unmet domestic needs." Clinton pledged to transfer savings from defense, "dollar for dollar," into "investment in the American economy."[1]

Unlike his opponent George Bush, Clinton seemed to appreciate the momentous challenge facing the country. The end of the Cold War, like the end of all great wars, is a crossroads in history. Fundamental choices must be made. For the United States, a key question is one of national priorities: With the evaporation of the Soviet threat, is the United States prepared to shift resources from the military to needs that have been too long ignored?

The stakes are immense. The country that watched in amazement as the Soviet Union collapsed has itself been sapped by the long Cold War. Under Ronald Reagan, the United States experienced the largest peacetime military build-up in history. In that period the United States spent roughly $8,700 on the military every second, while it slashed domestic spending and doubled the national debt.[2]

As a consequence, the cost of the investments not made and the needs not met is considerable. Inequality in the United States has reached record extremes. One child in five grows up in poverty and one adult in five is functionally illiterate. Our roads and bridges are in serious disrepair, adding thousands of dollars to the cost of doing business in America.

The need to reorient our priorities is no less great abroad. As the mists of the Cold War lift, the dawn of the postwar era has been dimmed by mounting unemployment, mass migration, and ethnic violence. Without a significant shift in priorities, the United States will find it difficult to galvanize support for the global initiatives necessary to ease the wrenching transition of the East or the growing desperation of the South.

The American public, moreover, is looking for dramatic change. By 1992, polls showed that most Americans thought the country was on the wrong track. Their choice of the little known governor from Arkansas over the experienced George Bush reflected that view. Bush credibly managed the Soviet collapse, German unification, and routed Saddam Hussein but offered no vision for the future. He had little interest or insight into the economic and domestic policy concerns that Clinton had mastered. In contrast Clinton made himself the messenger of "change," pledging a strategy to meet the new challenges to the nation's security. Now, at the end of Clinton's first year in office, there is a real danger that the president will squander the very historic opportunity that made his accession to the White House possible.

The Clinton Program

Once in office, Clinton announced his "Vision of Change for America," widely hailed as a bold, new economic plan. He called for $170 billion in new investments and tax incentives over four years, though these would quickly be overshadowed by his $500 billion deficit-reduction plan. The entire package was to be paid for by taxes, primarily on the rich, and by spending cuts, primarily from the military. Clinton's military plan sought $88 billion in savings over four years from the Bush projections.[3]

In the fall, Defense Secretary Les Aspin completed his "Bottom Up Review" of the U.S. defense posture. This was billed as the first comprehensive, threat-based review of military missions, doctrine, and budgets since the collapse of the Soviet Union. Aspin emphasized the wrenching adjustment the U.S. military would be required to make, including a budget projected to be 40 percent lower by 1998 than its Cold War heights.[4]

The armed services were said to be reeling from the scope and the pace of the cuts and reforms. Pundits worried that the defense cuts went too far, too fast. Conservative Democratic legislators warned about the return to a "hollow military." Republicans assaulted the administration, claiming, in the words of Senate Minority leader Robert Dole, that "Democrats under the leadership of President Clinton want to gut defense."[5]

Headlines broadcast the Labor Department announcement that an estimated 2 million defense-related jobs would be lost from 1987 to 1997.[6] Communities from Newport News, Virginia, to Oakland, California, were hit by base closures—with more yet to come. Economists noted that the loss of defense jobs was slowing the recovery. To address the fears of defense workers and communities, the president travelled to a Maryland Westinghouse plant that had begun to wean itself from defense contracts. There he announced a five-year, $20 billion conversion program. "I know today," he said, "that the world's finest makers of swords can and will be the world's finest makers of plowshares."[7] Polls showed the public concerned about the severity of the cuts and increasingly worried about a world that seemed to grow more violent with each passing week.[8]

But the brouhaha was misleading. Aspin described the administration's military plan as a dramatic adjustment to the threats of the post–Cold War world. Yet Clinton's proposed cuts amounted to a mere 8 percent of the projections that the Bush administration had cobbled together when the Soviet Union was still intact.

The administration plans to spend $1.3 trillion on the military over the next five years. The annual defense budget would decline to about $250 billion by 1997 and then begin to rise again. The celebrated 40 percent cut from Cold War heights comes from a military budget that had been pumped up by 50 percent in the early 1980s. Under the Clinton plan, military spending will remain at Cold War levels for the rest of the century.[9]

This is hardly an austere budget. Some 1.4 million men and women will remain on active duty. One hundred thousand of these troops plus their dependents will continue to be stationed in Germany, standing guard against a threat that no longer exists. All told, the Defense Department will employ about seven of ten federal government employees into the next century. Each of the four service branches will maintain its own

"Under the Clinton plan, military spending will remain at Cold War levels for the rest of the century."

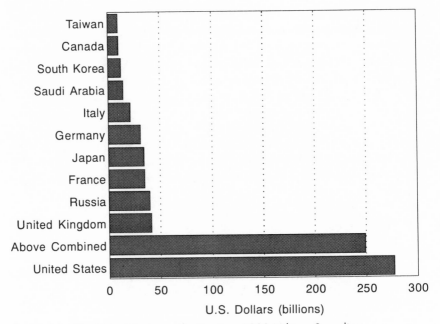

Figure 4.1   The United States vs. the Top Ten: 1992 Military Spending
Source: Campaign for New Priorities.

air force, with the Defense Department struggling to decide whether three or four new attack aircraft should be developed simultaneously. The navy is fighting to keep twelve aircraft carrier task forces, the same number it "required" throughout most of the Cold War.

Compared with the rest of the world, the disproportion is striking. The United States spends more on national defense than the next ten most costly militaries combined—and all of those either are or want to be our friends. While we plan to spend $1.3 trillion in five years, Britain, with the second largest military budget, will spend about $200 billion. Russia, Japan, Germany, France, and China will all spend less than that.[10]

Aspin touted the Pentagon review as a "threat-based" assessment but that too was misleading. The defense plan provided rationale, force structure, and weapons plans to fit the budget numbers already in the president's economic plan. As one official put it, "We're wrapping a veneer of strategy on a budget that's already been decided."[11]

The original Clinton numbers were derived more from the threat of Senate Armed Services Chair Sam Nunn than North Korean strongman Kim Il Sung. Clinton, burdened by his opposition to the Vietnam War, wanted Nunn's imprimatur on the campaign. To secure it, he agreed to limit defense cuts to $60 billion from the Bush base force plans. The additional savings in his defense plan came primarily from a lower estimate of inflation costs and the Pentagon's share of the wage freeze on government employees. In office, Clinton, at loggerheads with the military on the question of gay rights, simply did not want a pitched battle with the security establishment over budget levels.

Threat Inflation

This immense recommitment of resources to the military comes at a time when the United States finds itself remarkably free of any direct foreign military threat. As former Defense Secretary Dick Cheney, now a Republican presidential hopeful, put it, "America's strategic position is stronger than it has been in decades. ... There are no significant hostile alliances. ... [T]he strongest and most capable countries in the world remain our friends."[12] Robert Gates, Bush's hawkish CIA director, holds a similar view: "We do not expect direct threats to the U.S. to arise within the next decade."[13]

For over forty years, the military budget has been driven by the Soviet threat. Over half of the budget was devoted to the single mission of defeating a sudden conventional attack by the Warsaw Pact nations on Germany. Now the Soviet Union does not exist and the Russians want to join the North Atlantic Treaty Organization (NATO). In the words of Gen. Colin Powell, then-chairman of the Joint Chiefs of Staff, "the Red Army is no more."[14] Russian troops have been reduced to pawning weapons for food in neighborhood bazaars; last year, four Russian sailors died and dozens more were hospitalized from malnutrition.[15] According to estimates by the Central Intelligence Agency (CIA) and the Defense Intelligence Agency (DIA), even if Russia were to be taken over by a dictator, it would be more than a decade before that country could reconstitute a conventional military threat to the West.

The world, of course, remains a dangerous place. Any illusions about a new Kantian era of peaceful relations among democratic, trading nations have been quickly dashed by the spread of ethnic and nationalist violence, regional conflicts, and proliferating weapons.

Yet the United States, bounded by friendly neighbors and two oceans, is as secure from external military attack as anytime in its history. Ethnic violence in places like Bosnia poses hard questions to the international community but it requires a perfervid imagination—like Samuel Huntington's invocation of a global conflict of civilizations[16]—to transform the terrible slaughter in Bosnia into a direct security threat to the United States. As Jeane Kirkpatrick, Ronald Reagan's ambassador to the United Nations, has pointed out, "Horrible as they are, ethnic strife in Bosnia, Croatia and ... social breakdown in Somalia are not major military threats to the United States. They are not the kind of 'principal military concerns' that can reasonably determine major aspects of defense planning."[17]

Even the Pentagon strains to find justification for its budget. In their official review in 1992, the Joint Chiefs of Staff admitted that it was difficult to name a threat "without straining credulity." So they invoked the "threat of the unknown," which at least offered scope for the imagination if not for planning.[18]

During the Bush administration, the military responded to the threat of peace by becoming more active, giving new meaning to the term "volunteer forces." The army embraced drug interdiction missions that previously had been scorned; NORAD radars and jets struggled valiantly to intercept the Piper Cubs and prop planes of the drug trade while Panama was invaded in the most expensive drug bust in history. The navy volunteered help in humanitarian relief at home and abroad. The air force delivered food and medicine to the former Soviet Union. Kuwait—its oil in particular—was defended in the mother of all routs. And the marines landed boldly on the beach in Somalia in an expensive photo opportunity.

Seeking to demonstrate the point that the military was capable "of doing many, many things," General Powell brought a map to a hearing of the House Armed Services Committee to "just give you a flavor of the kind of things we have been doing over the past couple of years." The map listed fifteen military operations on five continents: "Just Cause," the bust of Noriega in Panama; Desert Storm in the Persian Gulf; "Operation GTMO," with its 1,700 troops in Guantánamo, Cuba, "caring" for Haitian refugees; drug operations in Latin America; "Provide Hope," delivering supplies to the former Soviet Union; rescue and relief missions in Zaire and Somalia; and "Firey Vigil," intimidating coup plotters in the Philippines. "Threat-based analysis," Powell contended, "is not enough for the requirements that our commitments put on our plate from day to day."[19]

In the Clinton administration, Defense Secretary Aspin argued that regional malcontents like Kim Il Sung and Saddam Hussein now drove the budget. The Aspin "Bottom Up Review" evaluated and accepted the regional warfighting scenarios that the Bush Pentagon had prepared. The mighty gorilla has been slain, testified CIA Director James Woolsey—making the case for a bigger CIA budget at the end of the Cold War—"but the jungle is filled with a bewildering variety of poisonous snakes."[20]

This is no doubt true, but since none of Woolsey's snakes has the ability to swim the oceans and strike the United States, it is far from clear why the United States need poke a stick at them. And even assuming our desire to get entangled with Woolsey's snakes, they are not potent

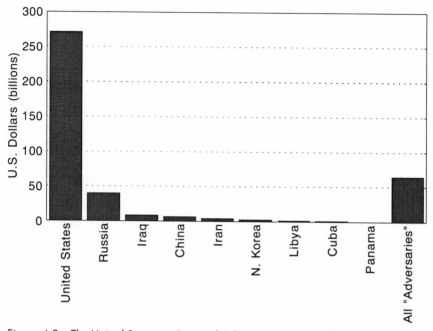

Figure 4.2   The United States vs. Potential Adversaries: 1992 Military Spending
Source: Campaign for New Priorities.

enough to justify the Pentagon's base force budget. None of the supposed adversaries spends more than $40 billion on its military, while the U.S. defense budget totalled roughly $290 billion in 1993.[21] In Desert Storm, the United States and its allies routed Iraq, with the fourth largest military in the world, in forty-three days using about 20 percent of its forces.

With not one of the regional powers that "drove the budget" sufficient to justify the force, the military chose to inflate the threats by adding them together. Aspin acceded to the military "requirement" that the United States alone be able to fight two regional wars "nearly simultaneously" (a reborn Iraq and a renegade North Korea is the most common scenario), while sustaining the capacity for a Panama-like intervention in this hemisphere, a Kurdish-level relief operation, reserve forces in the event that one of the regional wars is extended, and, of course, a "foundation" of strategic nuclear forces, continental forces, new weapons research and development, base troops in Europe, and top-level operations and training.[22]

But the Pentagon's requirements make little sense. Most of the new dangers—"major regional contingencies," or "MRCs," in Pentagonese— seem little more than the detritus of the Cold War. Desert Storm provided a force level and a mission—the defense of the feudal emirates and oil against Iran or Iraq—that no politician dare question. Yet one might wonder at the logic of spending $40 billion a year or more to keep oil cheap for Japan and Europe rather than investing in alternative energy and a sane energy policy.

Aspin estimated that over time a Desert Storm–like force would cost $90 billion a year. That would hardly sate the Pentagon's budgetary appetite. So in addition, the Pentagon designated forces to defend Europe against a reborn, aggressive Russia. Yet even in the last years of the Cold War it was clear that the Europeans were fully capable of defending themselves against the entire Warsaw Pact but were happy to allow the United States to bear much of the burden. Now with Germany united and Russia divided and isolated, it is bizarre to suggest that the United States must keep significant forces on guard to defend Europe from Russia. Even George Kennan, author of the containment policy in the early years of the Cold War, has called for the boys to come home: "The time for the stationing of American forces on European soil has passed and the ones now stationed there should be withdrawn."[23]

The standoff between North and South Korea represents another major regional contingency in the Pentagon's mind. At the dawn of the Cold War, North Korea was viewed as a Soviet and Chinese cat's-paw—a test of American resolve in the global conflict. Now the Communist monarchy is isolated and nearing collapse. South Korea has twice the population and ten times the economic production. The South Koreans maintain a standing military of over 630,000 troops that guard the most heavily defended terrain on earth. The South can defend itself against a conventional threat and President Clinton has bluntly warned the North that use of nuclear weapons would mean the "end of their country as they know it." The American conventional forces stationed there are an expensive hangover from a bygone era.

Some argue that American forces must remain on the Korean peninsula not to contain North Korea but to prevent South Korea and Japan from developing nuclear weapons. But both Seoul and Tokyo are already reassessing their policy, assuming American decline or withdrawal. With the end of the Cold War, sweeping reappraisals of security concerns are taking place across the globe. In this context, an aggressive nonproliferation policy and initiatives for sustainable growth are far greater priorities and far more likely to have an effect than the continued garrisoning of U.S. forces on the ramparts of the past. In the end, little but nostalgia and budget appetites lead the United States to station 60,000 troops and dependents in Korea and commit to reinforcements that Brookings analyst William Kaufmann estimates cost as much as $60 billion a year.

Most curious is the "requirement" that the United States maintain standing forces capable of fighting two major regional conflicts simultaneously on opposite sides of the world. This is a pure Cold War atavism, derived from the old theory that each regional conflict might be an orchestrated probe by the Kremlin. Yet even by the mid-1970s, budgetary constraints had forced Richard Nixon to move the United States from a two-war to a one-and-one-half war frame (a major war against the Soviet Union in Europe and a regional conflict somewhere else).

The new rationale assumes that a dictator like North Korea's Kim Il Sung, seeing the United States engaged in the Persian Gulf, might choose that moment to attack. But regional conflicts have their own dynamics, as violence in the Balkans, Georgia, Azerbaijan, and elsewhere has shown. They are unlikely to be either deterred or triggered by events elsewhere. A Kim Il Sung might just as easily fear that the United States would do something rash if it felt truly pressed.

It is inconceivable that the United States would actually choose to fight two major regional wars simultaneously. Consider the effort that Desert Storm required. Public, congressional, and international support were hard to rally, even with the control of oil, the sanctity of borders, and "jobs" allegedly at stake. The notion that a president would seek and gain public and congressional support for fighting a second Desert Storm on the other side of the world, with U.S. security only remotely threatened, is a planner's mad fantasy.

"In the end, the Pentagon budget rests not on the threats we face but on the imperial pretensions we have."

In the end, the Pentagon budget rests not on the threats we face but on the imperial pretensions we have. "We no longer have the luxury of having a threat to plan for," General Powell explained. "What we plan for is that we're a superpower. ... We have to remain engaged; it's expected of us. It's the role history has given us."[24] And those pretensions have thus far sustained a military budget far beyond our needs.

Opportunity Cost

President Clinton has made no serious attempt to call public attention to the wrenching transition required at home and abroad with the end of the Cold War. This failure to put forth a coherent vision and agenda for America in the world is a matter of choice, not capacity. On occasion Clinton has revealed his understanding of the historic moment. Speaking to a friendly audience at the National Education Association convention in the summer of 1993, for instance, he invoked a similar challenge of an earlier time:

> Forty-five years ago at the end of the World War II, President Harry Truman and a generation of visionary leaders realized we had entered a new age that demanded new policies and new institutions. They built NATO to deter Soviet aggression. They created international financial institutions to help to rebuild Europe and Japan and promote global economic growth.
>
> Now our generation after the Cold War must create a new vision, new policies and new agreements to enable the world's nations to prosper. ...[25]

But the president's political advisers believed that the public could not comprehend the end of the Cold War. The United States still seemed to be involved in every corner of a world ever more rife with violence. Moreover, the president had enough trouble with the military over his Vietnam dissent and gay civil rights. As in the campaign, the political advice Clinton received was to frame the administration's "stimulus package" in terms of the recession and its investment program in terms of the long-term decline of U.S. competitiveness and the failure of Reaganomics.

One result was that the investment deficit that Clinton had focused his campaign on went largely unaddressed once he assumed office. When the economy began to pick up, his token stimulus package was lost to a Republican filibuster. With no historic imperative for new investment, the president's new programs were an easy mark for Perot and Republican gibes about "tax and spend." Deficit reduction became the watchword and less than one-half of the president's very modest new investment agenda survived the process.

Clinton's program allowed for some redistribution; it raised taxes on the affluent and provided the working poor with an expanded earned-income tax credit. It also continued the trend begun under Bush for increased spending on Head Start and the Women, Infants and Children (WIC) nutrition program. But there was no meaningful relief for the cities. Real spending on education, the environment, and housing is slated to decline over the next five years. And discretionary spending will remain essentially frozen. No major commitments have been made to new public investments in mass transit, electric cars, and telecommunications. Military research and development continues to dominate federal budgeting, greatly limiting resources for the development of alternative energy, efficient manufacture, and sustainable "green" technologies that will surely dominate the markets of the future. As one Democratic bud-

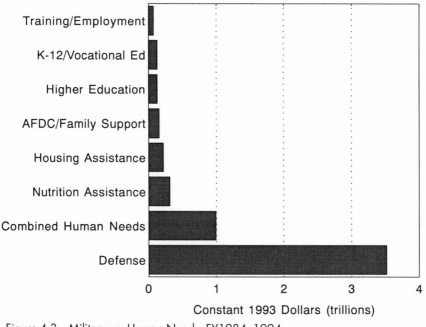

Constant 1993 Dollars (trillions)

Figure 4.3   Military vs. Human Needs, FY1984–1994

Source: Campaign for New Priorities.

get expert put it, "It's misleading of the White House to argue that there's significant additional [investment] money in the budget. Yes, they have tried to change some of the priorities, but they haven't significantly changed the amount of money for domestic discretionary spending that Bush approved."[26]

The lack of resources also crippled Clinton's conversion program. Bush had resisted planning conversion for defense industries in the belief that the marketplace would handle the problem. Clinton knew better and put aside funds to help displaced defense workers and impacted communities. Moreover, the number of workers displaced was relatively manageable. Despite all the attention given to base and plant closings, the Labor Department estimate of 2 million jobs lost over a decade amounts to about 1 percent of the workforce. The defense downsizing is slower and the layoffs relatively smaller than those that followed World War II, Korea, or Vietnam.[27]

But defense spending supports disproportionately the high-wage, high-skilled manufacturing jobs that the administration claims it wants to protect. For an administration deeply concerned about the country's manufacturing base, the conversion program thus leaves much to be desired. Most of the conversion budget is devoted to research and development to support "dual-use" technology programs controlled by the military. This money will enable contractors to get funds to keep some scientists and engineers employed but it hardly constitutes a jobs program for displaced defense workers.

The bulk of the remaining money is to be used for worker retraining, but defense workers might well wonder what jobs they are to be trained for. The civilian economy is shedding the very high-skilled, high-wage manufacturing jobs that have been lost in the Pentagon cutbacks. And the president's budget plan contained no commitment to the kind of long-term, significant public initiatives that would encourage defense firms to convert and enable skilled workers to find work: for instance, building mass transit and fast trains, creating a market for electric cars, or seeding the sustainable manufacturing techniques of the next century. If the initial results are any indication, the administration's plan may end up producing a corps of the best educated cab drivers in southern California.

Abroad, the administration's default is similarly costly. The unmet needs at home made it more difficult to rally resources for the post–Cold War transition needed overseas. The president found it difficult to pass even a shamefully inadequate aid program for Eastern Europe and Russia. The global recession—exacerbated by the convulsions and economic dislocations at the end of the Cold War—was much bemoaned but little addressed. The administration adopted a more muscular trade policy and tried to stimulate world trade talks, but bolder initiatives to restructure global financial institutions, limit currency speculation, and circumscribe transnational corporation have not yet been put on the agenda.

Instead, in its first months, the Clinton administration found itself consumed by crisis management. By trying to keep foreign policy on the back burner, it lost control of the agenda. The great problem with a $250 billion a year military is that it will find things to do and places to go, if only to look useful. By the middle of 1993, the U.S. military had 20,000 personnel in the Persian Gulf enforcing the UN embargo and two no-fly zones; U.S. naval and air force aircraft enforcing a no-fly zone over Bosnia; several thousand troops stationed in Somalia and Macedonia; special forces active in Georgia; and troops still standing guard over Germany, Korea, and elsewhere.

Ironically, the administration's caution may render its defense program more rather than less vulnerable. Hawkish defense analysts are correct to suggest that the projected force structure does not have the capacity to undertake all of the requirements the Defense Department says it must meet. Even the Bush base force lacked the transport capability to fight two full-scale regional wars at once. This need-capability gap provides explosive ammunition for a conservative assault on a vulnerable president.[28]

Present at the Creation

It is not too late for the administration to rally itself and the country to address the critical challenges of our time. Slow growth and high unemployment at home, the continuing recession in the industrial nations, the deepening crisis in the former Soviet Union, and a growing upheaval in the South provide the backdrop and impetus for a bold new set of initiatives.

> *"It is not too late for the Clinton administration to rally the country to address the critical challenges of our time."*

Without vision, the Bible teaches, the people perish. The president should begin there. He could deliver a major address that "names the age" and paints in bold colors the opportunities and the perils we face. Portraying the dangers of the global recession and upheaval, he could inspire Americans to be "present at the creation" of a new postwar order and, with the success of the post–World War II effort as inspiration, outline an ambitious reform agenda at home and abroad.

With the budget agreement setting the frame for deficit reduction, the program must begin with spending priorities. The president should reassert the pressing need to invest in areas vital to a decent society and a vibrant economy—in education and training, in twenty-first century infrastructure and communications, in sustainable manufacturing and alternative energy, in bringing our cities back to life. He should make clear the wrenching transformation that is taking place from the Cold War economy and emphasize that public investment is essential if the skills and technologies of defense workers are to be engaged in peace.

To find funds for new investment, the president needs to reopen the question of military spending. He could convene a panel of respected outside advisers—former high officials, reputable economists, business and labor leaders—to review the assumptions of the Aspin plan. The commission could provide rationale and authority for changing priorities, just as the infamous planning document, NSC-68, provided the justification for the Cold War build-up in the late 1940s.

Significant authority exists for far greater defense savings than those projected in the Aspin review. MIT scholars led by former MIT President Jerome Weisner have called for a build-down to about $115 billion over ten years. A range of establishment experts—former McNamara whiz kid William Kaufmann and, on occasion, Robert McNamara himself, former CIA director William Colby, former Reagan defense planner Lawrence Kolb—have all called for a reduction to about $150 billion a year.

A $150 billion yearly military budget is far from disarmament. It does not require a pacific world living under international law. A budget of $150 billion would sustain the most powerful military in the world. It would sustain roughly 1 million active forces, the most potent air force in existence, a navy with no rival, and the most lethal nuclear arsenal on the planet. It would be able to undertake a Desert Storm operation or contribute U.S. forces to six or seven peacekeeping operations of Somalia levels at the same time. The United States would still be spending about as much on new weapons each year as Britain does in toto for the second most costly military in the world. But it would save over $200 billion more than the Clinton plan in five years and $70–80 billion a year thereafter. Even in Washington $70 billion is serious money.

With these savings the president could fund vital domestic conversion and investments but also sow the seeds of a global "Putting People First" program for economic growth, moving away from crisis management to institution building. The president could use the global economic crisis to push for a new Bretton Woods that would restructure international financial institutions, both to expand the global economy and to limit international financial speculation. A significantly greater global initiative for investment and aid to the former Soviet Union and Eastern Europe nations is also critical.

The reduction of U.S. arsenals should be accompanied by a renewed effort to bolster and restructure the United Nations before it collapses beneath the new responsibilities it has assumed. At the same time, the administration can use its own arms build-down to push a global disarming initiative, extend the nuclear test ban, strengthen enforcement of the nuclear nonproliferation regime, and seek new restraints on the arms trade.

The world that is emerging from the Cold War faces monumental tests that have no easy answers. A dramatic change in spending priorities in the United States offers no solution to global economic displacement, entrenched poverty, growing environmental limits, and deep-rooted ethnic and nationalist conflicts. But without a dramatic change of priorities, the United States will end up expending lives and resources policing an unruly world while real security concerns are slighted at home and abroad.

Dismantling the
National Security State

MARCUS RASKIN

When Bill Clinton took the oath of office on January 20, 1993, he not only assumed responsibility for managing the nation's economic health. He also found himself in charge of a vast web of organizational structures that an Arkansas governor could hardly have imagined. As president, Clinton became head of the bureaucracy of the U.S. national security state—a netherworld of interlinked agencies that includes the Department of Defense, the Central Intelligence Agency, the National Security Agency, the Department of Energy, the Federal Bureau of Investigation, the Drug Enforcement Agency, and dozens of other entities that operate in secret and often are exempt from accountability.

As a candidate, Clinton campaigned on continuity with the past in foreign affairs.[1] He showed no interest in reexamining the labyrinthine national security state structure bequeathed to him, even though with the collapse of the Soviet Union that structure has lost most of its ideological underpinning. He showed no interest, either, in the price paid for maintaining the national security state—the costly drain on resources it imposes and the threat to democratic governance and international peace it represents. Like the moderate Democrat he is, Clinton's interest was only in making course corrections for the ship of state that he was now to direct. It was not to bring the ship of state home for an overhaul in accordance with changed global realities and new national imperatives.

Already since taking office, Clinton has endeavored to find new purposes for the instruments of the national security state. But the problems that have sprung up in the wake of the Cold War do not lend themselves readily to the "solutions" that this apparatus offers. The reasons for dismantling the national security state, therefore, are compelling. And despite Clinton's initial reluctance to take serious steps in that direction, the opportunities for doing so remain considerable.

The Roots of the Problem

The security state system Clinton inherited is not a recent invention. Its roots extend as far back into history as the founding of this nation. But the legitimation for its modern incarnation can be found in World War II, the National Security Act (NSA) of 1947, and attendant acts of that creative imperial period. It was then that the national security state was invented as the day-to-day governing structure of the United States.[2]

The term "national security" was not in fact defined in the NSA or any other piece of legislation. It was to acquire meaning through the positive action of those who had the power to introduce the term, as they rationalized their activities to themselves and to the public. Hundreds of pages of executive orders and congressional legislation protected and extended the power and authority of the national security state in so-called emergency legislation. Some of these laws and edicts no longer have validity; they were repealed after the Watergate revelations. Yet it is important to understand the original thinking behind this early Cold War policymaking since so many of the institutions it gave rise to remain in place.[3]

NSC-68, for example—the infamous policy statement of Harry Truman's National Security Council—is a textbook example of the use of the term "national security" to rally the bureaucracy and the nation behind the principle of continuous war. As Dean Acheson, Truman's secre-

---

"Clinton has shown no interest in reexamining the labyrinthine national security state structure bequeathed to him."

tary of state, put it, NSC-68 was meant "to so bludgeon the mass mind of 'top government' that not only could the President make a decision but that decision could be carried out." NSC-68 was to give the executive full sway in the Cold War; it was the articulation of what the national security state was about.[4]

The national security state was necessary, it was thought at the time, because the United States had an empire to protect abroad, known commonly as the "free world." The world itself was perceived to be in constant conflict and the national security state was to manage that conflict—fighting small wars, where necessary, while forever threatening to wage the big one. Further, the national security state would conduct covert wars as well as other clandestine activities, including bribery, assassination, and intelligence collection. And it would maintain control over the secrets of the state—variously defined—insisting, moreover, on loyalty to the cult of secrecy.

These activities were thought necessary for a number of reasons. One was the fear of rhetoric from the Soviet Union, which had cleverly expropriated the language of equality and justice to tempt the unsuspecting, including the world's poorer classes. To a lesser extent, these activities were also motivated by concern for the apparent strength of Soviet military forces, which were always inflated. According to our own political rhetoric, the Soviets were the "Enemy Other" that had to be contained or destroyed in a long battle for the soul of civilization. As NSC-68 stated:

> The Kremlin is inescapably militant ... because it possesses, and is possessed, by a worldwide revolutionary movement, because it is the inheriter of Russian imperialism, and because it is a totalitarian dictatorship. ... [It] requires a dynamic extension of authority and the ultimate elimination of any effective opposition. ... [The United States] is the principal enemy whose integrity and vitality must be subverted or destroyed ... if the Kremlin is to achieve its fundamental design.[5]

Such language ensured a huge buildup of U.S. conventional and nuclear forces without regard for the actual intentions of the Soviet Union or its own massive internal conflicts or needs.

The unspoken aim of the National Security Act was to manufacture and maintain consensus at home through internal security laws that controlled both action and speech. Such practices as loyalty oaths for government and defense workers and the classification of documents— even when there was no war—governed the nation's economic, scientific, and journalistic enterprises. Institutions of civil society such as universities, schools, clubs, banks, newspapers, radio stations, and publishing houses were informed that the geopolitical contest in which the United States was engaged required broad consensus and internal discipline. Those who were not part of the consensus could expect penalties in the form of status reduction, job loss, blacklisting, and even imprisonment.[6]

The national security state had economic justification as well. Throughout the Cold War there was a general but unarticulated belief that the United States averted deep depression and class division through the benefits of defense spending. From 1931 through 1939 the jobless rate never fell lower than 14 percent and for four years averaged 20 percent. The partial mobilization of 1940 brought the unemployment rate down to 10 percent.[7] For a generation that had lived through these experiences, there was a strong ring of truth to the economic rationale offered for the national security state.

The End of an Era

It was all of these fears and possibilities together that made the national security state a defining feature of the American nation during the Cold War. But now the glue that gave that structure cohesion is no longer there. The Soviet Union has disappeared, and the supposed need for internal consensus no longer exists. Nor can military Keynesianism any longer prime the economy the way it once did, with the defense sector having grown increasingly irrelevant to the civilian economy. Indeed, economic decline may be directly related to the *folie à deux* we conducted with the Soviet Union, accelerating the internal decay of both nations through the misapplication of public expenditures.

"The question of what to do with the national security state is not even on the political radar screen."

Now that the circumstances that gave rise to the national security state apparatus no longer pertain, the question of what to do with it is not even on the political radar screen. The original circumstances permitted the use of democracy as a fig leaf for imperial designs. Throughout the Cold War period, military force and other instruments of the national security state were used ostensibly to promote democracy—notably in southeast Asia, Panama, and Grenada. Today many assume that the "intelligence community," the military, and the structures of government formed in the past fifty years can be used in support of similar enterprises. Thus the Clinton administration has taken upon itself the task of justifying military intervention in terms of democracy and human rights.

Not only is the world substantially different today than it was in 1945 but so, too, is American society. Sexism and racism were protected by law in 1945. Virtually no attention was paid to the environment except as an object of use and plunder. In political terms the United States was not a multicultural society. The consciousness of the nation was narrow and parochial. In 1945 there were two black members of Congress and no women. Today there are thirty-nine members of the Congressional Black Caucus and fifty-five women members of Congress, most of whom do not embrace the Cold War shibboleths. This makes it possible, in principle, to reexamine root and branch the relevance or irrelevance of the national security state. Regrettably, though, there is little if any interest within the Clinton administration to undertake such an evaluation.

This reluctance may be linked to misplaced embarrassment on the president's part for having protested the Vietnam War and escaped the draft. Unlike Abraham Lincoln, who held his opposition to the U.S. war against Mexico as a badge of honor and did not fear his generals, Clinton's opposition to the Indochina war has put him at a disadvantage. He spent an enormous amount of time during his first year attempting to befriend military officers and the civilianized military. This posture led him to a most unfortunate position—negotiating openly with the Joint Chiefs of Staff over a question (gays in the military) that should have been decided directly by the president without fanfare and through an executive order. The negotiating process used by the president has only increased the military's formal role in politics, lessening his own authority as commander-in-chief and shaking the historic principle of civilian control of the military.

There is another, more direct reason for the Clinton administration's difficulties in the national security arena: the fear of economic dislocation stemming from military cuts. The administration estimates that it will eliminate $118 billion from projected defense expenditures beyond the $42 billion cuts recommended by the Bush administration over the next five years. However, the president does not have an overarching economic plan that will guarantee full employment and utilize the skills of national security workers to their full capacity. He has allocated only $18 billion in the 1994 budget for defense conversion over the 1993–1997 period—a period during which 700,000 defense workers and military personnel will be fired.[8]

The magnitude of the problem is not small, even though the defense cuts are. (The budget still makes provision for such anachronistic weapons systems as "Star Wars," the Seawolf submarine, stealth bombers,

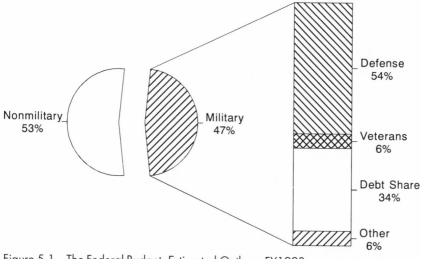

Figure 5.1   The Federal Budget, Estimated Outlays, FY1993
Source: Friends Committee on National Legislation.

and the C-17 cargo transport.) A further inhibition against cuts is that created by the institutions of defense, security, and intelligence themselves, which can be expected to play continuously on national insecurity and fears. They still hold to the original forms of imperial defense adumbrated in the 1947–1950 period. It is these assumptions that must be retired with the Cold War.

The present intelligence budget, a state secret, is estimated to be $28 billion a year, although one careful analysis suggests the figure is considerably higher.[9] Its purposes are not easily divined because of its secret nature. Missions are invented and new threats found. Thus, for example, a new multibillion dollar satellite system is being planned to eavesdrop on potentially hostile ships so that naval forces can pinpoint and interdict them. And some congressional voices have suggested that the CIA spy for American corporations, although this idea has not gained favor within the agency itself. (Throughout the Cold War CIA agents used international corporations as their cover. What benefits corporations derived from such patriotic service is not publicly known.)

These differing views of the proper role for our espionage capabilities miss the fundamental point: It may no longer be necessary or desirable, if ever it were, to monopolize the information gathered through these channels. The practice is at odds with a democratic society, which is predicated, in part, on the principle of shared knowledge. (Where knowledge and information are monopolized by the few, the democratic ideal is lost.) Indeed the very premises of the national security state are at odds with our national interests. These old assumptions keep us imprisoned in a conflict/threat mentality, which in turn limits our ability to work toward establishing a system of international cooperation. And they maintain a role for covert operations and clandestine interventions in violation of international and constitutional law. The national security system becomes the means to ensure that the nation lives in a constant state of low-level hysteria and war preparation searching for enemies, pretexts, and, of course, justifications for the national security state.

Transforming the National Security State

The United States must confront four major challenges over the next several years if it hopes to escape the chains forged in the Cold War.

The first is to identify relatively painless ways to move from a war-based economy to a civilian-based economy. The second is to change the ethos of the "intelligence community"—disbanding parts of it, opening its research to international use, and internalizing the Nuremberg war crimes judgments into domestic law. The third is to set in motion a comprehensive disarmament program of both conventional and nuclear weapons in which all nations take part. The fourth is to formulate policies that take account of the United Nations and the protean character of sovereignty, thus ensuring that groups and individuals other than states can be represented on issues from trade and the environment to human rights, transnational peacemaking, and international citizenship for the stateless. This direction is premised on the idea that what may have been defensible during war, and the Cold War in particular, is no longer either useful or warranted.

Transforming the national security apparatus will be no easy task. Soldiers, technicians, scientists, intelligence agents, and factory workers—as well as their families and their communities—are finding it very difficult to transcend the national security mentality. (At the height of the Cold War, at least 6 million people were employed directly in the business of anticommunism.) Jobs, careers, security, and status have all been part of the allure of the national security apparatus, whether the person happened to be a physicist working on "Star Wars," a welder building the Seawolf, or a spy in Thailand.

It is doubtful whether a postwar project of social reconstruction can generate the same enthusiasm and sense of national purpose and resolve as the Cold War did. It will be hard to find a moral equivalent to war in peaceful pursuits unless there is a commitment to a new covenant of equality and social and economic justice that can free up our latent spirit of cooperation and fairness. In the short term what is clear is that those who have been part of the national security system must now be allowed to benefit in ways similar to those who benefited from the GI bill, arguably the most important piece of social legislation to come out of World War II. Without such benefits millions of national security workers could become a very powerful reactionary force.

But the GI bill itself needs an overhaul. A substantial proportion of the armed forces are minorities. For them to leave the military in a period of economic stagnation would surely be against their interests. Because of the high level of racism in society this group would certainly be the hardest hit.

"A National Security Adjustment Act is needed to allay any difficulties workers will have in shifting to peacetime pursuits."

A National Security Adjustment Act is therefore needed to allay any difficulties workers will have in shifting to peacetime pursuits. It would be aimed at ending our economic reliance on armaments and the perpetuation of Cold War tasks that have outlived their usefulness. In their place would be substituted tasks identified through a national needs assessment program. The Act would seek to provide retraining, education, and technical and economic assistance to members of the national security establishment. They would be prepared for jobs that would help jumpstart a stagnant economy. The Act would also be aimed at skills-training for such pressing needs as environmental protection and nuclear and toxic waste cleanup.

The covert and clandestine functions of the CIA, moreover, should be disbanded because of the immense harm they have done over the Cold War period. Legislation should be drafted that incorporates the Nuremberg standards into American law, in particular the notion that no government official should be permitted to perform acts of war even under the orders of a superior unless there is a congressional declaration of war—and then only in accordance with accepted principles of international law. The effect of such legislation would be to ensure that international law is respected and not used as a perverse justification after officials of the state have acted illegally or criminally, as the United States was found by the International Court of Justice to have done with respect to Nicaragua.[10] It would also help national security officials develop alternative modes of behavior and encourage them to find legal, nonviolent solutions to difficult international issues. Attempts at the time of Watergate were made by a group of thirty-eight congressmen to pass such legislation. Had they succeeded, the Iran-Contra fiasco most likely would not have occurred.

Complementing this legislative initiative should be efforts to curb secrecy. Its cumulative effect on government and society is devastating since secrecy often protects illegal and criminal activity. Present levels of secrecy, surveillance, and security have taken on absurd proportions. Moreover, the intelligence comunity's purpose in a post–Cold War period remains vague, although CIA director James Woolsey seems to believe that all the "snakes" in the world ensure a continued need for the CIA. A far better use of information and communication is as an instrument for enhancing democratic control. In that context the CIA should become a public adjunct to the Library of Congress and the National Archives, with most of its files open to the public.

The National Security Agency—which, parenthetically, has no public charter—should turn its attention to problems of the environment and other basic issues relating to hunger, drought, and disease. Like the CIA, the NSA should also make its information available to the public, perhaps through the United Nations. Among other things the NSA should disclose its information about troop movements and weapons deployment. Whether the NSA should be disbanded and divided among other government institutions cannot be known because of the enormous secrecy that enshrouds its activities. Its utility can only be known if there is a public debate about its purposes and activities.

Since 1962 the idea and practice of disarmament has dropped out of the lexicons of government, universities, think tanks, and foundations. It has been replaced by the idea of arms control. Arms control represents an effort to manage the arms system; as such it is a prudent rationalizer of that system. Disarmament, in contrast, would mean actually dismantling the foundations of the national security state.

The United States is the world's largest arms dealer. It has the biggest defense budget by far. And it should have an interest in curbing the proliferation of arms worldwide because those arms contribute to profound instability and regional war. The United States should therefore take the lead in presenting an orderly plan for common security and general disarmament. Such a plan would seek, within a specified period of time, to achieve the abolition of nuclear weapons and conventional arms and the establishment of forces needed for the United Nations to properly carry out its peacemaking and peacekeeping obligations. The plan would also seek to establish an International Disarmament and Inspection Organization as part of the UN family of institutions.

There is no reason to leave disarmament entirely to the governing elites. The development of a worldwide communications network run by citizens would help ensure that disarmament is in fact taking place. Another "bottom-up" approach to disarmament would be a campaign to urge scientists and technicians to take a new Hippocratic oath and forswear work on weapons of mass destruction.

Such a program as part of an overarching strategy for general disarmament and common security would relieve other nations from the burden of armaments, a situation that very few nations can afford.

There is a chance to transform the national security state, provided the United States works toward sharing secret information with the world, ending reliance on conventional and nuclear forces, and undertaking to aid the national security workers of the Cold War. This would give American society, and other nations as well, the opportunity to redirect their efforts toward social reconstruction and the well-being of their people.

The Clinton administration has yet to propose such an agenda. Presently it only responds to and manages crises with policies and through a structure that are hopelessly out of date, antidemocratic, and often inimical to international law and human rights. If it wishes to escape the Cold War and its legacy, the Clinton administration will have to call for the revision of the National Security Act, for it reflects the assumptions and style of a time that does not fit with our present and future long-term needs. The Clinton administration has committed itself to "reinventing government." If this is to be more than a campaign slogan then President Clinton must realize that he cannot begin this task without dismantling the national security state.

DOMESTIC
ECONOMY

Investing in Our Future

GREG BISCHAK

The statistics tell us that the United States still has the largest economy and the highest productivity in the world. Americans can, on average, get more for their money than citizens of other countries. But anyone who has hit a pothole on an American highway, been delayed on an American train, lived among the bombed-out buildings of an American ghetto, or visited America's former steel and auto factories knows that our economy is in trouble. Compared with the reasonably prosperous and well-functioning societies of Europe and Japan, the United States is rapidly becoming a second-class country.

To meet the challenges of deteriorating infrastructure, stagnating growth, increasing global competition, and mounting environmental problems, the United States literally has to rebuild itself. Reaganomics unleashed the market to do this job. But a less regulated private sector has left the United States in a worse position today than twelve years ago. A different path must now be taken. To create sustainable economic growth, the American economy requires large-scale public investments. Yet the government's ability to provide that investment is constrained—both politically and economically—by a mountainous national debt that rises with each year's budget deficit.

Particularly since the end of the Cold War, military conversion has been offered as the magic wand that can simultaneously redirect billions of dollars from the Pentagon into public investments and alleviate the government's annual budget problems. Conversion is not, however, a simple technique, a cut-and-paste job that trims from defense and applies to the civilian sector. Military cutbacks are withdrawing an enormous amount of money from the U.S. economy. Jobs are being lost, entire industries such as aerospace and shipbuilding are threatened, communities dependent on defense contractors and naval bases have been thrown into chaos and despair. Conversion, in other words, can only work as part of an entirely new industrial strategy that profoundly transforms the U.S. government's role in the economy.

An astute politician with a good command of economics, Bill Clinton has certainly acknowledged the immensity of this challenge. To date, however, he has provided only marginal solutions. Even before the defeat of an economic stimulus program intended to sugar-coat the bitter pill of deficit reduction, the administration set aside too little money for meeting critical U.S. needs. This proposed public investment could not even balance the quite modest cuts in military spending the president has offered. And Clinton's conversion plans suffer from residual Cold War thinking that preserves Pentagon control over far too many resources.

A major transformation of the economy is needed to shift from debt-driven militarism to publicly supported efforts to meet Americans' needs equitably and sustainably. Clinton's approach to investment, deficits, and conversion, while heartening after twelve years of Republican-style borrow-and-spend policies, stops short of restructuring the U.S. economy to fit the global needs of the twenty-first century.

Public Investment

In his "Vision for Change" speech in February 1993, President Clinton unveiled a three-fold plan to rebuild America. He proposed a short-term job creation and stimulus program. He called for long-term public investments to increase the productivity of people and businesses. And he

---

"Military conversion has been offered as the magic wand that can redirect billions of dollars from the Pentagon and alleviate the government's budget problems."

---

offered a deficit strategy that included real reductions in military spending.

The economic strategy was subtle. The short-term stimulus would immediately boost the economy and the president's approval ratings. Over the long term, the administration assumed that the proposed $500 billion deficit reduction program would generate additional government revenues and more private-sector investment. Any short-run contractionary effects of these spending cuts and higher taxes were to be offset by lower interest rates that would stimulate business investment and consumer purchases of big-ticket items and residential housing.

The plan could not succeed, however, on subtlety alone. Political opposition emerged quickly and strongly. Congress gutted the economic stimulus package that was to have provided a temporary boost to the economy. Fiscally conservative politicians whittled $30 billion down to $16 billion and then to a few billion, leaving public investment at little more than what George Bush would have offered if reelected.

What remains after the heated budget battle of 1993 is the long-term program for economic growth, slated for 1994 to 1997. The administration has argued that public investments that enhance productivity and quality of life—on the order of $160 billion over the next four years—can have a dramatic effect on the performance of the economy. Other countries have already adopted a similar logic: Japan, for instance, increased public spending by $116 billion in 1993 alone to counteract stagnation.

This reinvestment program envisions shifting defense and discretionary savings into infrastructure and high-technology intensive fields—especially transportation, energy, and environmental restoration. In addition, new investments will be made in human resources and job training. These monies, combined with liberated scientific and technical resources, will stimulate development of new products, production processes, and markets. Not only will these investments compensate for reduced military spending, they will also improve the nation's competitiveness.

The administration is anticipating significant gains from such a reorientation. Military spending has imposed trade-offs on our budget priorities, leading the nation to make fewer productivity-enhancing public investments. The majority of federal funding—for instance, in research and development (R&D)—has gone to the military, rather than to basic research and civilian infrastructure.[1] Numerous studies have indicated that a reorientation of federal spending could generate more jobs and higher levels of economic activity.[2] Indeed, one study demonstrates that an annual transfer of $70.5 billion from the military budget to education, infrastructure, and other critical needs would generate an annual gain of nearly 477,000 more jobs on average over a four-year period. In this sce-

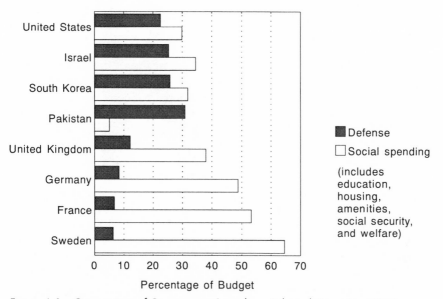

Figure 6.1   Comparison of Government Spending, Selected Countries, 1990
Source: World Bank.

nario, the gross national product would grow by an average of $17.6 billion annually.[3]

Although it relies on these sound economic judgments, Clinton's long-term approach to rebuilding America suffers from several key weaknesses. For instance, allocations for infrastructure repair will at best grow modestly, bringing the level of proposed nonmilitary investments only back to that of the mid-1970s.[4] Indeed, if the administration is to make good on its promise to rebuild America, it must triple or quadruple the increase in civilian infrastructure investment just to keep pace with its leading competitors, Germany and Japan.[5] Similarly, our share of federal R&D devoted to industrial development is so woefully inadequate that we would have to increase it forty-fold to replicate Japan's effort.[6]

Proposed new funding for alternative energy research is a significant improvement over the past but a far cry from what is needed to pioneer new technologies.[7] In the transportation field, conventional highway and auto-related technologies absorb most of the funding, leaving little for developing high-speed rail. In the Clinton budget, the military still controls 58 percent of proposed federal R&D—an increase of 1 percent from fiscal year 1992.[8] While the Clinton administration pledges to reverse the shares of military and civilian R&D, the current trend is not encouraging.

Meanwhile, the administration's reliance on monetary fixes is questionable. Interest rates are already at very low levels because of the dampening effect of the recent recession and stagnant recovery. There is little reason to believe further declines are in the offing, nor are there grounds to accept Federal Reserve Chairman Alan Greenspan's claim that a 1 percent drop in interest rates will boost the economy by $100 billion.[9]

Given the anemic recovery, front-loading many of the investment initiatives would have provided a much needed stimulus to the economy. Indeed, by front-loading $50–$60 billion of the $160 billion in new infrastructure and human resource spending proposed for the next four years, the administration could have guaranteed the economy an immediate boost. Instead, the administration made a critical mistake by separating its economic proposal into a short-term stimulus plan and a long-term investment program. Obviously, this budget strategy was a concession to the deficit hawks who wanted to see rapid implementation of the administration's deficit-reduction program rather than a "spend now, pay later" plan favored by some Keynesian economists. As a result, however, the long-term investment package may suffer the same fate as its short-term cousin, both victims of an overriding concern for cutting government spending.

The Deficit

The fiscal deficit of the federal government is the most prominent economic constraint on reinvesting the peace dividend. The conventional wisdom is well known. Excessive public borrowing for chronic deficit financing tends to crowd out private borrowing as the cost of capital increases. Thus, the only remedy is to trim public expenditures so that they eventually balance with government receipts.[10]

With its $500 billion in budget cuts over four years, the Clinton administration clearly adopted the logic of this position. Examined more closely, however, the president's budget takes a somewhat less draconian approach to the deficit. First of all, according to its targets, the administration will not begin lowering the federal deficit until 1995. Moreover, the Congressional Budget Office has forecast budgetary increases after 1997 that will continue until 2003. Thus, Clinton's best efforts only promise to slow the growth of the deficit. Even the most optimistic forecasts of the effects of deficit reduction estimate it will be five to seven years before the economy feels the benefits of a lower deficit and more robust private investment. Meanwhile, in the short run, the defense and other discretionary budget cuts will exert a drag on growth, consumption, employment, and investment.

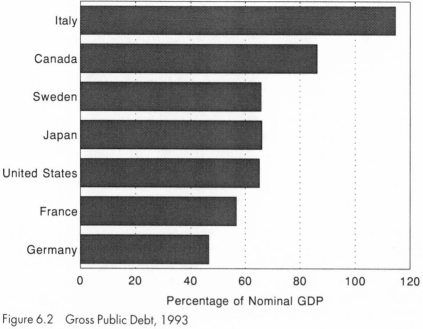

Figure 6.2   Gross Public Debt, 1993

Source: International Monetary Fund.

Some economists maintain that the deficit can be reasonably ignored for the time being. Public investments, they insist, will generate new economic activity, restore productivity, and lay the foundations for higher levels of economic growth.[11] Such investments should therefore be viewed as wealth-producing assets, rather than as simple public expenses.[12] According to this view, it would be short-sighted to use military savings exclusively to reduce the federal budget deficit while ignoring the nation's most pressing economic and social needs.[13]

One side says "cut," the other side says "grow." Beyond these conventional prescriptions for public finance lies the possibility that the current fiscal crisis is caused by the unsustainable way in which the public sector serves the private sector. Indeed, the pattern of public-sector spending and revenue generation may be predicated upon an outmoded assumption: namely that economic growth will solve all our problems.

From an ecological point of view, the fiscal crisis of the state reflects the cumulative social and environmental costs associated with the modern industrial system. In other words, the social and environmental side effects of the normal operations of the economic system may be swamping its capacity to finance a set of credible solutions. Solving the problems of the modern industrial state therefore requires confronting vested interests such as the auto industry, the military-industrial complex, the modern medical system, the real-estate moguls that define our nation's housing policies, and the energy companies that hold sway over our energy policy.

Herman Daly, an economist and adviser to the World Bank, has advanced similarly radical notions concerning the trade-offs between economic growth and environmental sustainability.[14] Society, he argues, must fundamentally change the nature of work, the distribution of income, and the control of investment resources. The composition of the usual "basket" of goods and services to which Western workers and wealth-holders have become accustomed must become the subject of open debate and discussion from an environmental point of view; otherwise hedonism and ignorance will lead to future impoverishment. The length of the working week should be shortened to four days to reemploy those affected by the slowdown in economic growth, the downsizing in defense, and the environmental restructuring of industry and agriculture. On a national and international scale, the gross inequality of income and wealth distribution must be corrected to relieve the overexploitation of the environment. The North therefore has to undertake a large-scale transfer of financial and technological resources to the South. Daly also sees the need for a profound reorientation of security policy that demilitarizes international affairs and redeploys the resources now used for making war.

"The gross inequality of income and wealth distribution must be corrected to relieve the overexploitation of the environment."

The Daly approach has important implications for how public investment and public debt are calculated. In general, the environmental damage associated with growth policies is not reflected in public-sector costs. A new form of "social accounting" would identify these hidden costs and establish an index of sustainability that maximizes economic welfare by minimizing environmental impacts. Such social accounting techniques, applied to the public-sector budget, would force a reevaluation of national policies, from agriculture and energy to transportation and military production. The true costs of current, misguided national investments would be revealed, as well as a more accurate picture of what does and does not swell the public debt. Once these costs are demonstrated, a clearer rationale for rebuilding America would emerge. Guided by the principle of sustainability, the administration would advance a new type of public investment in support of: redeveloping our manufacturing system, reducing emissions from energy production, establishing a more rational and environmentally benign transportation system, slowing deforestation, and creating an ecologically friendly agricultural policy.[15]

No longer can the problems of public finance be understood simply by "cuts" or "growth." Taking Daly's insights seriously, we cannot fall back upon rebuilding the old infrastructure or extending the old model of security.

Conversion

The key to rebuilding America—from the point of view of necessary investments, fiscal sense, and environmental sustainability—is to transform our permanent war economy. After the woeful footdragging of the Bush years, President Clinton is finally moving in the right direction. His task is two-fold: to cut back on defense spending and to find benign economic activities to replace the military-industrial complex.

Clinton plans to reduce military spending by $118 billion over and above President Bush's proposed defense budget.[16] Procurement will fall by 17 percent in 1994 as compared to the last Bush plan. Indeed, the Pentagon has identified over eighty-two separate procurement programs that will be cut by 25 percent or more in 1994.[17] Details are not yet available on the composition of proposed budget reductions for the 1995–1997 period, as the administration is awaiting the Pentagon's "bottom-up" review of defense needs. Yet, it is evident that military personnel, procurement, and R&D will be subject to further cuts.

Although modest when judged against the current international situation and the already inflated Pentagon budget, these military reductions nevertheless imply tremendous economic dislocation. Nearly 460,000 defense-industry jobs have disappeared since 1990. Under President Clinton's five-year defense plan, a budget reduction of about 18 percent adjusted for inflation will mean layoffs of almost 2 million employees. The prospect of even deeper reductions to the military budget will mean still more layoffs. The closing of more military bases—and the ripple effect of cuts on the local and regional economies of defense-dependent communities—will amplify the impacts.

The administration must also reckon with the other costs of demilitarization. The federal government estimates that costs for cleaning up the 24,000 federal facilities currently identified as contaminated will range from $100 billion to $400 billion. Mostly military-related, these sites will require decades of work to clean up. So great is the problem that the environmental legacy of the Cold War may consume the entire peace dividend.[18]

Just cutting the military is not enough, then. During his presidential campaign, Clinton promised a "dollar-for-dollar" reinvestment of defense savings in the economy to generate conversion opportunities. Thus far, his four-year $18 billion conversion program falls far short of that goal. Meanwhile, of the $160 billion proposed in the administration's long-term investment package, only $48 billion was proposed for high-tech, civilian R&D and infrastructure. Thus, it is doubtful that this reinvestment will offset the magnitude of the defense cuts, particularly for the manufacturing sectors. Perhaps more disturbing, the president's plan does not explicitly link the reinvestment program to its conversion efforts.

The response of the defense sector to this reorienting has been predictable. Defense contractors are, by and large, invoking the usual strategies of layoffs, plant closures, mergers and acquisitions, and arms exports as methods of dealing with lower military spending. Conversion has taken place in many small to medium-sized firms, and among some larger firms. But the predominant tendency has either been to "cut and run" or to "hunker down and get a bigger piece of a shrinking pie." Workers and communities have mostly been left to the vicissitudes of the marketplace.

While the Clinton plan does offer some assistance to workers and communities, nearly $3.9 billion is being spent on dual-use programs—technologies that ostensibly have both military and civilian applications. The major objectives of these dual-use programs are to preserve the defense industrial base, ensure military technological superiority, promote spin-offs from defense technologies to civilian use, and increase the use of advanced civilian technologies for weaponry to reduce costs. In theory, such technologies provide a bridge for military contractors to move into civilian markets while continuing to serve national security needs. For example, replacing costly, specially designed computer chips that meet rigorous military specifications with commercially designed chips could lower procurement costs.

In reality, with its dual-use program the Clinton administration is setting up dangerously inadequate half-way houses for Pentagon-dependent corporations. History has shown that firms interested in applying military technology to civilian purposes need to do the hard work of retooling plant and equipment, retraining workers, and restructuring the company itself. Managers and engineers accustomed to functioning in the performance-driven defense market must adapt to the cost and quality specifications that define commercial markets. Experience shows that defense firms that do not do this have failed in civilian markets. Requiring firms to straddle military and commercial production will inhibit this restructuring from taking place. Dual-use programs also betray a built-in bias to serve the demands of the defense market. Recent trends in military-industry consolidation suggest that major portions of the industry may become less flexible and more defense-dependent, while others may exit the industry altogether.

By attempting to preserve the military-industrial base that provides the United States with its superior technological capability, the administration has, with its dual-use strategy, failed to learn a critical lesson from the experience of World War II. The United States was able to launch the rapid build-up of a technologically superior war-fighting capability because it had a world-class industrial base, not because it had a dedicated defense-industrial capacity. Thus, calls for continuing high levels of military R&D in the name of preserving our military technological superiority are misplaced, especially since these dual-use programs will claim scarce dollars at the expense of civilian-oriented industrial programs.

The administration has created a bureaucratic maze by distributing its proposed programs across several agencies. Moreover, by locating a good portion of the conversion programs in the Pentagon, the administration has left the fox to preside over the restructuring of the chicken coop. Many conversion activists have proposed to remedy these problems by creating a "one-stop-shopping center" housed in the Commerce Department. The administration, responding to such suggestions, has proposed to create a package of community assistance programs drawing on the Pentagon's Office of Economic Adjustment (OEA), the Commerce Department's Economic Development Administration and Small Business Administration, and the Labor Department's Displaced Worker Retraining program. The aim would be to develop pilot programs for 1994 with a regional focus on industrial redevelopment at the firm level, particularly for small to medium-sized firms. At first, these demonstration projects would be coordinated by the Pentagon's OEA, but once established the program would be transferred to the Commerce Department.

Such an approach would help to streamline the application procedures, eliminate bureaucratic red tape, maximize the impact of assistance, and counterbalance the undue influence of the Defense Department. While a step forward for the administration, this proposal still leaves much to be desired. The influence of the defense sector remains dominant, and the conversion effort remains unlinked to major rein-

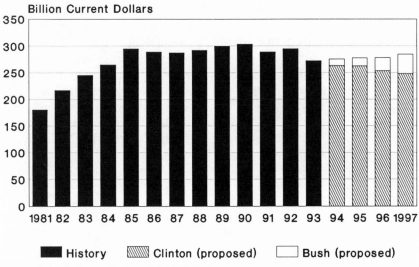

Billion Current Dollars

■ History   ▨ Clinton (proposed)   ☐ Bush (proposed)

Figure 6.3   Defense Budget, 1981–1997

Sources: FY 1994 U.S. Federal Budget Historical Tables and Council for a Livable World.

vestment initiatives in infrastructure, transportation, alternative energy, and environmental technologies.

In the end, then, the Clinton administration has neither cut enough from the military nor prepared for the dislocations that these modest cuts are causing. Its conversion programs are Pentagon-driven and, in most cases, Pentagon-directed as well. The permanent war economy thus remains essentially intact, even in the absence of any likely wars.

What Clinton Should Do

Bill Clinton is in a difficult political spot. He has promised short-term investment in the economy but has fallen back to a program focusing on deficit reduction that will keep the American economy stagnant or worse. He has promised a defense conversion process but has neither shifted sufficient funds to civilian programs nor offered enough public investment to compensate for the billions of Pentagon dollars withdrawn from the economy. His long-term investment plan will likely encounter as much political resistance as the recent stimulus package did. And he has clearly not prepared for the significant transformation of the U.S. war economy that new global realities require.

How can Clinton extricate himself, his administration, and the country from these economic traps? Unless he is content to be a caretaker president and suffer the political consequences, Clinton must recognize first and foremost the need for sweeping change. He must refocus his national investment policy toward the development of an environmentally sustainable industrial system. As Ann Markusen and Joel Yudken have argued, such a policy could construct a new regime capable of replacing the military-industrial complex.[19]

Such a transformation requires much deeper cuts in the military. Even reductions modeled on the rather conservative proposals of the Brookings Institution could yield additional savings of nearly $142 billion over and above those proposed by Clinton for the 1994–1998 period.[20] Such savings could be used to fund a more substantial public investment program.

The administration must also use federal research allocations as a tool for transformation. Reducing military R&D funding would stem the influence of the military on scientific development. Increased federal investments in civilian R&D would meanwhile promote the advance of human knowledge, strengthen basic and applied scientific research, and stimulate technological innovations that could enhance the quality of life and chart a path for environmentally sustainable economic development. The private sector has little incentive to invest in basic research because of the uncertain return from such long-term investment. In research areas such as environmental restoration and alternative energy, increased federal spending would compensate for the lack of market incentives for private R&D investments and assist the private sector in meeting environmental regulations.[21]

Targeted federal research funding for industrial R&D has traditionally been based on military requirements and other strategic objectives such as space exploration. Today, however, the economic and environmental dimensions of security are eclipsing military criteria as the principal determinants of the nation's future well-being. Targeted industrial research could support pollution-reducing production technologies, as well as productivity-enhancing research on manufacturing process innovations. Transportation technologies could go beyond the current vogue of magnetically levitated high-speed trains to explore multimodal transportation systems as well as hybrid automotive technologies like solar-electric, natural gas–electric, and hydrogen fuel–electric vehicles.

To explore these options, the administration will naturally have to confront serious vested interests. In the transportation field, the auto-oil-industrial complex has long resisted the expansion of public transportation alternatives to the automobile.[22] In the case of energy policy, the oil and gas industries and the nuclear power companies have benefited from a de facto national industrial policy that has encouraged and subsidized the "hard energy" path.[23] But a concerted federal approach can create new industries beyond the control of these vested interests that can serve as the building blocks for an environmentally sustainable industrial complex.

In its conversion program, the administration can institute some important interim reforms. With the prospect of an additional 150,000 defense industry workers affected this year by cuts, and perhaps another 200,000 next year, a key concern is getting early notification to workers and communities. By initiating a formal pre-notification process at the beginning of the budgetary cycle, the administration will be in a better position to get early intervention programs into place for workers and communities. Since the regional distribution of contract dollars can be determined in advance, businesses, workers, community leaders, and planners will have the information necessary to launch timely job retention and business development efforts.

The administration must also address the looming job gap between the declining defense sector and the still stagnant civilian sector. Bridging this gap will require several key policies. First, new enterprises must be created that can exploit technological innovations. Small enterprises built around new technologies like electric car components, alternative energy systems, and communications systems for intelligent vehicles can help maintain high-wage jobs in manufacturing (and also provide a foothold for union membership in new and emerging occupations). The administration should also provide economic incentives such as an investment tax credit to enable defense firms to move into these emerging new technology markets, converting their existing capacity and reemploying defense workers in civilian work.

"Small enterprises built around new technologies can help maintain high-wage jobs in manufacturing."

The administration should use educational grants to retrain engineers and managers for work in this high-tech civilian sector. In addition, educational loans should be provided for production workers who may wish to qualify for emerging opportunities in high-tech occupations or to pursue higher education. The retraining programs currently being revamped by the Labor Department should include income support and relocation benefits for displaced workers to ensure that they receive the long-term training necessary to get high-wage jobs. Such a program should go beyond mere extensions of unemployment insurance and should improve on the performance of the current trade adjustment programs.

Linking reinvestment with retraining and redevelopment efforts will require an interagency coordinating and planning body, preferably housed in the Commerce or Labor departments. Such a body is necessary to coordinate the various programs, streamline procedures to speed access and assistance, and counterbalance undue Pentagon influence. Finally, new sources of finance for enterprise development will be needed to encourage employee ownership, middle management buyouts, and community redevelopment projects. The Clinton plan puts very little money in community redevelopment assistance and provides little for financing new business development.

Steeper cuts in the military, reoriented research priorities, a more coherent conversion effort: these are elements of a new approach. Such an approach does not separate public investment, deficit reduction, and military conversion into three competing programs. This model of sustainability responds to the radical transformation now taking place in our understanding of international security, the global environment, and domestic needs. To overcome political resistance to a government-led initiative to transform the economy, the administration must demonstrate the linkages and lay out before the American people the price of missing this historic opportunity.

If we fail in this effort, the nation will lose the opportunity to revitalize the civilian economy and create the basis for sustainable economic development. Moreover, failure to successfully convert will create resistance to further reducing our military budgets and block the chance to develop a more enduring basis for international peace and security. It is Clinton's task to transcend the "cut" and "growth" schools and provide the vision so lacking in previous administrations.

Creating Decent Work

MARTIN CARNOY

Bill Clinton learned quickly what the main issue of the 1992 campaign would be in the grim faces of New Hampshire's unemployed: jobs, jobs, and jobs. When he triumphed over George Bush in November, Clinton also learned the fate of presidents who promise jobs but do not deliver them. The new Democratic president therefore knows that turning America's labor market around is crucial to his political success. But he has thus far sorely underestimated the difficulty of this monumental task.

To produce millions of new, high-paying jobs over the next four years, the Clinton administration initially had the support of significant parts of the business community for a private-public investment partnership. Once legislation was introduced, however, substantial resistance developed. American business has been reluctant to alter the Reagan-era labor policies that have led to the very problems the Clinton administration has been trying to solve. Yet major compromise on the jobs issue may mean serious political problems, not just for this administration but for others that follow. For if anything, studies suggest that to achieve his goal of more employment at higher wages the president should promote even greater changes in the workplace than he has so far proposed.

In general, the Clinton economic program needs to address five employment problems. The most immediate stems from the Bush recession. This current unemployment crisis is further heightened by the massive deficits of the Reagan-Bush era and the end of the Cold War, which limit government job-creation programs and cause substantial job displacement from declining military-based work. These two prob-

Figure 7.1   Growth of U.S. Employment, Productivity, and Real Wages, 1960–1990

Source: Economic Report of the President, 1993, Tables B-37, B-42, B-45.

lems are compounded by the slow growth in productivity (output per worker hour) over the past fifteen years, which simultaneously inhibits the growth of wages and jobs. A related productivity issue concerns the politics of the workplace—how labor and management are responding to new global economic realities. Finally, the Clinton reforms must deal with the increasing separation of inner-city youth from the workforce, which has been aggravated by structural shifts in the labor market and a consistent neglect of education, training, and jobs programs for disadvantaged teenagers.

Before putting forward his own solutions, the president had to confront the labor problems inherited from his predecessor. Although employment rose rapidly under Ronald Reagan, productivity grew slowly and real wages stagnated. This picture contrasts starkly with the 1960s, when employment, productivity, and real wages in the United States increased together. In the 1980s, by comparison, Europe and Japan had less job growth but their productivity and real wages increased more rapidly. European leaders in the mid-1980s envied the capacity of the less regulated U.S. economy to generate new employment. But the Reagan strategy had two major drawbacks.

First, a high percentage of net new jobs created in the 1980s were low-wage.[1] Moreover, many "high-wage" jobs went to women who, because of the pay-equity gap, actually received relatively low salaries. Only about 25 percent of the net increase in jobs have therefore been truly high-wage, and these went almost entirely to white, non-Latino males.[2]

Second, Reaganomics worsened the condition of the working poor, a result not only of the decline in manufacturing jobs for black males but also of the low-wage strategy and cuts in social services. Typical of Reagan policy was the decision to hold the legal minimum wage constant in nominal terms throughout his entire presidency. Even after two post-Reagan increases, the purchasing power of the minimum wage remained at its 1950 level of $1.00.[3] Accompanying this erosion of living standards for the working poor has been the decay of urban centers, which poses a threat to the cohesion of American society as a whole. Indeed, the United States seems to have cornered the market in the industrialized world on dire poverty in the midst of plenty.

This legacy means that to create more "good" jobs, the Clinton administration will have to do two things. On the one hand, it will have to increase high-wage opportunities by raising productivity in already high-wage jobs. This strategy requires rapid increases in demand for professional, managerial, technical, and sales personnel in high-wage industries. On the other hand, to improve the lot of most blacks and Latinos, the new administration will have to change America's investment strategy from expanding low-wage opportunities to increasing production that generates more middle-wage jobs. In part (but only in part), this can be promoted by increasing the training and retraining of workers who now have little access to skilled, well-paying work. But these middle-wage jobs still have to come from somewhere, whether from inner-city start-ups, expanding exports, or a construction boom.

These are not easy tasks in today's anxiety-ridden globally competitive economic environment. All the major industrial countries are facing slower economic growth and capital flight to lower-income economies. To overcome the legacy of the 1980s and adapt to the new international realities of the 1990s, the president will have to make some drastic changes in the way we think about job creation. Taking traditional macroeconomic approaches is just not going to work.

The "Putting People First" Strategy

The Clinton strategy to solve these employment problems is spelled out in the presidential campaign's bible, *Putting People First*—still perhaps the best overall reference to what the president is trying to accomplish even as he makes major alterations along the way. Its underlying philosophy—to "create millions of high-wage jobs" and "put America back to work"—translated into a national economic strategy based on comprehensive government-led programs of public and private investment stimuli.[4]

This strategy sensibly distinguished between the easier task of boosting employment in the short run and the more difficult challenges of increasing the number of high-paying jobs in the longer run and solving the conundrum of inner-city youth unemployment.

During the transition, Clinton favored giving the economy a shot in the arm through a stimulus package, reducing recessionary unemployment from 7.5 percent to the 5.5–6 percent range through the creation of about 2 million additional jobs. The follow-up package combined funding for education and training with longer-term private investment stimuli and direct public investment in new technologies such as fast trains, electric cars, telecommunications, and environmental innovations. These measures were designed to ease the transition from a military economy (solving the medium-term problem) and to raise productivity and create faster job growth in the longer term. The Clinton health-care reform would slow corporate America's fastest growing component of costs, with a net positive effect on overall employment (as health-care jobs expanded in the medium run before eventually tapering off). And the Clinton plan for the cities would create new kinds of employment and training for inner-city youth.

The approach was sound. Indicators suggested that the recovery from the Bush recession would be slow and that employment would therefore also rise slowly. A stimulus would have accelerated the recovery. Long-term interest rates might fall less as a result of such a stimulus, but the Clinton team seemed initially willing to take this risk. The Clinton approach to retraining defense workers also made sense, as did the focus on shifting government consumption (military spending, subsidies to farmers, growing Medicare costs, and untaxed Social Security and military pensions for high-income retirees) to government investment in lifelong learning and new technology to stimulate higher productivity. These were all serious solutions to well-defined problems, and they would have gone a long way toward creating a lot of new jobs.

But the president-elect soon got a different message from the financial community. Bankers and investors were far more concerned with the inflationary (long-term interest rate) effects of tighter labor markets and government spending than with the positive revenue effects of stimulating the economy and increasing public investment in human resources. According to their monetary model, the main stimulus to economic growth and employment should be lower long-term interest rates, which meant cutting the budget deficit first and raising public investment second. It also meant a longer, slower recovery.

Clinton clearly listened to this constituency. He appointed Robert Rubin of Salomon Brothers to coordinate his National Economic Council and named Lloyd Bentsen as secretary of the treasury. These nominations achieved their intended effect of calming the bond markets. Long-term interest rates fell steadily in the first months of the administration. By inauguration day, a subtle change had taken place in the "Putting People First" program. Bill Clinton still believed in education, training, and other public investments as long-run solutions to the employment problem. But lower interest rates, not federal spending, had become the main vehicle to short-term jobs growth.

This compromise on the short-term unemployment problem was just the beginning of a larger conservative assault on the fundamental concept of government's economic role as spelled out in the campaign. Republicans and conservative Democrats in both houses of Congress successfully translated business resistance to expanded government programs into common voter fears of "tax and spend" liberalism. Jobs and higher wages got lost in the fray. Clinton knew he was up against the American electorate's tremendous distrust of government; he simply underestimated the difficulty of making pro-active government look good as entrenched powers battled him at every turn.

> *"Clinton knew he was up against the American electorate's tremendous distrust of government; he simply underestimated the difficulty of making pro-active government look good."*

Congressional conservatives have not been the only obstacle to putting America back to work. Even assuming that the president faces less resistance to the productivity-increasing pieces of his economic program, a more serious long-term threat looms. The proposed program may not be able to overcome business practices that are increasingly resistant to hiring highly paid employees and to providing job security and training to production workers. The need to develop "flexible production" in an increasingly global market means that most firms are cutting payroll obligations to the bare bones. This does not bode well for creating masses of high-paying, secure jobs with accompanying training. It also implies that any administration hoping to solve the job problem in the long term must change current labor market practices, which the Clinton administration now seems unwilling to do.

Short-Term Jobs Stimulus

During the transition, the size of the stimulus—or even whether there should be one—became a major issue within the Clinton team. The original plan called for about $50 billion to give the economy a jolt and push unemployment down quickly. The main component—$30 billion—would have gone to infrastructure repairs already planned by cities. The nation's mayors supported this program element not only for jobs but also to begin a longer-term recovery program for urban areas. This larger version of the stimulus did not last long, however. It was viewed in financial circles as inflationary—a sure bet to drive up interest rates and the last thing the president would want to start off his first year.

The economic package that the administration sent to Congress in February 1993 contained only a very conservative $16 billion in short-term stimulus, still with some urban repairs and summer jobs programs but not much else. Although this minimalist approach found approval in financial circles—long-term interest rates fell steadily from the time the package was first announced—Republicans and conservative Democrats went after much of the remaining short-term spending on the grounds that it was pork barrel, contributed to the deficit, and meant more taxes.

By the time the Senate was done with the bill, its focus had changed from stimulus and public investment to deficit reduction. Sen. David Boren (D-OK) pushed for his own fiscal blend of twice as many spending cuts and half as many taxes. One Clinton adviser said of Boren's conservative counterproposal, "If a Republican had been the sponsor, we could have run against it forever."[5] The short-term stimulus thus became negligible: funds for improved urban infrastructure were completely cut, leaving only $1 billion for summer jobs.

As a result of this shift in emphasis, the Clinton package's effect on unemployment in the short-run came entirely from lower interest rates—which was nothing more than what Bush had proposed.

Declining Military Spending

The Clinton economic package contains development funds for communities hit by military base closings. It also includes funds for retraining workers displaced by current and anticipated cuts in military spending. Together, these programs total a proposed $1.7 billion for four years.

The legislation that originally made such "conversion" funds available was actually enacted in summer 1992 with solid backing from both Democrats and Republicans, and with good reason. The workers in question are all well-trained and can be easily absorbed into an expanding labor force if appropriately retrained.

If Clinton implements a larger, more serious conversion package—with a major research-and-development tax credit and other incentives to push some of America's massive array of defense contractors toward making new products—the transition would be more effective, at least in keeping highly paid defense workers in good jobs. Even so, the reduction of military contracts is bound to lower engineering and technical pay in the electronics sector over the next five years. And, as Seymour Melman and other analysts have noted, conversion of most defense contracting firms is unlikely because their management is unwilling and probably unable to reorganize for private market competition. As these companies downsize or disappear, workers from that sector will also have to be retrained.

Retraining displaced workers (or soon to be displaced workers) is becoming one of the major employment issues of the present phase of America's economic development. The "permanent" job, where a person finds work in a firm in his or her twenties and stays until retirement, is being replaced by a work system that is much more flexible for firms but less secure for employees. In the new system, firms change location more frequently, and their core work force is smaller, augmented by "temporary" labor or subcontracted work to other firms. Increased full-time temporary labor and a higher percentage of employment in small and medium-sized subcontractors means greater job instability. Should government therefore expand its role beyond unemployment insurance? Is unemployment insurance even the most appropriate form to handle these more frequent displacements?

Currently, retraining is largely state or locally funded, with community colleges often providing the adult training and certification for career change. Special state agencies, such as the California Employment Training Panel (ETP), are involved in short-course job retraining. ETP focuses on established workers recently laid off or in danger of being displaced. Started in 1982, ETP contracts with existing training institutions and with private companies to provide the training. It is set up to be 100 percent performance-based: it only pays training providers for participants who complete training and are retained on a related job for ninety days.

ETP is supported by contributions to the Employment Training Fund—0.01 percent of wages contributed by each private, for-profit California employer. In fiscal 1991–1992, this tax generated over $80 million to be used to retrain about 49,000 workers. However, in the 1991–1992 recession and current weak recovery, 50,000 workers is only a small portion of those displaced in California.

This is where the federal government could help. Yet in the Clinton economic package, less than $2 billion is available annually for the training of displaced workers. At California costs per retrained worker, this amount would cover 600,000 workers annually nationwide, only about 30 percent of the newly unemployed in the 1990–1992 period. A much bigger and more innovative program is therefore needed. The case of ETP suggests that unemployment insurance should be replaced by a system of training funds to be used before actual displacement, with training plus maintenance for workers suddenly thrown out of work.

The Clinton economic package does not move very far on the larger issue of job displacement. To his credit, the president is considering expanding "lifelong education" aimed at providing new skills for displaced workers. Yet what may be needed is a totally restructured system of training and unemployment insurance that would encourage firms to help retrain workers rather than lay them off.

Raising Productivity

Raising productivity to put the American economy on a more secure track—creating more jobs with greater real wages—is the most important part of the president's agenda. An increase in the productivity of U.S. workers is the only sure way of improving the American standard of living. The Clinton administration approaches the productivity issue through increasing investment per worker. That increase in investment is to be achieved by stimulating private sector spending on new machinery and training, and by shifting government consumption to government investment. Clinton's argument is that net domestic investment generated by the free market during the 1980s was too low and that federal spending was highly concentrated in transfer payments and military industry, both of which were largely government consumption. Crucial public investment in human resources, research and development (R&D), and infrastructure—such as improving roads, bridges, sewers, transportation, environment, and telecommunications—was much less than needed to raise the productivity of both labor and private capital.

The new administration initially proposed to take three major steps as part of its investment stimulus program. It sought to stimulate private investment through lower long-term interest rates, a permanent investment tax credit (ITC), and an R&D tax credit. It also proposed to increase direct public investment in high-tech R&D and infrastructure. And it looked to improve the quality of the American labor force through educational reforms and greatly expanded in-firm and out-of-firm training programs.

Interest rates did fall in the early months of the administration, mildly increasing private investment and productivity. The permanent ITC was scrapped because most economists and business leaders felt its negative revenue impact was greater than its benefits. The R&D tax credit amounts to $4.3 billion over four years. Recent analyses suggest that it will yield $2.00 of added investment in R&D for each dollar of lost tax revenue, a substantial impact over the long haul.[6] The final economic package provided for roughly $120 billion in long-term public investment. In addition to increasing academic standards in high schools, the educational reform program would reform vocational education to include new "career academies" and cooperative industry-school programs in high schools, combined with apprenticeships and an additional year or two of post-secondary career education.

The *direction* of the Clinton package is laudatory, but its impact on investment, productivity, and job growth over and above what Bush's more laissez-faire program might have achieved will probably be limited. On the one hand, the Clinton package does little to push private industry to change its investment habits; on the other, the amount of additional public investment is being severely constrained by the Senate's anti-inflation bias. Whereas in the past it was possible to mobilize nationalistic sentiment for the defense budget as a major source of high-wage employment and industrial policy, the end of the Cold War makes it much more difficult to gain consensus on comparable government spending for new jobs.

> ## *"The president has shown himself highly sensitive to conservative pressures."*

Furthermore, the president has shown himself highly sensitive to conservative pressures. He seemed ready, early on, to keep financial institutions and the business sector happy by a minimal stimulus and an emphasis on deficit reduction. To his surprise, they kept the pressure on him throughout the year, continuing to paint him as a tax-and-spend liberal even as his program turned increasingly away from job creation measures.

The ideologically most well-defined piece of the Clinton program is the emphasis on raising productivity by improving human resources. Secretary of Labor Robert Reich argues in *The Work of Nations* that the main role of nation-states in the new global information economy is to create highly productive labor through quality educational and training systems.[7] Trainable and trained workers make private capital investment more productive, hence attracting it from all over the world. Recent growth models stress the primary role of "endogenous" technology, the result of qualified workers, technicians, scientists, and managers constantly innovating in the workplace and creating new knowledge that increases productivity.[8] In other words, increasing the quality of the work force improves the possibility for developing new knowledge, which in turn increases productivity and growth.

The administration's commitment to such a model is clear in a number of bills sent to Congress. The economic package included funds for retraining. The educational reform bill stressed increasing enforceable standards on what high school students had to know in order to graduate. The administration brought the college loan program back under direct control of the federal government with the intention of expanding the amount of credit available to potential college students. The president also proposed a largely symbolic national service program that would enable college students to fund a large portion of their education by serving in a volunteer corps or in other public service capacities after graduation.

Probably the most innovative of the legislative packages presented to Congress was the reform of vocational education intended to improve the transition of America's youth from school to work. This apprenticeship proposal is based loosely on the highly successful German dual-apprenticeship system. More than 60 percent of German youth enter apprenticeship programs in firms—paid for by the firms—while continuing to attend government vocational schools on a part-time basis and ultimately being state-certified as skilled workers. The Clinton version is much more limited, aiming to induce more non-college-bound youth into career programs in high school, to keep them in school for at least one year beyond high school, and to provide them with job training in firms as they continue in school. The hope is that such training will make them much more employable, more certifiably skilled, and more productive than under the present system.

This is a valuable initiative, and in the best-case scenario it will induce states to propose realistic plans of integrating non-college-bound students into the workplace. The initiative's potential success, however, could be severely constrained by the job market. States and local communities can build career programs, but the success of such programs depends on the existence and growth of good jobs with good wages and further training opportunities. A better educated work force will only "create" better jobs over the long haul, and employers' response over the long haul is conditioned by other factors, such as regional free trade agreements, world economic growth, and the state of the U.S. economy. Even the more successful school-to-work transition systems, as in Germany, are running into serious trouble in today's labor markets. Only a few of the apprenticeship programs, such as in electronics, offer good job opportunities. And these programs are filled by the better non-university-bound students, with the rest relegated to careers of much less promise.

This educational program could also suffer because the large-scale spending needed for both the public and private sides of the equation will not be forthcoming. On the public side, the most important part of the proposal is the tie between the high school career programs and post-secondary institutions. Apprenticeship programs have the best chance to succeed at the post-secondary level, where they already exist in some places. As those who have worked on this legislation realize, preparing youth for high-skilled jobs and moving them into jobs through apprenticeships is going to take more than just finishing high school.[9] This makes the program much more expensive than the states can currently afford and is far different from the high school dropout antidote program the president envisages.

On the private side, the program ultimately depends on employers' willingness to hire youth as apprentices. Consequently, employers not only have to be hooked into the career programs in high schools and community colleges but also have to be willing to allocate significant resources to employing and training young people in their firms. German firms spent $50 billion on apprenticeships in 1990, an amount almost as large as the entire $60 billion public budget for all levels of German education (including university).[10] Compare this with the American Society for Training and Development estimates that America's private employers spend about $30 billion a year on *all* training (most of it going to management training) for a labor force more than three times as large as Germany's.[11]

Sometime during the Clinton transition, the notion of inducing employers to increase training through the "play or pay" 1.5 percent payroll tax was dropped from the economic package. According to this concept, already highly successful in France, employers can either show that they spend that percentage of their payroll on in-firm training ("play") or contribute to a fund used by states to provide appropriate on-the-job training to workers ("pay"). "Playing" can be defined to give more credit for each dollar spent on training production workers rather than on management, and more credit for training apprentices rather than existing workers.

"Play or pay" would have pushed firms solidly toward increased training and toward hiring apprentices. Giving up the proposal leaves the administration with the limited option of "jawboning" firms to do more training. Such federal persuasion may or may not work. If not, much of the Clinton emphasis on more training, greater cooperation between high schools and local employers, and apprenticeship programs will fall far short of what is needed to raise the skills and employability of America's workers.

Other initiatives in the larger Clinton program bode ill for more investment in the training of U.S. low- and middle-skilled workers. The North American Free Trade Agreement (NAFTA), for instance, will undoubtedly increase the demand in Mexico for many high-skill-intensive goods produced in the United States. But with improved sourcing, more political security, and foreign exchange stability in Mexico, even more of U.S. auto manufacturing and a whole host of other middle-skilled and capital-intensive industries could move south. When workers at the state-of-the-art Ford engine plant in Chihuahua, Mexico, can be brought by special training programs to higher levels of productivity than Ford workers in Detroit and Canada, yet receive one-eighth the wage, it is likely that most new U.S. auto investment and worker training will end up in Mexico. NAFTA could produce many benefits for certain groups of U.S. workers, such as those with college degrees. But as Mexico's standard of living rises and with it the demand for U.S. products, NAFTA could also hurt Clinton's efforts to increase average wages in most core middle-level U.S. jobs.

The NAFTA discussion suggests a broader problem for increasing high-wage employment through traditional macroeconomic policies in the present world economic situation. In theory, Reich's conception of creating a labor force of symbolic analysts would move the United States to much higher productivity and wages as practically everyone becomes employed in high value-added knowledge-producing jobs. Rather than being the world's breadbasket or world's automaker, the United States would become the world's knowledge producer, processor, and communicator.

But that route to higher wages is already being short-circuited by the growth of alternative sources of high-value knowledge at much lower wages in places such as India, China, and Russia. These countries have masses of underemployed, highly trained scientists and engineers eager for jobs in world-class companies. Reich is right, of course, that we have little choice but to invest heavily in education and training just to stay slightly ahead of the game. But our expectations of how quickly we can raise employment and wages simultaneously should not be very high. The number of good jobs may increase, but not quickly enough to create the kind of social mobility America enjoyed in the immediate postwar

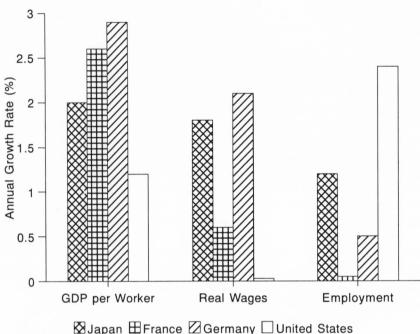

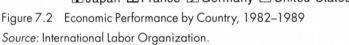

Figure 7.2   Economic Performance by Country, 1982–1989

Source: International Labor Organization.

era. Much more likely, increased productivity will result in higher wages for those in the core labor force, while a large number of workers will remain in low-paid temporary jobs, in low-wage subcontracted jobs, or in almost permanent unemployment.

At the Tokyo Summit in July and later in the fall at a conference of labor and education ministers of the seven largest industrial nations, participants attempted to coordinate their economic and labor policies to get the largest possible employment effect from increases in investment. Although very vague, their initiatives reflect an awareness that coordination rather than competition could soften the rising tendency to hold down wages, reduce employee security, and prevent employment increases in the name of greater flexibility, higher profitability, and economic growth.

Yet the real coordination needed to resolve these issues is not among the already developed countries. Rather, communication and interaction between the North and the South must be enhanced. Retaining jobs in the North may mean keeping Southern growth lower, and that could lead—in the absence of the mutual exploration of alternatives—to even greater global economic problems.

Labor-Management Reform

The Clinton administration is also moving toward reorganizing production to improve productivity. Such reorganizations require changing the way American management and organized labor deal with each other, and providing incentives for greater participation in employee ownership and management. Secretary of Labor Reich has organized a task force to develop labor-management committees in firms to increase productivity through greater cooperation.

A good deal of controversy surrounds these attempts to forge a new partnership between labor and management. Some unions charge that the administration simply wants to dilute the power of organized labor. Indeed, the task force's ten members include only one union official, the United Auto Workers' Doug Fraser, and he is retired. Other unions, meanwhile, have wholeheartedly embraced these new ideas, in part to improve their bargaining power with the administration to win on the strike-replacement bill and a revised NAFTA.[12]

In any case, greater employee involvement (EI)—particularly in conjunction with employee ownership—probably does increase productivity and profitability. Indirectly, this involvement would also lead to greater job security, successful worker training, and increased wages—all key objectives of Clinton's economic package. Most important, EI seems to have helped save certain manufacturing industries, such as steel, and might help save other sectors that cannot seem to compete under the present managerial system.

EI's big payoff is not necessarily in harder work, but in the improvement of production methods through employee suggestions, team problem solving, and a clearer and more integrated system of skill development. The highly successful GM-Toyota plant in Fremont, California, for example, pays employees for suggestions that reduce costs, improve product quality, or enhance worker safety. Through the production teams, the firm also does a lot of informal training that yields many such suggestions for cost savings. Both the employees and the management have compromised at this successful auto plant. The union and employees have accepted less control over job classification, higher penalties for absenteeism, and more responsibility for enforcing employees' obligations. Management has given way on employment security, training obligations, and some shared decision making. Work effort has increased because the production line is down less often and absenteeism has declined.[13] The Fremont case suggests that unless both management and unions compromise, productivity gains are minimal. If management uses EI as a means of dismantling union influence or breaking the union, organized labor simply prevents the EI scheme from moving forward.

Employee ownership, when combined with employee involvement, has a much greater impact on productivity and profits. Such ownership schemes include profit-sharing plans, employee stock-ownership plans (ESOPs), and cooperatives in which employees collectively own the company in which they work. ESOPs where workers own a majority of the stock also fall into this last category.[14]

The schemes that seem to work well in raising productivity and providing greater employee security and higher wages (tied to higher employee performance) are those that involve the greatest EI. Particularly successful are gain-sharing plans, in which rewards are team-based and related to indicators other than profits (e.g., labor cost savings or machine down-time). Good examples of such plans, which can be promoted without worker ownership or control of equity, include Fremont Toyota-GM, Hewlett-Packard, and most large Japanese companies.

But ownership that goes hand in hand with involvement works the best. Corey Rosen, at the National Center for Employee Ownership, claims that in a careful study of ESOPs before and after they began their plans, companies that combine ESOPs with EI grow 8–11 percent per year faster than they would have otherwise. According to Rosen, neither ownership nor participation alone has much long-term impact.[15]

Despite Reich's task force, the Clinton administration is a long way from seriously considering changes in the organization of production to increase productivity. Yet such reorganization may ultimately be necessary to raise low wages, increase employment, and improve the low level of employee training in U.S. firms.

The Difficult to Employ

Although many new jobs created during the 1980s were high-wage and high-skilled, they were distributed very unevenly among the populace. A disproportionate number of these high-wage jobs went to white males and females. Whereas African-Americans got about one out of seven of all new jobs, they only got one of sixteen high-wage jobs and more than one of five low-wage jobs.[16] African-American unemployment rates remain two to three times higher than for whites. With real wages falling in already low-wage jobs, many less-educated young blacks and native-born Latinos have chosen simply not to work.

The Clinton administration's task of turning around this low end of the labor market is enormous. One essential part of the solution is to create higher-paying jobs in areas where African-Americans and native-

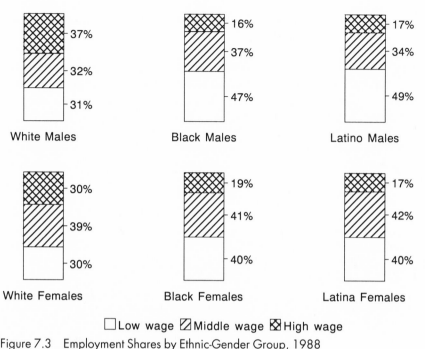

White Males   Black Males   Latino Males

White Females   Black Females   Latina Females

☐ Low wage ▨ Middle wage ⊠ High wage

Figure 7.3   Employment Shares by Ethnic-Gender Group, 1988

Source: U.S. Department of Commerce, Bureau of Census.

born Latinos live—primarily inner cities—and tie these jobs to training programs inside and outside schools. The key is providing incentives to employers to hire and help train people from the areas themselves. Since such jobs should not be dead-end, a system is required to give an opportunity for further training to workers who show they can hold down a job.

A second part of the Clinton solution is to increase substantially the proportion of African-Americans and Latinos who finish four-year colleges. It is almost impossible in today's labor market to get a high-paying job without a college degree. Efforts must also be expanded to improve nutrition, child care, preschool education, and public education in low-income areas. The post-tax income of the poor, regardless of ethnicity, must also be increased. The earned income tax credit (EITC) for the working poor was designed to move in this direction, but that, too, was scaled back by the Senate's heavy emphasis on deficit reduction. Colleges should expand grants to genuinely low-income students by enough to cover at least part of their forgone wages while attending school, and improve the academic support for these students in college to make sure that they complete their studies.

A third part of the Clinton solution was to legislate a $1.00 increase in the minimum wage to $5.25 per hour. Even this increase would only bring the purchasing power of the minimum wage to the level of 1960. Recent studies show that such an increase would not reduce youth employment: the double increase in minimum wage in California in the late 1980s had negligible impact on youth employment but did raise lower-end incomes significantly.[17] Even so, the administration has backed off the $1.00 increase and has settled for a much smaller amount.

The president appears to be well on the road to expanding programs for young children in poverty and increasing the resources available to poor working families through the EITC. Both these efforts could help reduce the worst effects of poverty on future generations. But to move large numbers of minority young people into college while raising productivity and increasing jobs for low-income young people on the scale required will demand much more public support than the president seems able (or willing) to generate at this point.

An Alternative Package

The Clinton administration began with a conceptual package of reforms that could have improved employment in both the short and long run. Those reforms ran into opposition from the financial community and conservatives in the Senate. Between the two, much of what was innovative and progressive about employment creation and productivity enhancement in the economic package fell by the wayside. Far fewer jobs were created in 1993 than might have been, and those that were came from lower long-term interest rates and the slow cyclical rebound from the Bush recession. Although the financial community feels much more comfortable with slow growth and very low rates of inflation, consumer confidence suffered and an opportunity was lost to change profoundly the way America does business.

If short-run employment creation engenders so much opposition, meaningful long-term reforms will be even more difficult. Increased training at the workplace and improved educational opportunities—ensuring higher-wage employment—requires an entirely new strategy for American management and labor unions. Increased public investment would help, if Congress cooperated in pushing through such investment.

But in the longer run, the president also has to convince the U.S. business community that creating high-wage jobs is more profitable than keeping wages low—a difficult row to hoe when firms are downsizing, increasing "flexibility," and facing increased international competition. The Clinton administration must be willing to undertake more creative

---

"The president has to convince U.S. businesses that creating high-wage jobs is more profitable than keeping wages low."

---

measures than currently planned—or else it will find that the United States in 1996 might be more financially sound than when the Democrats took power, but good jobs will be hard to find.

The Clinton administration should continue to move along the path of shifting public consumption to public investment as outlined in *Putting People First* and as incorporated in a series of bills put before Congress during the past year. The effort should not stop there, however. The administration should reconsider some level of payroll tax as a "play or pay" incentive for firms to foot the bill for training. Jawboning firms to change their training ways and to invest in apprenticeships is unlikely to work, but tax incentives will.

Present government safety-net programs such as unemployment insurance have to be rethought in terms of the effect they have on firms' employment and training practices. Based on California's experience with unemployment insurance reforms, Claire Brown and Michael Reich at the University of California (Berkeley) propose that employees should be eligible to receive unemployment insurance if their work week is shortened.[18] Such a plan reduces layoffs, helps keep the work force intact, and protects workers' skills from depreciating. Under certain conditions, unemployment insurance funds should be used to help companies retrain workers so that they are not laid off.

The president should also be much more aggressive in improving job markets and training programs in cities. Unless a major change takes place in the *conditions* under which firms do business in the inner city, enterprise zones or other tax incentive schemes to induce capital to bring businesses and hire workers in cities will only be a token of the investment needed to make a difference.

Clinton should also promote a change in worker-employer relations by helping the growth of ESOPs. This could be done without much fanfare by supporting existing state programs and promoting a few simple changes in ESOP regulations regarding hostile takeovers. A total budget of $2 million for state programs would have a large impact on the incidence of ESOPs and also appear to increase the degree of employee involvement.

In addition, the administration could beef up the Bureau of Labor-Management Relations and Cooperative Programs in the Department of Labor to promote EI/employment security efforts both in companies that have employee ownership and those that do not. Clinton should also create a U.S. Productivity Center that would develop longer-term programs and policies for companies and unions to increase productivity, particularly through employee involvement and training.

To keep manufacturing in the United States, the Clinton administration should closely explore employee buy-outs. Any incentives that give employees a majority ownership in running companies will likely discourage companies from closing down and moving offshore. In the steel industry, for example, buy-outs have saved a number of smaller companies through employee takeovers. ESOPs have been the mechanism for many of the buy-outs. Additional financial help is still needed for ESOPs to borrow the capital necessary for taking over not only companies on the rocks but successful firms that might otherwise move.

Promoting employee buy-outs would probably have a much greater effect on preserving jobs in the United States than a successful coordination of the employment-trade policies of the largest industrialized nations, even though the two strategies are not mutually exclusive. Ultimately, coordinating macroeconomic policies could help increase growth rates worldwide but still may not solve the underlying moves by private firms to reduce their permanent core labor force in developed countries.

The Clinton administration, for its own political good as well as for the good of the country, must turn around America's job market. The political price for neglecting these issues was paid by George Bush in 1992. The economic price is being paid every day by the American people.

TAXATION

Sharing the Burden

RALPH ESTES

While the attention of politicians, pundits, and the public has focused on government spending, America's national tax system has drifted into incoherence. It fails to accomplish its primary tasks of raising revenue and redistributing income fairly. Its recent overhauls—the most significant in 1986—have only further skewed the system in favor of corporations and the wealthy. And instead of getting simpler, the tax code has simply become more complex.

Even before taking office, Bill Clinton recognized these problems, particularly the issue of revenue shortfalls. But his first proposals for economic reform, while they may have represented a dramatic change of direction from Bush administration policies, have not really begun to solve the problems. And when Congress subsequently diluted even these modest proposals, Clinton went along.

In order to restore fairness to national tax policy and raise sufficient capital for government programs, the Clinton administration will have to work harder to reverse the trends of the Reagan-Bush era. Over the long term, it will have to raise taxes on the wealthy, eliminate corporate loopholes, and simplify the code. In the short term, it should enact a personal wealth tax, a corporate wealth tax, and a higher inheritance tax. Only then will our democratic system have an equally democratic tax structure to keep it solvent.

A Flawed System

Our present tax system does not raise enough revenue. The annual budget shortfall is now over $300 billion. Spending may or may not be too high, but that is a different matter. The fundamental purpose of the tax system is to raise the revenue required to run the government. Our tax system no longer does that, and it hasn't since 1969, the last year the federal budget ran a surplus.

These deficits have continually added to our national debt, which is now nearly as large as our gross domestic product—the total output of our economy. Even if we reduce the annual budget deficit, systematically and progressively, the national debt will still grow. The only way to reduce the debt, by even one dollar, is to have a budget surplus. Some economists believe that we will never again see a surplus and that the national debt will never be lower than it is today. Based on their performance so far, neither Clinton nor Congress is likely to correct these budgetary problems by raising taxes to a fiscally sufficient level.

What may be worse for our democracy, however, is the serious and obvious inequity of the tax system. Progressive taxes should be based on ability to pay. With a progressive tax, people with lower incomes pay at lower tax rates and those at higher income levels pay at higher rates. The higher the income, the higher the tax—both in actual dollars and as a percentage.

In 1972, the personal income tax was rather progressive. The highest tax bracket, the "marginal tax rate," was 70 percent. The lowest bracket was 14 percent on the first $1,000 earned, then 15 percent for the next $1,000, 16 percent on the next $1,000, and so on with the income brackets widening at higher levels. Before 1972, the federal income tax was even more progressive. The highest bracket was 94 percent in 1944 when we were at war; it fell to 91 percent in the 1950s and stayed at that level until 1964.

In the 1980s, however, the tax system shifted the burden decisively from the rich to the middle class and the poor. As the House Ways and Means Committee described the changes:

> The highest income one-fifth of the population paid a smaller percent of their income in taxes in 1990 than in 1977; the bottom 80 percent paid more of their income in taxes in 1990 than in 1977. Taxpayers in the very highest income categories (top 1 and top 5 percent) showed the largest reduction in taxes as a percent of income.[1]

This 1 percent with the highest income had an effective average tax rate in 1977 of 39.2 percent, after all deductions, exemptions, and credits.

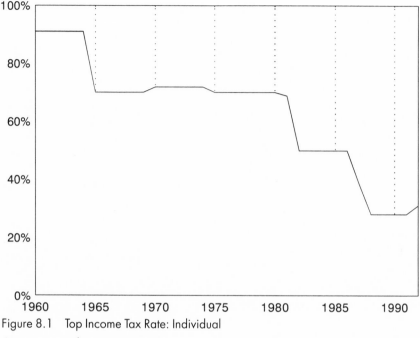

Figure 8.1   Top Income Tax Rate: Individual

Source: Internal Revenue Service.

By 1988 that rate had dropped 25 percent to 29.3 percent. The changes for everyone else were minimal.[2]

According to a joint study by the Federal Reserve Board and the Internal Revenue Service, the very wealthiest Americans—the top 1 percent—held 31.3 percent of all wealth in 1983. In just six years, with the help of economic and tax programs put forward by the Reagan and Bush administrations and accepted by a willing Congress, they increased that share to 37.1 percent.[3]

If this rate of wealth redistribution were to continue unabated, in only thirty-five more years the richest 1 percent would own all of the wealth in America. No one else would own a home or a car, have a pension plan, or hold any share of American business. Presumably we will never get to that point. But then, who would have imagined such a concentration of wealth in only six years?

While the average American is paying more taxes, corporations are paying a lot less. In the 1950s, businesses were responsible for 39 percent of the U.S. income tax burden; individuals, 61 percent.[4] Now businesses contribute only 10 percent; individuals make up the other 90 percent.[5] To reduce their burden, corporations have taken advantage of a number of special tax favors: lower rates, accelerated depreciation, special first-year asset write-offs, investment tax credits, and the foreign tax credit.

---

*"If the present rate of wealth
redistribution were to continue
unabated, in only thirty-five years the
richest 1 percent would own all of the
wealth in America."*

Of all the tax favors granted to corporations, the worst is undoubtedly the foreign tax credit.[6] Here's how this credit works: Suppose the ESTES Corporation has a plant in San Diego, California, and paid $100 million to that state in income taxes. Total corporate income before deducting this $100 million was $500 million. So ESTES has federal taxable income of $500 million minus the $100 million deduction—or $400 million. Its federal income tax bill at the 1992 rate of 34 percent would be $136 million.

Now suppose ESTES moves the plant out of the country, perhaps just across the border, and pays $100 million in taxes to another country. The tax deduction now becomes a tax credit. A tax deduction is a subtraction from the amount of income on which the tax bill is calculated. A tax credit, on the other hand, is a subtraction from the tax bill itself.

On taxable income of $500 million ESTES's federal income tax before the credit would come to $170 million. It can now deduct a $100 million foreign tax credit against this bill, just as if that amount had been paid to Uncle Sam, and simply pay the remainder of $70 million.

So the ESTES Corporation pays federal income taxes of $136 million if its plant is in California and only $70 million if it moves out of the country. Our tax laws, in other words, give this corporation a $66 million bonus to move its plant out of the country. And that is where many of our jobs have gone.

Tax shelters are also a large part of the problem, since they favor those with higher incomes. And the higher the income, the greater the favoritism. Several tax shelters were eliminated by the Tax Reform Act of 1986, but major ones remain. A retirement plan with tax-deductible contributions is a very important example. Within defined limits, the contributions of both employee and employer are not presently taxable until the funds are withdrawn, which may be years in the future. The employee has meanwhile deferred the tax payment, and for someone with high income that can mean a significant savings. Low-income workers who must spend all of their earnings on living costs cannot, of course, take advantage of this tax shelter.

One of the most accessible tax shelters, for someone with capital, is an investment in corporate stocks, especially growth stocks. These generally pay low or even no dividends, which would be taxable as income when received. The investor's return comes from growth in the market price of the stock—the capital gain. And capital gains for higher income taxpayers are taxed at a rate lower than that for ordinary income.

You must have capital to get capital gains. Over nine out of ten American taxpayers—93 percent of the people—receive no capital gains, so they do not get the special benefits from the way capital gains are taxed. Since virtually all taxable capital gains come from stock investments and speculative real estate, most of the capital gains, 72 percent in fact, go to just 1 percent of the taxpayers.[7]

In fact, a fairly large share of capital gains never get taxed at all—those that are passed on by gift or inheritance. When assets are inherited, the cost or basis to the heirs is the assets' market value at the time of the original owner's death. In technical terms, this is known as a step-up in basis, which means that the basis or cost on which capital gain is calculated is "stepped-up" to the market value at the time of death—thereby permanently sheltering often substantial gains from taxation.

To illustrate: a taxpayer might buy common stock for $1,000, hold it for years while the value increases substantially, and bequeath it to her son at death when the market value of the stock has risen to $500,000. Since the mother never actually sold the stock, she neither owed nor paid any tax on the $499,000 gain, and neither did her estate. If the son immediately sells the stock for $500,000, he registers no gain and therefore owes no tax—because the stock's basis to him is taken to be $500,000. This loophole costs all other taxpayers, in taxes not collected on this type of capital gain, over $43 billion a year.[8]

There are, of course, federal taxes on estates, but effectively they do not apply until the estate is over $600,000, or $1,200,000 for a couple. In fact, it has been estimated that this tax affects only 0.5 percent of all estates.[9]

A corporation can also provide a tax shelter. The highest tax rate for corporations is now 34 percent, although many pay considerably less because of provisions like the foreign tax credit. Smaller businesses pay lower rates—15 percent for taxable income up to $50,000, 25 percent for income between $50,000 and $75,000.

Since these rates may be lower than their own marginal rates, many high-income individuals set up corporations to have a portion of their income taxed at the lower corporate rates. And a lot of personal expenses get run through these nominal corporations. Although the issue becomes somewhat complicated with consideration of present values

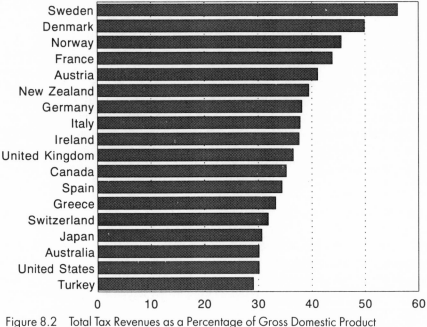

Figure 8.2   Total Tax Revenues as a Percentage of Gross Domestic Product

Source: U.S. Department of Commerce, Bureau of Census, 1992.

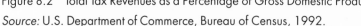

and ultimate disposition of the funds, every accountant understands the corporation's value as a shelter.

With all these special benefits that primarily favor corporations and wealthy individuals, taxes in the United States are among the lowest in the industrialized world. The only such country with a lower overall tax burden is Turkey.

The major problems with our present tax system are thus clear: it does not raise enough revenue and it unfairly favors corporations and the wealthy. It is also too complex for many taxpayers to understand; it changes too often, requiring taxpayers (and their accountants) to constantly learn new rules; and it costs too much both administratively for the IRS and in taxpayers' time.

Unfortunately, the Clinton administration has proposed minimal improvements at best. Despite the president's campaign theme of "change," most of these proposals would only maintain the status quo.

The Administration's Proposals

The Clinton administration has put forward a set of tax proposals that, in the aggregate, will do little to restore the fairer, more progressive tax system this nation had prior to the Reagan-Bush era. Some reforms go in the right direction but are inconsequential. Others go in the wrong direction, several with significantly negative consequences.

The best of the administration's proposals in terms of fairness and revenue productivity is the increase in tax rates on corporations and higher-income individuals. Unfortunately, though, the changes are more symbolic than substantive. For instance, the maximum rate for individuals would go from 31 to 36 percent for incomes over $140,000, with a 10 percent surcharge on incomes over $250,000 (producing an actual maximum rate of 39.6 percent). This reform, although a good start, would not begin to undo the 1980s raid on the national treasury by the wealthy.

The administration's plan originally included an energy tax based on British Thermal Unit (BTU) content. Reducing our dependency on fossil fuels is a laudable goal, but this tax would have been unfair to working people because it is regressive—it takes a higher percentage from the earnings of the middle- and lower-income groups and a lower percentage from those with higher incomes. Replacing the BTU tax is a 4.3 cent per gallon gasoline tax that is similarly regressive and is frankly too small to ensure energy conservation. We should address our energy problems, but with more direct policies that do not penalize taxpayers who have already been hit so hard by the avaricious policies of the 1980s.

A token increase in the top corporate rate, from 34 percent to 36 percent, was first proposed but then compromised down to 35 percent. This rate would apply only to income above $10 million. While a step in the right direction, this modest increase is essentially tokenism. The top rate was lowered from 46 percent to 34 percent in 1986 and was even higher prior to Reagan. Corporations receive great benefits from our society, and they impose substantial costs on public services and facilities. They should pay a fair share of taxes.

Rather than restore fair taxes on corporations, the administration unfortunately is offering handouts to the business sector. For instance, Clinton has advocated the establishment of enterprise zones—a notion that gained currency during the Reagan-Bush years—as a stimulus to economic development in depressed areas. These zones have been tried in most states, but objective studies, by academic scholars as well as the General Accounting Office and the Department of Housing and Urban Development, have found little evidence of significant effect. Enterprise zones have served mainly as vehicles for the transfer of monies from individual taxpayers to corporations, with no accountability required and no measurable economic impact. Fortunately the administration has allocated only modest funds for this program.

The administration earlier undertook to provide additional largess to corporations through the resurrection of an investment tax credit. This attempt to reward business for additional investment was shot down by Congress, and with good reason. A tax credit for further capital invest- ment will not benefit the economy because business is now operating at only about 80 percent capacity. The problem is not ability to invest, but rather that consumer demand is lacking. Business will not expand with- out a demand for products. Hence this credit would have gone almost entirely for investments that would have been made anyway: a gift to business with nothing for taxpayers in return.

The administration also proposed limiting the tax deductibility of ex- cessive executive compensation. This symbolic gesture means nothing in tax revenue, but it does send a positive message about the impropri- ety of executive greed to corporate America.

Two administration proposals concern Social Security. In an excellent partial step, the administration has eliminated the ceiling on earnings to which Medicare withholding applies. Now the White House and Cong- ress should take the much more important step of removing the ceiling on earnings subject to Social Security withholding. Ceilings on Social Security and Medicare withholdings make these taxes regressive, as lower income taxpayers pay both taxes on 100 percent of their earnings while those with high incomes are taxed on only a fraction of earnings.

The administration also seeks to tax more of the Social Security pro- ceeds received by elderly persons with other income. While not neces- sarily a bad idea, this is the wrong approach to dealing with the issue of the wealthy who receive Social Security benefits. The right approach is to establish a means test under which elderly persons with sufficiently high incomes receive no Social Security benefits; this would make it possible to lower the Social Security withholding rates to which working people are subject.

One tax not included in the package sent to Congress is a veritable 800-pound gorilla hiding in the bushes. This is the value-added tax, or VAT. President Clinton has said more than once that this tax might be necessary, and it has been mentioned recently as a way of funding the overhaul of the health-care system. Senate Republican Majority Leader Robert Dole has indicated a strong preference for a value-added tax as a replacement for the income tax.

"The value-added tax is a veritable
800-pound gorilla hiding
in the bushes."

Dole's view represents a frontal and outrageous attack on tax equity. The VAT is equivalent to a national sales tax and is essentially regressive. Consider a family with income of $15,000 a year. They spend virtually all of it on food, clothing, and purchases subject to a 6 percent sales tax. So they pay roughly $900 in sales tax for the year. That amounts to 6 percent of this family's annual income.

Now consider a wealthy family with income of $500,000 a year. They do not need nearly that much to actually live on, so perhaps they spend $100,000 on purchases subject to the tax. They would therefore pay $6,000 in sales taxes. The wealthy family pays more tax in dollars, but of course they have a lot more money to begin with. As a percentage of income, then, they are paying only 1.2 percent, less than a fourth of the poorer family's bill, percentage-wise.

In this example, the family with the lower income pays 6 percent of their income in sales tax, while the person with thirty-three times as much income pays 1.2 percent. And the percentage of sales tax to income continues to fall as income rises—thus a regressive tax. It takes a bigger percentage bite out of the total income of those with the lesser ability to pay.

Advocates of a value-added tax claim it can be made less regressive with exemptions for the poor. They would probably start with a low rate and exempt most necessities including food, medicines, clothing, rent, and utilities. This is exactly what happened in a number of states. But a short time after the tax was enacted, one and then another and then another necessity was removed from the exemptions, until eventually all purchases were subject to the tax. The history of taxation is all too clear on this point: exemptions to make a regressive tax less so will eventually be lost. You just can't make a progressive silk purse out of a regressive sow's ear.

Long-Term Policy Goals

A tax system provides the means for paying for social programs. It raises enough revenue to fund the activities and programs that Congress adopts—to fund what the people, through their elected representatives, say they want government to do in society. Some deficit between expenditures and tax revenues may be tolerable or even good policy. But this amount should be set by explicit policy and not arrived at haphazardly because Congress does not have the nerve to impose the taxes to fund the programs it wants.

Next, the tax system should be fair. If it is not fair, people will not support it. History demonstrates that citizens are liable to revolt when taxes are used to exploit working people for the benefit of the well-to-do.

Tax Bracket

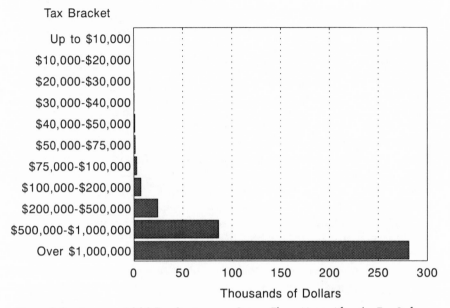

Figure 8.3   Average 1989 Tax Savings per Return Three Years After the Tax Reform Act of 1986

Source: Adapted from Donald L. Barlett and James B. Steele, *America: What Went Wrong* (Kansas City: Andrews and McMeel, 1992), p. 6.

Tax fairness certainly does not mean that everyone, rich or poor, should pay the same amount, but rather that everyone "feels the bite" in much the same way. The upper-, middle-, and lower-income taxpayers should all pay taxes in proportion to their ability to pay. With a progressive tax, people in lower-income brackets pay at lower tax rates and those in higher brackets pay at higher rates. The higher the income, the higher the tax, both in dollars and as a percentage.

Through the machinations of the Reagan-Bush era, our system has become decidedly less progressive and less fair. And the people know it: In a 1992 poll more than three out of four Americans said that upper-income people were not paying a fair share of federal taxes.[10]

To restore fairness to national tax policy the tax burden that was lifted from corporations and high-income individuals should be shifted back. This can be done largely through higher rates for higher incomes, accompanied by the elimination of deductions that favor the wealthy (home interest deductions, state income and property taxes, special corporate depreciation provisions). Capital gains should be taxed at the same rate as gains from labor, i.e., as ordinary income.

The third policy goal should be simplification. Citizens cannot challenge a tax system they cannot understand; this undermines our democracy at its foundation. Furthermore, taxpayers have to spend far too much time dealing with their taxes or far too much money to pay someone else to attend to them. According to the Internal Revenue Service's own estimates, a reasonably complete individual return requires nearly forty hours of labor each year. This hidden cost is equal to an entire week's pay.

Simplification made the flat tax advocated by Democratic presidential hopeful Jerry Brown appealing, even though that tax would have been terribly inequitable (for the same reasons the VAT is regressive). Simplification is necessary and attainable, but it should not come at the expense of progressivity and fairness.

Stability should be a fourth goal. Frequent changes in tax laws require citizens to go through a new learning process virtually every year, at substantial cost in time and anxiety. The broad tax rules should be hammered out and then left alone. Changing revenue requirements could be handled through periodic changes only in the rates.

Realization of these four long-term policy goals will empower citizens and restore our tax system to its proper role in our democracy.

Short-Term Policy Goals

In the short term, progressives should concentrate on a limited set of concrete goals.

First, to raise revenue and to make the system fairer, we should institute a wealth tax. The very wealthy can live at least partially off their wealth. They thus require less current income and can arrange their affairs to avoid income taxes. They are not paying taxes in relation to their ability to pay, which is required according to the fairness principle. And they are not paying their fair share in terms of the demands they place on public services and the benefits they obtain from our economic and social system.

A personal wealth tax of 4 percent with a generous individual exemption of $500,000 per adult could raise $225 billion a year—almost half of what is now raised by the income tax. Yet a husband and wife with assets of $1.5 million would pay only $20,000 a year.

We should also implement a corporate wealth tax—a tax on gross corporate asset holdings—to supplement the income tax. It should tax gross assets instead of net asset holdings because that is a better measure of the size of the corporation, the resources it controls, the spread of its influence, and the burden it places on public services and our national infrastructure. Using gross assets would also avoid favoring debt over stock as a source of capital financing, a problem with the present corporate interest deduction.

Both the corporate wealth tax and the personal wealth tax should be based on the value of the assets and not on the figures accountants now put in balance sheets. Wealth is measured in today's values, not what something might have been worth years or decades ago.

Second, we should raise the inheritance tax. There is no good economic or social reason for great wealth to be concentrated in a single family's lineage for generations—what could be called "blood welfare." We learned early on in this country that royalty—government by right of family lineage—does not produce good government. And we know by now that it does not increase economic productivity either. We need to tax estates at death and put those resources back to work in the economy.

Estate or inheritance taxes do exist at the federal and state levels. But they are too low, and they still result in enormous wealth being reserved for the exclusive benefit of heirs who may have done nothing to earn it.

After allowing a fair, even a generous, exemption—perhaps $500,000 or $1 million—to let a home or farm or small business stay in a family, the inheritance tax rate should be increased substantially, especially for the largest estates. Of course the present rule that the entire estate may pass to a spouse untaxed should be retained. Huge estates should, however, be heavily taxed after both the husband and the wife pass on. And if Congress does not have the courage to raise inheritance taxes significantly, it must at least eliminate the so-called step-up in basis for capital gains.

"We should stop trying to bribe corporate America to do good with special benefits like enterprise zones, investment tax credits, and accelerated depreciation."

Third, we should stop trying to bribe corporate America to do good with special benefits like enterprise zones, investment tax credits, and accelerated depreciation. Instead of contributing to the economic wealth of the country, these measures simply transfer the tax burden from businesses to individuals. Meanwhile we should eliminate the corporate foreign tax credit. Taxes paid to other countries should be deductions, not credits, just like taxes paid to states.

These short-term changes will move us substantially toward the long-term policy goals presented earlier. Those goals, in turn, will give us a "good" tax system that raises enough revenue to operate government and is both fair and simple. Once it is in place, the overall structure should be left alone, although rates and amounts can be adjusted occasionally.

As Oliver Wendell Holmes once remarked, "Taxes are what we pay for civilized society." A democracy must be supported by a democratic tax system. That means a system citizens can understand and support, and can, when appropriate, confidently criticize. It means a system that, as far as possible, is fair to all. And it means a system that works, in the sense of providing the revenue required to conduct the people's government. Our system is, at present, broken. Implementation of the proposals given here will go a long way toward fixing it.

Achieving Sustainability

BARRY COMMONER

The basic environmental problem that Bill Clinton confronted in his first year in office was the legacy of recent political history: the fact that for all but four of the first twenty-three years of its life, the U.S. environmental program was controlled by Republican presidents.

By 1993, under that leadership, the program had failed dismally to reach its legislated goals of environmental improvement. It was governed by a flawed remedial strategy that guaranteed a conflict between environmental quality and economic development. Its cost, in public and private money, was over $130 billion a year and rising. And its chief instrument, the Environmental Protection Agency (EPA), was saddled with a managerial staff that for the past twelve years had slavishly followed the environmentally hostile dictates of the Reagan-Bush administrations.

As a result, President Clinton's call for "change" applied as much to environmental regulation as it did to the economy. However, while Clinton has at least made an effort to deal with some of the economy's structural weaknesses, he has thus far ignored equally fundamental flaws in the nation's environmental program. The consequences of this error are potentially far-reaching: Because of the strong connection between the environment and the economy, Clinton's environmental failure could very well undercut his efforts to revive the economy.

A Tale of Two Strategies

The environmental program that the Clinton administration inherited was created in the early 1970s in response to intense public concern, dramatized by Earth Day 1970. The first legislative product borne of that concern was the National Environmental Policy Act (NEPA). It established a policy that not only called for repairing the nation's badly polluted environment but specified how that goal was to be achieved: through efforts to "prevent or eliminate damage to the environment and biosphere."[1]

Somehow between NEPA and the implementation of the Act that followed, the emphasis shifted from a strategy of prevention or elimination of pollution to one of reduction or control of pollution. The EPA determined that remediation could be accomplished by appending control devices to the sources of pollution—for example, by attaching catalytic converters to automobile exhausts or scrubbers to power plants.

The twenty-three-year effort to improve the environment has tested the capabilities of these two strategies, albeit inadvertently. The attempt to improve air pollution has relied almost entirely on control devices that seek to trap or destroy pollutants after they have been produced. Only lead, among the standard pollutants, has been subject to efforts to prevent its emission altogether, mainly by removing it from gasoline. The different results each strategy has achieved are striking: Between 1975 and 1990, annual emissions of lead decreased by 95 percent while during that same period the average for the remaining pollutants fell by only 18 percent.[2]

The same story can be told for DDT, PCBs, mercury, phosphates, and Strontium 90. In each case significant remediation (70 to 95 percent) was achieved by preventing the generation of the pollutant in the first place rather than by attempting to trap or destroy it after it has been produced. Thus DDT and PCBs have been banned; mercury is no longer used in electrolytic chlorine production; the use of phosphates in detergents has been severely restricted; and the end of atmospheric nuclear bomb tests has curbed strontium 90 emissions. But these are the exceptions; most pollution emissions have been reduced by only 10–20 percent and some not at all.

Even Lee M. Thomas, Ronald Reagan's EPA administrator, has had to acknowledge the shortcomings of the control strategy. On January 19, 1989, on his and the president's last day in office, Thomas wrote a remarkably candid evaluation of the agency's past performance—a kind of bureaucratic last will and testament. For the first time a top environmental official stated publicly that EPA's effort "had been on pollution control rather than pollution prevention." More astonishing still was

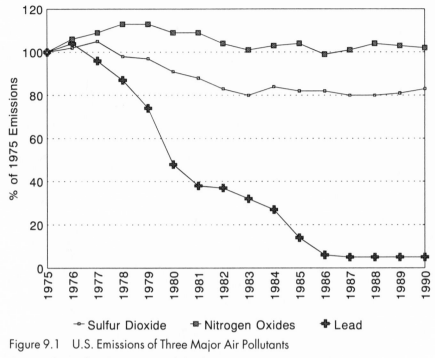

-•- Sulfur Dioxide   -■- Nitrogen Oxides   -♦- Lead

Figure 9.1   U.S. Emissions of Three Major Air Pollutants

Source: Council on Environmental Quality.

Thomas's admission that the control strategy had failed. "EPA realizes that there are limits as to how much environmental improvement can be achieved under these [i.e., control] programs, which emphasize management after pollutants have been generated," Thomas stated, with customary bureaucratic delicacy.[3]

Not only have control strategies failed to satisfy the stated objectives of national environmental policy, they have also imposed an unnecessary burden on economic development. Indeed, the oft-lamented conflict between the economy and the environment is not an ecological imperative but a result of the attempt to improve the environment by means of control devices. The failure to grasp this point, we will see, has serious implications for Clinton's environmental policy.

A control approach to environmental improvement is inherently self-limited. As the efficiency of a control device increases so does its cost—exponentially. For example, the cost of improving the efficiency of sulfur-dioxide controls at coal-fired power plants increases from $50 a kilowatt at 70 percent efficiency to $2,200 a kilowatt at 95 percent efficiency. Extrapolated to 100 percent efficiency, this relationship reaches a control cost of $4,270 a kilowatt, which is about ten times the cost of the power plant itself.[4] The net result is that the degree of environmental improvement that a control device can achieve is sharply limited by its cost.

Moreover, because the device does not reduce emissions to zero, its practical effect is diminished as the pollutant-generating activity increases. Thus, although the overall efficiency of nitrogen-oxide control in U.S. transportation improved by 38 percent between 1975 and 1990, annual emissions decreased by only 16 percent because the vehicle-miles traveled per year increased by 52 percent.

In contrast to control strategies, prevention requires the use of technology that does not generate the pollutant in the first place—whether that means unleaded gasoline in automobiles, the substitution of semipermeable membranes for mercury in electrolytic chlorine production, or the elimination of toxic pesticides from agricultural production. Indeed, preventive remedies for the major environmental problems we face are now well known and the necessary substitute technologies are already in hand. For instance, coal-fired power plants—major contributors to global warming and air pollution—can be replaced by renewable, solar energy generated by photovoltaic cells or wind power. And the automobile, whose internal combustion engine produces a number of noxious pollutants, can be replaced by a nonpolluting electric car.

The strategy of prevention cures the conflict between environmental quality and economic development that is inherent in the control strategy. Since prevention eliminates pollutants—reduces emissions to zero—it allows the relevant economic activities to expand without inducing a concomitant increase in pollution. And it allows capital that would otherwise be used for control devices to be used for more productive investment. Indeed, pollution prevention can be implemented through new productive activities that are often more economically efficient than the activities they replace.

But pollution prevention can be fully implemented only by undertaking extensive transformations of systems of production: energy, transportation, agriculture, and major industries—the petrochemical industry in particular. Such a transformation, though costly, would release the huge sums of money now spent on the futile effort to control pollution for new productive investments. This in turn could help trigger the economic renaissance and the new jobs that Clinton has promised.

Thus, properly understood, the country's environmental problem is intimately linked to the economic difficulties that Clinton pledged to confront. The linkage is a fundamental one, for it raises the issue of whether economic development is to be guided by social interest—for example in the form of industrial policy—or is to remain the haphazard outcome of "free market" forces. We can judge how well Clinton has met the challenge of improving the economy *and* the environment from the administration's record thus far.

Clinton's Successes

In a sense, the Clinton administration was born with an environmental success to its credit—the selection of Al Gore as running mate. Gore's book, *Earth in the Balance,* had established him as a thoughtful and committed environmental advocate, whose influence on Clinton's grasp of the issues was evident during the campaign. As vice-president, Gore has been more heavily involved in technology, a natural transition given the emphasis in his book on "the development of environmentally appropriate technologies that will abet sustainable economic programs and that can be substituted for the ecologically destructive technologies currently in place."

With respect to its actual performance, since taking power the Clinton administration has successfully settled several longstanding environmental controversies. In the Northwest, the standoff that pitted the timber industry against environmentalists—the one defending the owners' profits and the workers' jobs, the other the spotted owl's habitat—has apparently been resolved by a compromise. Some areas of the old-growth forests have been set aside for the spotted owl and protected from human incursion, and the loggers have been given the right to cut 1.5 million acres instead of the 5 million acres previously allotted to them. In California, a similar compromise has partitioned the coastal areas inhabited by another threatened bird, the gnatcatcher, between this original resident and the developers who wish to build houses there.

Here the issues are very different from those raised by pollution. Pollution not only damages the environment but is a direct threat to human health. The control strategy is an effort to minimize the damage and to reduce the threat without altering the human productive activity that generates these hazards. In contrast, the prevention strategy eliminates these hazards by changing the technology of production consistent with ecological principles. In both cases, however, the human activity that is the source of the problem—production—is not done away with. Cars run and electricity is generated, but the means of producing these goods are slightly modified (control) or basically changed in design (prevention).

In the Northwest's old-growth forests and on the California coast, the ecological conflict can be neither controlled nor prevented. There is no way to "control" lumbering to minimize its effect on the spotted owl. If you cut down an old growth tree, it is gone and with it, the bird's habitat. Nor is there any way to "prevent" the ecological consequence of logging. As long as timber is produced, trees must be cut down and the spotted owl displaced.

In sum, the spotted owl and gnatcatcher controversies deal with conservation, which protects the natural world—ecosystems free of people
and their works—from human intrusion. Conservation pits *any* human
activity, however benign in its ecological effect, against the natural, nonhuman world—two inherently incompatible spheres that can more or
less coexist but never together in the same space. Environmentalism,
unlike conservation, includes the human technosphere and considers
how human productive activities can be conducted in ways that are sufficiently compatible with the ecosphere to avoid damaging the lives of
its human and, insofar as possible, its nonhuman inhabitants.[5]

In the United States, conservation preceded environmentalism, inspired by huge tracts of virgin land wrested from its Native-American inhabitants and, by conquest, turned into land publicly owned by the federal government. It reached its peak with Teddy Roosevelt and Gifford
Pinchot, and left a political heritage institutionalized in the Department
of the Interior. Since its inception, the department has sought to defend
the wild public lands, especially in the west, from private, human incursion. In the New Deal, under Harold Ickes, the department's scope was
considerably expanded and oriented toward protecting public lands
from corporate raiders. In the Reagan-Bush regime, especially in the
hands of Reagan's secretary of the interior, James Watt, the department
was notorious for abetting attacks on public lands and the environment
rather than defending them.

Clinton's secretary of the interior, Bruce Babbitt, has clearly set out to
change course. Soon after he took office, Babbitt proposed a dramatic
increase in the prices charged to private operators for the use of public
grazing and forest land. These charges had been so far under the government's maintenance costs that the U.S. Forest Service, for example, lost
some $5.6 billion on sales of lumber rights over a ten-year period. Under
fierce opposition, however, the administration initially backed off and,
despite Babbitt's objections, tabled the plan to modify pricing practices.
By August, however, Babbitt had persuaded the White House to agree to
more than doubling the grazing fee—perhaps because the votes of western Democrats on the budget bill were no longer needed.

Babbitt also played an important role in the resolution of the spotted
owl and gnatcatcher issues. Until he intervened, these issues were simply pitched battles, with neither side willing to give ground. Through negotiations, the Clinton administration was finally able to arrive at the
only reasonable outcome of the conflict: a compromise that partitioned
the areas between people and nature. In another wise and unprecedented move, the administration provided a fund of $1.2 billion to aid
the communities affected by the loss of jobs in the Northwest timber industry. In achieving these results, Babbitt had to argue not only with developers and the timber industry but with President Clinton as well.[6]

On the other hand, Clinton's decision to sign the International Biodiversity Treaty, the crucial conservationist measure so rudely scorned by George Bush, was apparently his own. Although the treaty originated with efforts to conserve endangered species, its final form and its real significance reflect the fact that the endangered species are in developing countries and the conservationists who want to save them are largely in developed countries. As a result, basic North-South issues are embedded in the treaty. It speaks, therefore, of both conservation and the sustainable use of biological diversity; it provides funding to help developing countries protect endangered species; and it ensures that revenues from access to biological resources will be fairly divided between the sources (developing countries) and the developers (industrial countries).

"Bruce Babbitt deserves credit for resolving seemingly intractable environmental controversies."

All told, Clinton—or more accurately, Bruce Babbitt—must be credited with resolving these seemingly intractable controversies. All this good work has earned Babbitt an ironic tribute. His value to the Department of the Interior and to the environmental movement generally was so great as to convince Clinton that he could not afford to elevate Babbitt—apparently his preferred candidate—to the Supreme Court.

Clinton's Failures

Like Babbitt, Carol Browner, the new EPA administrator, also inherited an agency heavily conditioned by Reaganism. But unlike the Department of the Interior, EPA has done almost nothing to shake off this debilitating disease. There is in fact little to distinguish the work done by EPA under Browner thus far from its actions during the Bush administration, when major policies were dictated by the Office of Management and Budget and Vice President Dan Quayle's Council on Competitiveness.

The persistence of environmental delinquency is especially evident in the ongoing battle over a hazardous waste incinerator in East Liverpool, Ohio. The incinerator is meant to destroy mixtures of chemical wastes that contain highly toxic compounds such as dioxin and polychlorbi-phenyls (PCBs). EPA's Region 5 authorized Waste Technology Industries (WTI) to build the incinerator despite the fact that it is located within 1,100 feet of a school and situated in a low-lying site along the Ohio River that is frequently subject to air stagnation. Some sense of what is wrong at East Liverpool can be gained from the remark made by Valdus Adamkus, the administrator of EPA Region 5 who had approved the permit, when he was recently confronted by incinerator opponents. "Personally, in my heart, when I saw the location, I was shocked," he said.[7]

Adamkus's curious position—aware that the facility is environmentally unacceptable but nevertheless willing to approve it—turns out to be typical of the EPA middle-managers involved in the WTI controversy, most of them Reagan-Bush holdovers. This was clearly demonstrated by the litigation that an East Liverpool residents group, the Tri-State Environmental Council (TEC), with the help of Greenpeace and volunteer scientists, has forced on WTI and EPA. The legal battle came to a head in February 1993 when a federal district court judge, Ann Aldrich, agreed to hear testimony on a Greenpeace/TEC request to bar a test burn that, according to EPA regulations, was required in order to show that the incinerator's toxic emissions would meet environmental standards. Although the test, which was eventually allowed, would last only eight days, EPA had ruled that the incinerator could then continue to operate for a year while the results were analyzed and a final decision was made on an operating permit.

The opponents had criticized the Region 5 permit because it was based on the outmoded idea that exposure to the incinerator's dioxin emissions would occur only through the lungs. Current research, in fact, shows that the intake of dioxin-contaminated food may be far more important. The permit risk assessment concluded that the maximum risk of cancer from the incinerator's dioxin emissions would be ten in 1 million over a seventy-year lifetime, which is considered an acceptable risk by the EPA. The contemplated one-year initial operation, according to this reasoning, would thus involve a risk of only one-seventh in 1 million. But when Judge Aldrich ordered EPA to assess the risk of *indirect* exposure to dioxin, the resulting EPA document confirmed the opponents' position: It estimated that indirect exposure through food was 1,000 times greater than that due to inhalation.

One might have thought that this information would be enough to put an end to the controversy. In the hands of William Farland, the EPA manager who supervised the preparation of the report and presented it to the court, however, it turned into a defense of the EPA decision to allow the test burn *and* one year of operation. This was achieved by a statistical sleight-of-hand. Farland, who came to the EPA in 1979, acknowledged that home-grown beef eaten by a nearby farmer—chosen as representative of the highest possible risk of exposure—would contain enough of the dioxin emitted by the incinerator to result in a cancer risk of forty-two in 1 million for one year of operation, well above the risk that EPA considers acceptable. Nevertheless, Farland's report concluded, "Actual risks are likely to be less and may even be zero."

How was Farland able to reach such a conclusion? Farland resorted to the vintage Reagan-era practice of ignoring or grossly distorting scientific facts to justify a preconceived pro-industry policy. Indeed, Reagan's Office of Management and Budget (OMB) had gone out of its way to invent a new way to corrupt the crucial relationship between scientific fact and environmental policy. In a 1987 document, for instance, OMB pointed out that environmental risk assessment had traditionally been based "on the risk to a hypothetical individual who is assumed to be exposed to the worst possible combination of exposure circumstances" and argued that, instead, the assessment should be based "on risks that are usually found for the entire exposed population."[8] OMB decreed that henceforth risk assessments were to be governed by something called the "best estimate." What this meant, simply, was *average* risk.

It is true that the acceptability of the risks associated with hazardous pollutants has been routinely expressed in terms of the risk encountered by a person exposed to the *highest* level of the pollutant over a seventy-year lifetime—as well it should be. If the standard is based on some statistical average such as OMB's "best estimate," it will protect people exposed to an average risk or less—that is, *half* the population. On the other hand, if the standard is based on the population at highest risk, it will protect the most vulnerable people and everyone else as well. This is the moral imperative that governs preventive public health policy: that the health of all people, not half of them, should be protected by basing standards on the most vulnerable part of the population at risk. Farland's bland assertion—that "[a]ctual risks are likely to be less and may even be zero"—is a posthumous manifestation of the Reagan OMB's "best estimate."

Unconvinced by Farland's reasoning, Judge Aldrich rejected the EPA's claim and found for the plaintiffs on this issue, stating in her ruling, "[T]his court finds it clear that the operation of the WTI facility during the post trial burn period clearly may cause imminent and substantial endangerment to health and the environment."[9] The maximum cancer risk from a lifetime (seventy-year) exposure to dioxin engendered by operating the incinerator beyond the one-year period after the trial burn would, of course, be very much larger—at least 2,800 per million. This risk is far in excess of EPA's one to ten per million standard; in a verbal comment Judge Aldrich characterized it as "enormous."

Thus the court decided that EPA had failed to draw the correct policy conclusion from its own data and standard of "acceptability." In effect,

EPA was ordered by the court to do its job: the development and enforcement of environmental policy soundly based on the facts. In this respect, the performance of Clinton's EPA has been indistinguishable from that of Reagan's or Bush's.

"The performance of Clinton's EPA has been indistinguishable from that of Reagan's or Bush's."

The application of this statistical maneuver to the WTI case has created a dangerous administrative precedent. The senior official ultimately responsible for deciding the fate of the WTI incinerator is Robert M. Sussman, the deputy administrator appointed by Clinton (Carol Browner having recused herself from the issue). In July 1993, Sussman wrote to Terri Swearingen, the East Liverpool resident who has led the fight against WTI, to explain why EPA had decided to allow the incinerator to operate despite its own evidence that this would violate the one to ten per million maximum cancer risk that the agency had until then imposed on trash-burning and hazardous-waste incinerators. "Even with conservative assumptions," he wrote, "the estimated potential cancer risk from *average* dioxin emissions to a *typical* resident was determined to be approximately one in 10,000,000, a level well within the range of risks considered acceptable by regulatory agencies."[10] (emphasis added)

Here, consciously or not, Sussman has drastically changed the basis for regulating incinerator dioxin cancer risks, which, again, have always been based on the maximum rather than the "average" or "typical" exposure. In effect, Sussman has decided that the operative dioxin cancer risk at WTI is not forty-two per million but 0.1 per million. This maneuver—a kind of statistical detoxification of dioxin—makes the standard of acceptability at the WTI incinerator 420 times less rigorous than that applied by EPA to other similar facilities in the past. On its face, this decision is applicable to every assessment of the risks generated by incinerators, toxic dumps, and other emitters of chemical pollutants. Allowed to stand, it would massively degrade the already inadequate protection from the assault of toxic pollutants on the environment and health.

That the WTI incinerator issue has achieved such a troublesome notoriety symbolizes some of the Clinton adminstration's generic problems. One of them is Clinton's pattern of breaking campaign promises in the name of politically expedient compromise—as in the case of failing to lift the ban on gays and lesbians in the military or abandoning his initial jobs-creation initiative. The WTI incinerator is probably the earliest episode of this sort. During the campaign and again in December 1992, Clinton and Gore promised to block the operation of the incinerator. But as early as February 1993, only a few weeks into the new administration, the *Wall Street Journal* reported that Carol Browner, "in an apparent reversal of Clinton administration policy," suggested that the EPA would not block the WTI test burn.[11] With Sussman's later decision to permit at least one year of operation, and his revisionary approach to risk standards, there seems to be a good deal of truth to the caption at the top of another *Journal* article that appeared in July 1993: "EPA Chief Carol Browner's First Months in Office Echo the Approach of Her Bush-Era Predecessor."[12]

Where Is Clinton Headed?

Apart from serving as a portentous bureaucratic battleground, the WTI incinerator also symbolizes the intrinsic conflict between environmental quality and the chemical industry, which produces the hazardous waste that the incinerator is supposed to render harmless. For years these wastes have been accumulating in dumps around the country. The Superfund program, designed to clean up these toxic waste dumps, stands as one of the great failures of the national environmental program; thus far it has detoxified only a few percent of the tens of thousands of dumps extant. Meanwhile, the industry continues to emit into the environment some 100 million tons per year of chemicals officially designated as hazardous, all of them the industry's products or derived from them. The industry's constant toxic output is likely to create Superfund sites faster than they can possibly be cleaned up.

Enormous costs are involved. The Office of Technology Assessment has estimated that it will cost at least $500 billion, over fifty years, just to clean up the existing chemically contaminated sites. Some idea of what it would take to destroy the 100 million tons of hazardous waste produced annually can be gained from the cost of incinerating—and yet not completely detoxifying—one ton of hazardous waste: $100 to $1,000, depending on the nature of the material.[13] At $100 per ton, the total cost would be $10 billion, a figure considerably larger than the chemical industry's annual profit; at $1,000 per ton, it would amount to $100 billion, about one-third of the industry's total annual sales.

All this is to signify that however troublesome, the problems created by the attempt to incinerate toxic waste are minuscule in comparison with the problem of preventing it. That would require not merely a drastic restructuring of the petrochemical industry but greatly reducing its size, for many of the products that it sells are themselves toxic or become so when incinerated.

Thus, the disposal of hazardous waste is not just another of the numerous issues of environmental pollution. Rather, it is a problem inherent in the structure of the petrochemical industry. Hazardous waste-burning incinerators are essentially control devices attached to the end of the complex stream of chemicals, many of them toxic, that the industry produces. Like other control devices, they are costly and will inevitably become more so as increasingly expensive additions are needed to overcome their environmental defects. (For example, when the recent test burn at the WTI incinerator revealed that dioxin emissions were well above the allowable limits, EPA required WTI to add a costly carbon-injection system—itself of dubious efficiency—to the plant.)

"The petrochemical industry's assault on the environment will never be materially reduced by control devices. The only workable remedy is pollution prevention."

The industry's dangerous assault on the environment will never be materially reduced by control devices. The only workable remedy is pollution prevention, which means halting the manufacture of the industry's numerous products and inadvertent byproducts that are incompatible with the environment. The industry was recently forced to confront this issue when the U.S.-Canadian International Joint Commission that monitors the environmental problems in the Great Lakes called for a ban on the use of chlorine in manufacturing.[14] Incorporated into organic molecules, chlorine is responsible for a large proportion of the toxic chemicals in the environment, most of them produced in manufacturing processes such as paper and petrochemicals.

There is no sign that the Clinton administration is willing to confront this intimidating issue. Instead, as symptoms such as the WTI controversy surface, compromises are sought that seek to minimize the environmental hazards—but more often the objective is to contain the political fallout. For example, when the administration learned that a forthcoming National Academy of Sciences report would substantiate that children are at a considerably greater risk than adults from toxic pesticide residues in their food, the White House announced that it would persuade farmers to use fewer pesticides. That is, of course, a good idea. But it hardly confronts the origin of the problem and hence its only lasting solution: the elimination of petrochemical pesticides from agriculture. Together with the parallel problem of eliminating the environmental hazards of chemical fertilizer, this would involve basic structural changes in the system of agricultural production—essentially a transition to organic farming.

If government policies favored organic farming instead of the heavy use of chemicals, the farm economy would improve. (Studies show that organic farmers can obtain the same economic return per acre as conventional farmers and with a lower debt burden.) If American auto manufacturers moved rapidly into mass production of electric cars, they might recapture their pre-eminent position in the world market. If the United States produced enough reasonably priced photovoltaic cells to satisfy the potential domestic market and the huge existing market in developing countries, new enterprises for decentralized power production would be created and our balance of trade improved. If a moratorium on trash-burning incinerators were established, communities would have a chance to bring recycling up to its full potential, creating numerous jobs in recycling-based industries.

These are big "ifs." What is the Clinton administration doing to turn these contingencies into realities? What could it do? The answer to the first question is: not much. The answer to the second is: a great deal.

One of the few such policies that the administration has initiated on these issues is the establishment of a moratorium on the construction of new hazardous waste incinerators. However, the moratorium applies to only a few states that have not yet taken over the regulation of such facilities. It also fails to address the problem of preventing the production of wastes.

Another administration initiative is the establishment of a "Clean Car" task force for the purpose of "linking research efforts of relevant [federal] agencies with those of U.S. auto manufacturers."[15] However, action on this urgent issue, for example to put electric vehicles—the only workable answer to urban air pollution—on the road, appears to be a long way off.

Yet there is a way to act now on this problem, without waiting for a research "breakthrough." For example, rather than imposing a "backbreaking" (to quote Clinton) gasoline tax, a federal procurement program could accomplish much more for both the environment and the economy by creating a demand for enough electric cars to justify the auto industry's investment in the necessary manufacturing facilities. Without this action it is unlikely that electric car production could get off the ground, at least soon enough to fend off foreign competition. For example, after producing a prototype electric car, GM announced that the vehicle would not be manufactured unless it could sell 100,000 cars a year (the demand sufficient to justify the necessary capital investment). But since the car is not being manufactured, there is no demand.

As a recent study by the Center for the Biology of Natural Systems (CBNS) shows, this gridlock could readily be broken by a government purchase program. For among the nearly 75,000 cars, vans, and light trucks purchased annually for federal use, about 55,000 are operated in conditions for which electric cars are already suitable (fleet use to facilitate battery recharging and about 60–120 miles of urban travel each day). An executive order by President Clinton to require government departments to purchase electric vehicles, together with similar orders by state and local governments, which would amount to an additional 80,000 vehicles annually, would break the gridlock. The expanded production would quickly bring the present prohibitive cost of essentially hand-made electric vehicles ($25,000 to $100,000) into competition with conventional vehicles.[16] These same vehicles, equipped with new high-capacity batteries, would compete in price and convenience with the ordinary family car. This one act of leadership would open up a broad, worldwide market, revitalize the declining auto industry, reduce gasoline consumption and its contribution to global warming, and help lift the pall of smog that is smothering our cities.

Another CBNS report shows that federal purchase programs could rapidly expand the capacity of the small languishing industry that manufactures photovoltaic cells and increase the market for its goods. This simple device turns sunlight directly into electricity and eliminates the pollutants associated with current power production, including those responsible for global warming. Photovoltaic units are already cost-effective in a number of applications, such as roadside emergency telephones. A government procurement program to provide photovoltaic power for several suitable operations (including recharging the batteries in the government's fleet of electric vehicles) might cost about $2.7 billion. A well-established "learning curve" shows that this progressive expansion of the industry's capacity would reduce the present cost of photovoltaic electricity by two-thirds. It would then compete with the cost of environmental utility power in southern California, greatly increasing demand, further reducing the cost, and opening up the huge residential market to solar electricity. Moreover, as the CBNS report shows, the government's $2.7 billion investment would be a bargain: it would create new industrial activity that, through its "ripple effect," would total approximately $10 billion per year.[17] With this one move, therefore, the government could trigger the creation of a new ecologically sound industry that would help restore the country's economic vitality and begin to eliminate the electric utility system's drastic impact on the national and global environment.

Such an economically constructive approach to the environment would have equally important international implications, for it would enable a new approach to sustainable development in Third World countries. Developing countries are, of course, desperately in need of economic growth and increased production. As a result, as pointed out in the Brundtland Commission report, "[T]he industries most heavily reliant on environmental resources and most heavily polluting are growing most rapidly in the developing world, where there is more urgency for growth and less capacity to minimize damaging side effects."[18] This predicament is the inevitable outcome of the ecological unsuitability of conventional production technology. It engenders a clash between economic development and environmental quality, which, as we have seen, is only exacerbated if control devices are used to minimize environmental impact.

Thus even more than industrialized countries, developing countries need to base their economic growth on ecologically sound production technologies such as electric vehicles and solar electricity. If the Clinton administration were to take the leadership in establishing these new industries and bring prices down to compete with conventional vehicles and power plants, Third World countries could avoid the frustrating conflict between economic development and environmental quality. The benefits would be global, for given the rate of economic development in Third World countries, *they* rather than industrialized countries will soon become the major source of greenhouse gases and other global pollutants if they continue to rely on the present, ecologically unsound technologies of production.

Thus there are powerful lessons that the Clinton administration could learn from the massive two-decade effort to improve the environment:

- Efforts to recapture pollutants after they are produced have largely failed. Environmental pollution is an essentially incurable disease; it can only be prevented.
- To prevent pollution, the production systems that generate it must be replaced with nonpolluting technologies.
- A successful environmental policy is therefore an *investment* policy to transform energy production, transportation, agriculture, and industry along ecologically sound lines. Such a policy would create new opportunities for environmentally sustainable economic devel-

opment and growth, here in the United States and in Third World countries as well.

President Clinton has had the political misfortune of being elected in a time of undramatic crises. The crises are real enough: an economy unable to keep people at work; a health-care system that most Americans cannot afford; a manufacturing sector that is shrinking like the Cheshire Cat; a world in widespread upheaval. But no single threat is so palpable and so urgent as to elicit both the leadership and the popular support needed to generate decisive action. The environmental crisis is no exception. The crisis is just as real as it was in 1970, but the repeated alarms about toxic hazards, global warming, or the Earth's collapsing ozone shield—and the lack of a meaningful response—have become commonplace. Earth Day is no longer a powerful impulse to action. Yet the need for action is greater than ever, for now the remedial governmental machinery, EPA in particular, is strategically misdirected and riddled with managers still under the malignant spell of Reagan's anti-environmental philosophy.

What can Bill Clinton do? In a sense, the first step is the easiest because it is so routine: the replacement of the previous administration's

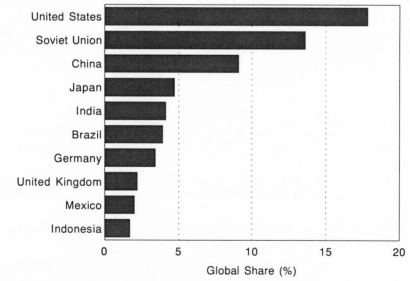

Figure 9.2   Percent Share of Global Greenhouse Emissions, 1989
Source: Intergovernmental Panel on Climate Change.

managerial personnel. This is long overdue at the EPA, where, as we approach the end of Clinton's first year in office, most of the new appointments below the rank of deputy administrator have yet to be made. The second step is much harder but can be facilitated if the new appointees are chosen for the purpose of carrying it out: a thorough, principled reorganization of the EPA program. The necessary administrative rubric has already been created; Vice President Gore heads a task force mandated to "reinvent the government." Given Gore's credentials, what better place to start than the EPA.

There is a danger, of course, that the new invention would be only a smaller, less well-funded, and therefore "more efficient" version of the old agency. If that were to happen, it would trivialize an opportunity of historic proportions. We now know that a successful environmental policy is, in effect, an industrial policy: what is produced and by what means can and should be determined with a livable environment in mind. Bill Clinton still has the opportunity to translate this hard-won wisdom into action.

10

Providing
Comprehensive Coverage

ELLEN R. SHAFFER AND PAUL D. WELLSTONE

In 1992 the dismal state of the health-care system became a front-burner issue in electoral politics. With the recession, the health-care horror stories reached a critical mass. It seemed as though everyone was touched by the crisis. A friend is involved in a car accident while she is between jobs and without insurance; the resulting hospitalization costs put her in debt for the rest of her life. A parent discovers that Medicare does not cover the home nursing care he desperately needs. A co-worker who suffers a heart attack is turned away from the nearest hospital, with fatal consequences, because she is not insured. Even for those of us who have avoided such catastrophes, we must still deal with the burden that escalating health-care costs have inflicted on the U.S. economy.

Health-care reform is perhaps the most explosive political issue now gripping the country. The Clinton administration has promised to make such reform a central part of its campaign to rebuild America. Its proposed solution—a hybrid version of "managed competition"—does not, however, do enough to cure our twin ills of skyrocketing health-care costs and plummeting access to care.

Sixty years of analysis by academic researchers, government commissions, and public advocates—and twenty to thirty years of actual experience in Canada—have convinced progressives and many other observers that a publicly financed single-payer system is the better alternative. Such a system, while preserving the current network of private hospitals and other health-care providers, would budget how much

151

those providers are paid and would severely limit the role of the insurance industry.

The single-payer proposal would assuredly draw enough attacks from vested interests and their congressional allies to make the Clinton administration's early budget battles look like a friendly game of badminton. Winning with the single-payer alternative would mean reaching out and mobilizing the public as a countervailing force to the health-insurance industry and other powerful concerns. An unknown element in the equation is the role of congressional Republicans. If they choose to stonewall and filibuster, particularly in an area where the public is clearly looking for change, Clinton may be able to score a decisive victory—provided he is willing to take on Republican obstructionism more vigorously than he has in the past.

The Democrats' ability to maintain a majority in Congress in 1994, and to keep the White House in 1996, will hinge in part on steering a winning course on health-care reform. If lost this time, the opportunity for meaningful reform could vanish for years.

The Scope of the Problem

Some 37 million Americans are uninsured. But even this staggering figure is deceptively low. Over the course of any given year, one-fourth to one-third of all Americans may experience periods without insurance because of job loss, employer cuts in benefits, or even, ironically, bouts of illness.[1] Most of the uninsured are employees and their dependents, creating a new middle-income and enfranchised constituency for change.

Many have found that they have to prove they do not need health insurance in order to get it. The insurance industry, trying above all to maintain profits by avoiding exposure to the risks against which it is supposed to be insuring, routinely denies coverage to those with "pre-existing conditions"—ranging from diabetes to cancer to depression. (And this process is not left to chance: A Boston data bank tracks the medical records of over 15 million Americans for the industry.)[2]

Tens of millions more are underinsured. Their plans do not cover the kind of care they need, or they cannot afford the out-of-pocket payments to hospitals and doctors that many plans require. The federal Medicare program that covers 35 million elderly and disabled people pays for neither prescription drugs nor long-term care. Payments to doctors and hospitals are so low under the state/federal Medicaid program that many doctors will not even see Medicaid patients.

Lack of coverage means lack of care. In 1993, millions of Americans did not seek care because of financial constraints; in many cases, the un-

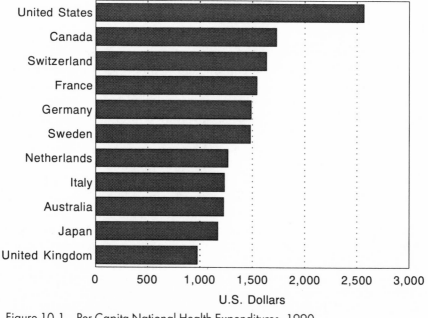

Figure 10.1   Per Capita National Health Expenditures, 1990

Source: Organization for Economic Cooperation and Development.

treated conditions turned out to be fairly serious or very serious.[3] A recent study has shown that uninsured people were twice as likely to die over a fifteen-year period as people with insurance.[4] Federal and state governments had to pass laws during the 1980s to prohibit hospital emergency rooms from "dumping" uninsured people on the street, yet there are signs that the practice continues.

Uncontrollable health-care costs are an oft-quoted fact of life in the United States. Per capita spending on medical care in 1991 was $2,868, compared with $1,962 in 1987.[5] Health-care expenditures were estimated to come close to $1 trillion for 1993 and are consuming an additional 1 percent of gross domestic product every year, for a total of 14 percent in 1992. Health-care inflation has risen at two to three times overall inflation throughout most of the 1980s and 1990s.

For the first time in 1992, the federal government, through its Medicare program, paid over 50 percent of the nation's hospital bills. Contributions to Medicare and Medicaid alone account for 13.5 percent of the annual federal budget, and other health-care expenses such as medical research and Veterans Administration benefits raise the total to 16.1 percent.[6] Obligated to provide some services to the poor and sick through the state/federal Medicaid program, states are also devoting about 12 percent of their budgets to health care, an allocation second only to education.

The administration cites this growing drain on public coffers as a major incentive for comprehensive reform. Congressional Republicans have meanwhile called for a cap on "entitlement" spending, meaning primarily Medicare and Medicaid. This position is not only politically untenable but would do absolutely nothing about the underlying problem of escalating health-care costs. Government programs have actually succeeded in controlling costs to some extent.

This is not so in the private sector, however. Unconstrained by regulation, facing losses for treating the ever-growing number of uninsured patients, and suffering reductions in payments from the government, private health-care providers have turned around and shifted these charges onto private-sector health-insurance plans. Such "charge-shifting" means that while the cost of health care was increasing at 6–9 percent a year in the late 1980s, the price of a health-insurance plan was increasing by 15–25 percent or more.

These costs have become a sore spot for many private employers, especially unionized companies obligated to provide coverage. Chrysler, not usually a bastion of socialism, reported a few years ago that health insurance cost the company $700 per car (now up to $1,000) and pointed out that its international competitors do not face a similar burden. A recent study by the Congressional Budget Office shows that for many employers the lion's share of the cost increases has actually been passed on to employees, who have sacrificed cost-of-living increases and other benefits to maintain their health coverage.[7]

Administrative excess is a primary culprit in America's cost crisis. Because we do business through 1,500 insurance companies, all of which market numerous health plans, administration eats up 25 percent of every U.S. health-care dollar, compared with about 11 percent in Canada. In addition to wasted dollars that go to weeding out potentially unhealthy people, the insurance companies and the providers who bill them have hired legions of people over the past six years to go through multiple duplicated procedures, such as checking the eligibility of the claimant for a particular plan and for particular benefits. Even hospitals that are part of health maintenance organizations (HMOs) show the same high rate of administrative expense. Requiring these companies to use uniform claim forms as both Presidents Bush and Clinton have proposed, although saving $4 to $8 billion a year, would merely touch the tip of the iceberg.

While some would argue that the health of our people is worth any amount of money, our health status in fact ranges from mediocre to appalling—a circumstance made all the more distressing because of the vast sums expended. By 1990, we had dropped to nineteenth in the

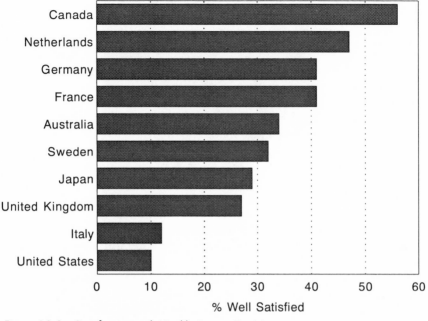

Figure 10.2   Satisfaction with Health Care in Ten Nations
Source: Adapted from *Health Affairs,* Fall 1989.

world in infant mortality, behind such nations as Singapore, Ireland, Hong Kong, and Spain.[8] For low birth-weight babies, the United States shares the thirty-first rank along with Albania.[9] U.S. life expectancy lags behind Japan, Canada, Italy, and Cyprus.[10]

Inequality is a primary factor in health status, and income level is the greatest predictor of health. Even so, our health-care system does not provide adequate care even for diseases that predominantly strike well-to-do white males. Survival rates following heart attack, a key measure of the system's ability to respond to a medical crisis, are worse in the United States than in most other industrialized nations.

As people watch their kids leave college and fall off the family's insurance plan, as their parents go bankrupt paying for nursing homes, and as their neighbors are overwhelmed by poorly timed catastrophic illnesses, a general mood of insecurity has settled in. Polls show that 66 percent of Americans would prefer the Canadian system to ours, and that satisfaction with the U.S. health care system is the lowest of ten industrialized countries (limping behind Italy, which spends about a quarter as much on health care as we do).[11]

All of these countries, and every other industrialized country in the world, already have national health-care systems of some sort that guarantee coverage to everyone. All do better on access, cost, and quality.

Roots of the Crisis

In the five years after World War II, every industrialized nation, with the exception of the United States, made the following two basic decisions. The first was that health care is a social good, not a market good. The right to be born healthy, to patch a wound, and to revive from a heart attack is as fundamental as the right to breathe. The second, flowing from the first, was that the government, not the market, has the primary role in setting and controlling health-care spending to keep it affordable for everyone.

Every other system in the world controls the amount that health-care providers are paid. Under Canada's single-payer system, provinces negotiate with doctors to set rates and with hospitals to set global annual budgets. Multiple-payer systems like those of France and Germany also set fees, though heavily regulated workplace-based insurance companies play a role along with the government in negotiating and enforcing rates. Britain's national health service pays hospitals and hires doctors and nurses directly.

Only the United States stands outside of this consensus. Although presidents from Woodrow Wilson (who favored Argentina's system) through Roosevelt, Truman, Kennedy, Johnson, and Nixon called for national health plans, political opposition has stymied the change at every turn. While Europe was moving forward in the late 1940s, the American Medical Association (AMA) was launching red-baiting campaigns that claimed that national health care was a Communist plot (to its credit, the AMA has moved far from that position in recent times).

The United States instead got an employment-based, private health-insurance system that enriched Prudential, Aetna, Metropolitan Life, and other major insurance companies by paying them a percentage of every medical bill. If health-care bills went up, the insurance company

"The U.S. health-care system is rigged for uncontrolled medical inflation."

just raised its rates and pocketed a bigger piece of change. The system never provided any mechanism for controlling costs. In fact, as workplace health insurance became more widespread, providers raised their own rates and treated insurance payments as an extra windfall. Because they were paid more for every additional test, procedure, and office visit, practitioners had a financial incentive to order ever more, whether necessary or not.

Unlike any other market-based enterprise, health-care providers control both supply (their own medical skills) and demand (the services, tests, and procedures they prescribe). The system is rigged for uncontrolled medical inflation. In fact, it would be hard to enforce even set rates, given the charge-shifting that goes on to cover the uninsured and underinsured as well as the sheer number of different entities that pay bills in the United States—private insurance companies, individuals, self-insured employer plans, union-management Taft-Hartley trusts, and the various levels of government.

Our system bears the marks of its perverse financial incentives. It pays far too much for expensive, specialized medical care once people are ill and not nearly enough for the kind of care that would keep them healthy in the first place. Preventive services such as prenatal care and nutrition education for pregnant women are underemphasized, as is primary care, which includes visits to a health professional early in the course of a disease. Insurance plans, including Medicare and Medicaid, offer broader coverage and pay higher rates for hospital care than for other kinds of services. Many plans do not even cover childhood immunizations, routine check-ups for children, or preventive screening tests that are particularly critical for women.

Mainstream economists often cite an aging population and expanding technology as important factors that drive up costs. While certainly these are factors, they do not explain the difference between the spending in the United States and in other countries, where similarly aging populations receive a much wider array of benefits. Rational distribution of our proliferating stock of sometimes harmful high-tech equipment could reduce costs and would improve quality.

Other countries with national systems in place are able to limit the number of specialists trained, invest rationally in new technologies, and emphasize primary and preventive care. One test of reform in the United States is whether a successful package will overcome professional turf battles and allow advanced-practice nurses and other primary care providers to expand their duties. This will be particularly critical in underserved rural and inner-city areas, where few doctors are willing to practice.

The Market Option

Managed competition forms the basis for much of the Clinton health proposal. It is an unproven, untested theory that presumes that the market will work to regulate health-care costs, if only we can make health care look like a market. The Managed Competition Act of 1992, introduced into Congress by Reps. Jim Cooper (D-TN) and Thomas Andrews (D-TX), reveals the fundamental problems any market-based proposal would face. The brainchild of the Jackson Hole Group, managed competition would combine the worst of bureaucratic regulation with the voraciousness of the market system.

Organized by Paul Ellwood, an early proponent of health maintenance organizations, and Alain Enthoven, who began his career at the Pentagon and has long been a business professor at Stanford, the Jackson Hole Group represents the cream of the insurance, provider, and managed-care industries, along with some Fortune 500 employers. Together they have sought to put their own unique spin on a remedy for what they see as the major problems with health care. Enthoven's proposal promised to expand coverage marginally, while letting the industry continue to reap handsome profits. Like rival compromises of the era, such as the employer-mandated "pay or play" plans, neither Reagan nor Bush ever bought it.

Under both the Managed Competition Act and the Clinton plan, most people would pay through work for "accountable health plans." To keep market forces active, these plans could charge different amounts of money. Employees who want a more expensive plan could pay a higher premium, out of pocket. Employers would pay about 80 percent of the average premium in the area, employees about 20 percent. There would be a cap on the percent of income that lower-wage employees and small businesses would have to pay for the average-priced plan.

The insistence that plans must compete for patients based on price, not just on the quality of their care, is a fundamental flaw. The market proponents argue that the lowest priced plans would be the best and most efficient, and that competition will actually drive prices down. In fact, experience with market forces in health care indicates that the opposite is true. Given the opportunity, some plans will offer better coverage or better services to those who can pay more and who are likely to be in better health. Low-income people will have one choice only, regardless of quality: the lowest cost plan. We would perpetuate our multi-tiered system of care and spend billions trying to regulate out the side effects of this discrimination.

The other market argument for having plans compete based on price, as well as for making individual consumers pay part of the premium and

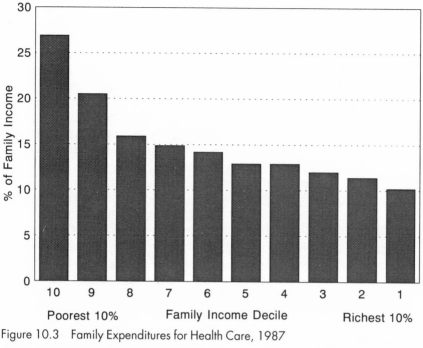

Figure 10.3   Family Expenditures for Health Care, 1987
Source: Economic Policy Institute.

maintaining co-payments and deductibles, is to cut down on "frivolous visits" to the doctor. Although Americans pay more out of pocket for health care than residents of any other nation, managed competitors would have us pay still more to become responsible consumers of cost-effective care. Compared with other countries, Americans do not make excessive office visits, and initial office visits are not responsible for the nation's high health-care bills. In fact, they may prevent costlier complications down the road.

High costs are driven by providers, not consumers. The provider, not the patient, orders the expensive diagnostic tests, prescriptions, and surgical procedures that swell Eli Lilly's income and consumers' health-care bills. Any system that does not control provider rates more directly is bound to fail to control costs.

Although managed-competition schemes offer some choice of different health-care plans, they encourage enrollment in what are known as "managed-care plans." Managed care refers very generally to networks consisting of a limited number of providers, who are under certain constraints to control costs. Originally, many health maintenance organizations, with roots in group practices formed decades ago by doctors who wanted to work collaboratively, often included significant consumer control. Today, however, managed-care plans are generally owned and run by insurance companies, and driven primarily by cost considerations, not concerns for quality of care.

Overall, managed care's record in holding down costs has been equivocal, while problems of undertreatment and quality of care continue to surface. To earn profits, plans may understaff, not answer phones, limit appointment slots, or simply not pay enough attention to enrollees, who will get frustrated and pay out of pocket to go elsewhere if they can afford it. Creating a health-care system where the bottom line is the only line is ultimately counterproductive, in terms of service and cost.

According to the Managed Competition Act, employers would evaluate a number of competing health-insurance plans and offer the best of them to employees to choose. The theory holds that for health care to operate like a market, consumers need adequate information to compare products. Since hospitals and doctors often shroud medical information in mystery, research on medical outcomes and reports to consumers on general health-status indicators can play an important role in empowering consumers and in identifying and improving the quality and efficiency of health care. But it will be some time before this information is sufficient either to guide medical decisionmaking or health plan choices. With expertise primarily in the bottom line, employers are not the best qualified to select their employees health plans. And if enrollees cannot afford to buy a better plan, documenting the poor quality of the plan they belong to is little help.

Clinton's proposed plan improves on this formulation by creating a public or nonprofit health alliance to serve as a clearinghouse for all the health plans in a region. Employee and employer premium contributions would go to the health alliance, which would in turn pay the health plan chosen by the employee. There would be one health alliance in a given area—at least one per state—that would negotiate rates with all providers in the area. It would also give residents enrollment and quality information about the health plans. Alliances would monitor data from the plans to ensure that quality is adequate, especially in the low-cost plans, and that the high-priced plans are not over-charging. Regulations and their enforcement would be left to the states.

These alliances will not offer comprehensive care. An early version of the Clinton plan mandates, for instance, 50 percent co-payments for mental health and substance abuse services, which would discourage access to timely care. Dental care would extend to children only. Limited coverage would be offered for long-term care, shunting expensive cases out of the hospital and into systems where the burden falls on the individual.

Moreover, under the proposed Clinton plan people who enroll in fee-for-service plans would have to pay more. There would be a $200 deductible for each individual ($400 per family), plus a 20 percent co-payment for all services (preventive care may be excluded). Families would not have to pay these fees after they hit $3,000 in a year. The plan would also severely limit Americans' traditional ability to choose their own health caregiver. It would discriminate against people who live in rural or inner-city areas, which are often lucky enough to attract any providers and cannot support a managed-care network.

What about the unemployed, retirees, and others not eligible for a workplace-based plan? What about low-income workers and small businesses who might have trouble paying even for the lowest priced health plan? The Clinton plan would give them subsidies to pay their insurance premiums. Yet, the financing for these subsidies remains one of the black holes of the proposal. The administration has argued that it can pay for this care through a variety of cost containment savings and perhaps a tobacco tax. Analysts were eagerly awaiting the numbers to prove it.

In a blow to cost control and equity, the administration announced that large employers (now defined as 5,000 or more employees nationally) could opt out of the system and continue to offer their own self-insured plans, as long as they meet health alliance criteria for benefits and prices. This opens the door to charge shifting, from health alliance to employer plans and back again. It would also set the stage for discrimination on many levels, giving both employers and health plans incentive and opportunity to screen out employees with medical conditions.

The Clinton plan fails because it gives markets one more chance to solve America's health-care problems. Markets by definition create inequality. When market forces are dominant, as in managed competition, they construct elaborate administrative mechanisms to distinguish the healthy from the sick. The public sector is then faced with the task of constructing bureaucracies to control discrimination. Such a system is not conducive to either controlling costs or providing quality care.

The Single-Payer Alternative

The leading legislative proposal for a single-payer system is the American Health Security Act of 1993 introduced by Sen. Paul Wellstone (D-MN), Rep. Jim McDermott (D-WA), and Rep. John Conyers, Jr. (D-MI). The most fiscally conservative and cost-effective of the health-care reform alternatives, the American Health Security Act (AHSA) meets all the basic criteria set out by consumer advocates for health-care reform.

It would provide universal coverage, with no employers allowed to opt out. There would be one tier of coverage, with the same benefits extended to all, regardless of income, health, employment, or location. Coverage would be comprehensive: all necessary services would be pro-

---

"The Clinton plan fails because it gives markets one more chance to solve America's health-care problems."

---

vided including preventive and long-term care, mental health and substance-abuse care, rehabilitative services and prescription drugs, hospital and health professional charges.

Costs would be effectively contained through the elimination of bureaucratic waste, needless care, and excessive use of technology. There would be no deductibles and no balance billing. Progressive financing would ensure affordability for all and most Americans would ultimately pay less. Single-payer advocates assert that a single-payer system could easily shave $107 billion off the nation's health bill by having one public-sector entity pay all the bills and making everyone eligible for the same benefits.

Consumers would choose from providers, including managed-care plans. Competition would be based on quality not price. Because the entire system would be administered by a nonprofit public entity, accountability would be guaranteed. Finally, the plan would deliberately create what competition cannot generate. It would allocate funds to medically underserved rural and urban areas, encourage training for primary-care physicians and advanced-practice nurses to improve the availability of primary care, and establish a consumer-provider commission on the quality of care.

The system would be publicly financed, primarily through payroll and income taxes. It would also transfer some of the hidden taxes that now go to pay for health care, including Social Security taxes that are part of Medicare payments. Local property taxes, which now support county health services, could be reduced. Because they would no longer pay insurance premiums and various other taxes, 95 percent of the nation's taxpayers would pay on average $1,500 a year less than they do currently.[12]

Annual health-expenditure budgets, global budgets for hospitals, and set rates for health professionals would be enforced to keep growth in spending in line with growth in gross domestic product. Administrative expenses would shrink dramatically, from the current 25 percent to about 7 percent. Studies by the General Accounting Office and the Congressional Budget Office have consistently shown that a single-payer plan would save the most money of any proposal.[13] In contrast, a July 1993 Congressional Budget Office report showed that the Managed Competition Act would add $214 billion over five years to national health expenditures and would still leave 25.3 million uninsured.[14]

Under the single-payer alternative, hospital and health-professional practices would operate just as they do now—as private or public enterprises. They would not be run by the government. However, they would be free from mounds of paperwork and the burdens of cross-checking every clinical decision with an insurance company.

The AHSA faces some tough issues head on. It would sharply limit the role of the health insurance industry. It would finance the system progressively through public funds at a time when the public has shown itself to be wary of taxes. Health care is not free now, and it will not be free after these reforms. But it will be vastly more affordable and accessible, more responsive to human need, and a great improvement over the status quo.

"Public support for a single-payer system, and for government involvement in the health-care system, has grown consistently."

Public support for a single-payer system, and for government involvement in the health-care system, has grown consistently as the reform debate has progressed, and the administration has consequently courted single-payer constituencies. Clinton understands the value of single-payer unions and groups like Citizen Action, Consumers Union, and the American Public Health Association in mobilizing grassroots support for health-care reform. Consumers see health care as a basic right, they believe that government should play a strong role in creating equal access to health care and in controlling costs, and they can understand the difference between a government-financed system (which this is) and one where government runs health services (which this is not). They are fed up with the insurance industry and would gladly remove it from the picture. Their trust in the government has been undermined by years of bashing and the deliberate undermining of services. But if there is any hope of governing, of coming together as a nation to surmount the difficult obstacles ahead, that trust must be renewed.

Support is not confined solely to the general public. Health-care providers also welcome a system that would remove perverse financial incentives either to overtreat or undertreat, as well as the intrusions of insurance industry bean-counters second-guessing their clinical decisions. Many are ready and willing—as long as they have a seat at the table—to discuss reasonable standards of care and reasonable rates of reimbursement.

Scenarios

The Clinton administration, by not addressing the public's health-care concerns, risks losing in Congress with its market-driven proposal. The right will charge that Clinton's plan is too redistributive; the left will not mobilize public opinion if the administration proposal is not sufficiently different from the status quo.

Defense of the status quo is masked as outright opposition to any proposed method of paying for anything, including taxes, premiums, or employer mandates. This can sound like an attractive option to legislators who sense an anti-tax mood. But it misjudges what Americans really want, which is some relief from the medical bills they have and the fear of more. Just saying no to health-care reform can do for the Republican Party what opposition to reproductive choice did for George Bush's 1992 campaign. The administration should not lose an important opportunity to take on a beatable opponent and build support for a Democratic alternative.

The Clinton administration's strategy has been to build a broad coalition for health-care reform—perhaps too broad—including providers, businesses, consumers, and some insurance companies. It bowed to pressure from business to permit large employers to opt out of the system, opening the door to continuing cost-shifting, administrative nightmares, and discrimination. The president is inclined to agree with providers that rate-setting should be avoided unless the market fails. This is bad news for universal, one-tier coverage, for effective cost containment, and thus for the viability of the system.

On the other hand, if the financing of the administration's ultimate proposal is progressive and its benefits are comprehensive, single-payer supporters will have to grapple with the age-old question of health-care politics: Are we reliving 1965 or 1978? Should we compromise for half a step now and keep fighting, as we did with Medicare and Medicaid in 1965, and risk that the other half step may be decades in coming? If the insurance industry remains in the picture, and a few large companies consolidate their grip, the other step may never be taken. Or should we hold out for something better, as in the late 1970s, and risk getting nothing at all? It remains to be seen how hard the vested interests will fight, how intransigent the Republicans will remain, and how vigorously and successfully the White House will bring the message to the American people. Compromise is possible, but only if the principles of universality, comprehensiveness, affordability, freedom of choice, and public accountability are preserved.

The fight for health-care reform is a test case for democracy. Health care is an issue people find personal and compelling. It has walked right into their living rooms and become a high priority issue. It is different from any issue the administration has tackled to date. There is a real opportunity to mobilize people around a proposal that is honest, exciting, and effective. It is the job of leadership to energize and empower the American public, to break the noose that the special interests have drawn around the Beltway.

The administration gets strong marks for knowing what needs to be done in the area of health-care reform and deserves encouragement for finding the will and the political smarts to initiate the process. But success will ultimately require that the president and his talented team face the health-care challenge head on, without blinking.

THE DISENFRANCHISED

11

Eliminating Poverty

TERESA AMOTT

On January 20, 1993, the poet Maya Angelou ushered in the Clinton presidency by declaring that "each new hour holds new chances for a new beginning" for all Americans, from the privileged to the homeless.[1] The privileged, who had benefited so richly from the policies of the past three administrations, toasted Clinton's ascension that evening at one of the fourteen official inaugural balls. In crumbling cities and impoverished rural areas, meanwhile, America's less advantaged were desperately awaiting their own new beginning.

Thirty-six million people—one in seven U.S. residents—live below the official poverty line. More than 14 million of America's poor are children, almost 6 million under the age of six—giving the United States the dubious distinction of inflicting poverty on a greater portion of its children than seven other Western industrialized countries. More than 2 million people over the age of fifteen work full-time, year-round, but are still unable to earn enough to raise their families above the poverty line. Under less stringent—and more reasonable—estimates of poverty, nearly one in four people living in the United States is poor.[2]

The new president faces a daunting challenge. Poverty has been rising in the United States for two decades, as impoverishing forces in the economy and inadequate, and sometimes harmful, public policy responses have combined to place an ever greater share of the U.S. population at economic risk. Combatting this rising poverty will require a reversal of public policy, a willingness to challenge the constraints of the global economy, and the political leadership to unify the country in the service of its most marginalized and disenfranchised sons and daughters.

After one year in office, the Clinton administration is moving in the right direction—but somewhat tentatively and with a considerable degree of caution and ineptitude. Progress is blocked by internal barriers as well as external constraints. Perhaps the most important internal barrier is the president's desire to establish himself as a "New Democrat" willing to meld liberal and conservative policies and rhetoric into a pragmatic consensus. This consensus has not, however, been achieved, and the administration has yet to produce any coherent anti-poverty strategy on a scale required by the times. Another internal barrier was created when Clinton succumbed to a deficit reduction mania that has vitiated any progressive spending initiative.

The external constraints are even more daunting. Two decades of economic, demographic, and political trends have impoverished ever greater numbers of families.

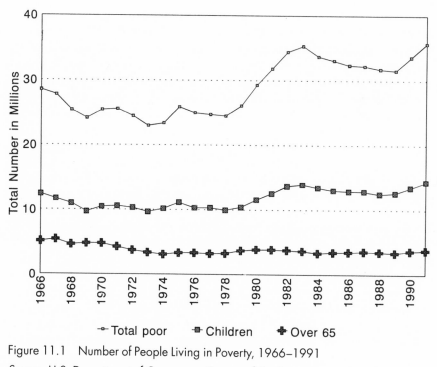

Figure 11.1   Number of People Living in Poverty, 1966–1991
Source: U.S. Department of Commerce, Bureau of the Census.

Rising Poverty

Rising poverty has its deepest roots in the economic stagnation that began sometime in the early 1970s as U.S. companies faced greater international competition and their profits leveled off. In response, corporate America restructured work in ways that contributed to growing poverty: rampant union busting, the replacement of full-time employees with part-time and temporary workers, and the transfer of capital to low-wage regions in the United States and to lower-wage countries abroad. Manufacturing was particularly hard-hit by foreign competition, and deindustrialization drained the life out of communities across the country. At the same time, women's participation in the labor force continued its centuries-long upward trend, bringing large numbers of lower-wage workers into the labor market. Some analysts, such as Chris Tilly, have argued that services grew throughout this period precisely because women were so readily available.[3]

Thus, manufacturing diminished and services grew—all at great cost to the average wage level. By some estimates, more than half the jobs created during the 1980s paid wages below the poverty level for a family of four.[4] As a result, according to Census Bureau estimates, nearly one in every five full-time year-round workers earned less than $12,195, the four-person poverty threshold in 1990.[5]

At the same time as wages stagnated, growing numbers of people abandoned traditional family structures. Younger people deferred marriage, gays and lesbians established new types of living arrangements, states introduced no-fault divorce laws, and more and more women chose to parent without husbands. In 1970, for instance, 82.3 percent of people lived in married-couple households; by 1991, that share had fallen to 68.5 percent. The number of single-parent families grew from 3.8 million to 10.1 million.[6]

Public policy has lagged far behind these dramatic lifestyle changes, with catastrophic effects for single parents and their children. In contrast to most Western industrialized countries, for instance, the United States lacks any form of family allowance, nationalized child care, or housing subsidy for single parents. Our child support system transfers far too little income to custodial parents. And we have not learned from Sweden that in most cases the state should simply advance child support payments to the custodial parent and worry about enforcement later. As a result, public policies in 1986 lifted fewer than 4 percent of poor children in single-parent families out of poverty.[7] Government benefits from the Aid to Families with Dependent Children (AFDC) program have dropped consistently since 1970. The "feminization of poverty" was inevitable as more and more women became the sole financial

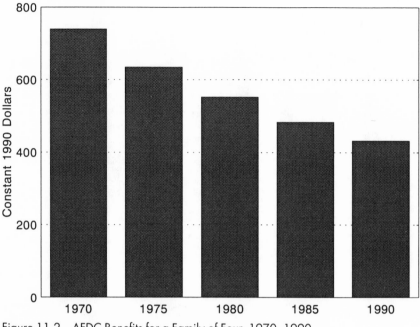

Figure 11.2   AFDC Benefits for a Family of Four, 1970–1990

Source: Committee on Ways and Means, U.S. House of Representatives.

support of their families—in a country whose implicit family policy assumed that Ozzie brought home the bacon and Harriet cooked it for the family dinner.

By the early 1980s, a near-total relinquishing of federal government responsibility for fighting poverty aggravated these trends. Appropriations for subsidized housing fell 82 percent during the Reagan-Bush years. According to census data, there were 4.1 million more low-income renters in 1989 than apartments they could afford (in 1970, the mismatch had been only 400,000).[8] While housing took the biggest beating, funding for other programs such as education, job training, public service employment, and a variety of public health programs was also cut back severely. For instance, employment and training programs aimed at the poor lost nearly two-thirds of their purchasing power. Between 1981 and 1993, spending on programs specifically targeted at low-income people fell by more than 45 percent on a per capita basis after correcting for inflation: from $3,107 per poor person to $1,697.[9] At the same time that the government slashed benefits, it froze the minimum wage. Between 1981 and 1990, the purchasing power of the minimum wage dropped nearly in half.[10]

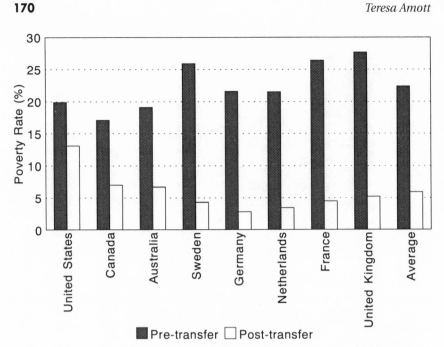

Figure 11.3   Impact of Taxes and Transfers on Poverty in the Mid-1980s (for all people)

Source: Luxembourg Income Study.

The United States does very little to lift its citizens out of poverty. In an eight-country comparative study conducted during the mid-1980s, the United States had the lowest transfer system effectiveness: that is, public policies in the United States lifted fewer people out of poverty—through taxes and transfer payments—than in the other seven countries studied.[11]

The states, mired in recession for much of the 1980s, were unable to pick up the slack. The Reagan policy of "New Federalism" burdened states with new responsibilities while diminishing their financial resources through cuts in federal revenue sharing and federal block grants. At the same time, a full-fledged taxpayer revolt at the state and local levels, fed by tax-cutting rhetoric from the federal government, prevented most localities from developing their own revenue base.

Stagnant wages, changing family forms, and government abdication of anti-poverty policy all contributed to swelling the ranks of the poor. During the 1981–1982 and 1989–1991 recessions, poverty grew especially rapidly. The subsequent recoveries were too weak, and too concentrated in the upper reaches of the income strata, to bring about any substantial declines in poverty. Even though poor people worked more hours during these recoveries, their wages declined so rapidly that the recovery failed to improve the lot of many low-wage workers.[12]

Who Are the Poor?

The federal poverty threshold differs by family size, varying from $6,932 for a single person to $13,924 for a family of four in 1991.[13] A close look at the individuals living below the official poverty line in 1991 (the most recent data available) confirms some popular beliefs about poverty but contradicts others. As is by now well-known, nearly 40 percent of the poor are children, a testament to the failure of AFDC and to the success of the Social Security and Supplemental Security Income programs in raising the incomes of senior citizens. Anyone familiar with the entrenched racial and ethnic discrimination in schooling, hiring, promotion, and housing could easily predict the degree of racial-ethnic differences in the poverty rate: far higher for African-Americans (32.7 percent below the poverty line) and Latinos (28.7 percent) than for non-Latino whites (9.4 percent). Still, non-Latino whites make up about half the poor.

More surprising, only one-third of the poor live in areas of high poverty concentration (defined as a census tract with a poverty rate of 20 percent or more). Despite popular stereotypes that unwed mothers constitute the vast majority of the poverty population, families with a female head of household make up 54 percent of all poor families, with married couples accounting for most of the rest. Nearly 40 percent of poor persons aged fifteen and over worked at some time during 1991 (compared with 72 percent of the non-poor), and 9 percent worked full-time year-round. Only 43.6 percent of all poor persons received any cash assistance, with more than 27 percent receiving no assistance of any type. Poverty has become deeper as it has spread across the population—by 1991, over one-fourth of the poor lived at half the poverty level. The average poor family was $5,515 below the poverty threshold.[14]

These data do not, however, begin to convey the social devastation that has been visited upon poor communities. In some areas, capital flight has systematically robbed the younger generation of any opportunities for meaningful, stable employment. In others, violence has escalated to war-zone levels, and mothers and children share a single aspiration: to live until the following week. Childhood diseases such as measles and rubella have returned, along with the new plague of violence fed by guns and drugs. In some areas, AIDS fills a majority of hospital beds, and gunshot wounds account for a majority of emergency-room admissions. In rural areas, the need for jobs is so intense that communities welcome hazardous waste incinerators and federal prisons. In cities and rural areas alike, some families send every available adult and child into the growing underground economy to work for sub-minimum wages. Homeless people push grocery carts full of scavenged belongings past people who have increasingly learned not to see them. Everywhere, communities have responded with organizing and charitable efforts, but none of these efforts are commensurate with the scale of the devastation.

Putting People First?

Clinton's campaign gave some promise of a concerted attack on poverty. In speeches, position papers, and in the Clinton-Gore book *Putting People First,* the needs of impoverished people and regions were often highlighted. Clinton vowed to "make work pay" by raising the minimum wage and increasing the Earned Income Tax Credit (EITC) so that compensation for full-time work would be sufficient to bring a family of four above the poverty line. He proposed a network of community development banks to provide capital for micro-enterprises and other business ventures in poor rural areas and inner cities. He also suggested establishing new types of savings accounts for low-income people, with special tax treatment and matching contributions from the federal government.

At the same time, however, Clinton's Democratic Leadership Council (DLC) leanings were evident in his calls for "responsibility" on the part of poor people. Perhaps most symbolic of the DLC interpretation of traditional welfare state themes was Clinton's intention to "end welfare as we know it, and lift the people on welfare by providing more responsibility and more opportunity."[15] Arguing that "welfare should be a second chance, not a way of life," Clinton urged a two-year cutoff in welfare recipiency. The plan, as he articulated it, was to provide help to welfare recipients in the form of education and training for two years, along with child care and other supportive services. At the end of two years, however, the recipient would be forced off the rolls and into private employment or a public-sector job.

For all its forcefulness, however, the rhetoric remained vague. Was Clinton proposing to provide public-sector employment for all those still on AFDC after two years? Or was he alluding to workfare, a plan by which recipients "work off" their benefits in unpaid jobs in the public sector or with nonprofit organizations?

Playing the "welfare card" by calling for a two-year cutoff is, of course, a time-honored campaign trick in U.S. electoral politics. In essence, Clinton was striking a bargain with the devil—the Reagan Democrats whom he wished to lure back into the party—by appropriating much of the analysis and rhetoric of the Reagan years, but with a twist. Yes, he would be tough on welfare recipients and force them into the work force, but he would also provide them with the necessary tools to succeed. This, then, became a part of the New Covenant. But this campaign promise would return to haunt the president months later as he attempted to devise a welfare reform plan that would pass a divided Congress. Conservative thirst for punitive policies against welfare recipients was whetted by the possibility of a two-year cut-off. But Congress did not anticipate the high cost of the added supportive services required to ensure that those stripped from the rolls would not be condemned to utter misery and homelessness.[16]

Clinton's urban policy also relied heavily on a reworking of the enterprise zones so dear to previous Republican administrations. Under these plans, businesses locating within poverty-stricken areas are promised tax breaks and other perks. Clinton's version—renamed "empowerment zones"—differs somewhat in that he promised to tie tax breaks and deregulation to a requirement that employers hire local residents. Unfortunately, the evidence on enterprise zones, by any name, suggests that they lower taxes for business without creating new jobs.[17] In many cases enterprise zones simply transfer jobs from one impoverished region to another, from a South Bronx to a Newark, New Jersey. Perhaps the most damaging example of all is south-central Los Angeles, clearly not a center of job creation and economic renewal despite its current status as an enterprise zone.

"Any serious, progressive analyst of U.S. poverty recognizes that substantial expenditures are required to address the results of two decades of neglect."

Where Clinton's plans for impoverished families and communities involved greater federal spending or declines in tax revenues, they were jeopardized by his allegiance to deficit reduction. Flanked by Ross Perot and George Bush, candidate Clinton was forced to make promises on deficit reduction that would return to haunt President Clinton. Any serious, progressive analyst of U.S. poverty recognizes that, the deficit notwithstanding, substantial expenditures are required to address the results of two decades of neglect. For instance, economist Paul Davidson has suggested that Clinton "put into effect as rapidly as humanly possible an annual spending program of at least $50 to $60 billion on infrastructure, while benignly neglecting the deficit for the next few years."[18] But the political opportunities for such spending have been closed off by "deficit hawkery," since Clinton appears unwilling to propose cuts in military spending or taxes on the wealthy on a scale sufficient to offset the needed anti-poverty spending.

The 1994 Budget

The budget package President Clinton brought to Congress in early 1993 contained several elements of a progressive social policy that would expand people's capacities to participate meaningfully in U.S. society.[19] Public and social investment appeared as thematic and programmatic emphases. Full funding of important entitlement programs was proposed. Low-income households were to receive a tax break on earned income, resulting in the most progressive tax initiative in decades. Upper-income households were asked to take on an increasing share of the cost of universal entitlement programs. Moreover, several initiatives would expand the nation's physical and technological infrastructure, improve education and job training, and redress environmental degradation. Investments in infrastructure were designed to bring needed jobs, services, and structures to impoverished areas.

The Clinton budget clearly reversed the direction of twelve years of Reagan-Bush policies on poverty. The proposed plan increased low-income nonentitlement program appropriations by 5.5 percent (these programs include financial aid, compensatory education, Head Start, programs for homeless people, operating subsidies for public housing, the Special Supplemental Food Program for Women, Infants and Children [WIC], programs for maternal and child health, Job Corps, Legal Services, and the Community Services Block Grant). By contrast, these appropriations fell 39 percent, after correcting for inflation, between fiscal years 1981 and 1993.[20]

Finally, the budget made a few steps toward tax equity, most notably with a major expansion of the Earned Income Tax Credit that would make the tax structure more progressive. The credit also represented a step toward fulfilling a campaign promise that the federal tax structure would not push a full-time worker earning the minimum wage below the poverty line. (Full realization of that promise will require indexation of the minimum wage and an expansion of participation in the food stamp program.)

Despite these important initiatives, the president's plan failed to address any of the underlying causes of impoverishment with the appropriate *scale* of policies. No serious effort was made to grapple with longer-term job-creation questions, for instance. The economic stimulus proposed by the administration would have been almost indiscernible in the light of a nearly $6 trillion gross domestic product. Nor did the plan go far enough to address the needs of devastated communities, both rural and inner-city. Progressive economists have urged spending on the order of $50 billion annually in infrastructure investment alone.[21]

Still, the administration's plan met with fierce resistance in Congress—led by Republicans and joined by moderate, mainly southern, Democrats—where it was subordinated to an overall concern for deficit reduction. The budget reconciliation process provided slightly less tax relief to poor wage earners, made deeper cuts in Medicare and Medicaid, and abandoned any pretense of economic stimulus. And yet, despite this resistance, most of the anti-poverty spending initiatives survived the process intact. Some critical programs, including Head Start, food stamps, and childhood immunization, will receive large increases in funding. Slated for $21 billion over four years, the expanded EITC will provide a maximum refund of $3,370 to a minimum-wage worker supporting a family of four. Over 10 million low- and moderate-income families and 5 million childless workers will receive a tax cut from the EITC expansion, making it arguably the largest federal anti-poverty initiative in decades.

The greatest threat to the administration's anti-poverty program, however, lies ahead. Congress adopted new spending caps for fiscal years 1996 through 1998 that will deeply compromise any additional domestic discretionary spending in the future. These caps, in effect, freeze domestic discretionary spending for the next five years. Any new spending must be "paid for" by cuts in either defense or nondefense spending. Thus, the administration must attempt to carry out new elements of its domestic agenda, such as expansions in health-care coverage, while wrapped in a fiscal straitjacket.

Welfare Reform

In late June, the president appointed twenty-six government officials to the inter-agency Working Group on Welfare Reform, Family Support, and Independence, charging them with making recommendations to "end welfare as we know it."[22] Although the Task Force's report will not likely be available until early 1994, the broad outlines of the plan are already clear from the content of the campaign and from previous writings by David Ellwood and Mary Jo Bane, two welfare policy experts appointed by Clinton to the Department of Health and Human Services.

The administration sees welfare reform as a package, with the EITC as a central piece to supplement wages for former recipients joining the work force. Another key element is universal coverage in a national health-care plan. Many welfare recipients, after all, will lose their Medicaid benefits when they take paying jobs, and some economists have estimated that only 15 percent of new hires receive health benefits from their employers.[23] In addition, the administration will most likely request additional funding for education and job training—and for supportive services such as child care and transportation—so that the first two years on welfare can provide recipients with some necessary tools.

These progressive carrots in the plan are coupled with a stick: a time limit of two years after which recipients will be forced to take jobs. At this stage, there is still no more clarity than there was during the campaign about the nature of those jobs. According to its advance material, the Working Group will consider community service employment, but the language is sufficiently vague as to be compatible with either public jobs creation or workfare.

The plan also contains tougher rhetoric on child support enforcement, for example calling for the establishment of a national "deadbeat databank" to facilitate interstate tracking of noncustodial parents who are behind on their child support obligations. Such a databank, however, would probably not bring a substantial number of families receiving AFDC out of poverty, since the fathers of children on AFDC typically are unemployed or earn low wages.[24] In lieu of checks from the noncustodial parent, such children can be assisted only by a government-guaranteed child support payment.

"It is hard to imagine any realistic job-creation scenario that would provide more than 1 million new jobs for former welfare recipients."

Most analysts of the Clinton plan believe that a two-year cutoff would throw approximately 1.5–2 million people into the labor market. There they will join approximately 8 million officially unemployed workers and perhaps another 4 million workers who are involuntarily employed part-time or who are discouraged and have left the labor force. It is hard to imagine any realistic jobs-creation scenario that would provide more than 1 million new jobs for former welfare recipients. Nor is it easy to imagine that Congress and the administration could agree to appropriate the billions of dollars needed to create new public-sector jobs on a scale hitherto unknown. When President Carter proposed to create 1.4 million new minimum-wage jobs in his 1977 welfare reform initiative, "Program for Better Jobs and Income," Congress considered the cost prohibitive and subsequently lost interest in the plan.[25]

That leaves the workfare option, in which recipients continue to collect AFDC benefits but work a specified number of hours in unpaid community service jobs. Even that plan is enormously expensive on the scale contemplated by the proponents of time limitations. Each workfare placement costs at least $3000—for a total cost of between $4 and $6 billion.[26] Such funding would come on top of $13 billion in federal AFDC funds and another $11 billion in state funds for cash assistance.[27] The public, of course, anticipates that welfare reform will lower costs not raise them and is unlikely to support major expansions in welfare spending. Most important, no good would be accomplished by this expenditure, since the program evaluation literature suggests that participants in workfare programs gain little in the way of marketable skills and show only minimal gains in employment rates and earnings as a result of their investment of time and energy. Worse, much damage is done: workfare takes mothers away from their children, creates no new jobs, and displaces public-sector employees.[28]

These halting steps illustrate Clinton's basic dilemma. Trapped in the neoliberal paradigm, the administration moves erratically between fundamentally conservative propositions such as workfare and essentially progressive proposals such as full funding for Head Start. A coherent anti-poverty strategy has yet to emerge. Important progressive initiatives such as an increase in the minimum wage and universal health-care coverage have been delayed, pending improvements in the political climate. Deficit reduction renders any important spending initiatives impossible. So the administration is forced to shift existing funds around in a budgetary shell game, arguing that different spending is as good as more spending. Meanwhile, the economy drifts, job creation is at historically low levels, poverty worsens, and the social decay of impoverished communities deepens.

What should the administration be doing instead? Five years ago, the Coalition on Human Needs, a Washington, D.C.–based organization that lobbies for anti-poverty programs on Capitol Hill, surveyed poor people around the country to learn how they would remedy poverty. Their answers were clear. Ensure that jobs are available and improve their quality. Raise benefit levels and relax eligibility rules for government safety-net programs. Increase funding and improve the quality of education and training.

In other words, there are three basic components to an anti-poverty agenda: raise poor people's access to higher-paying jobs; stretch poor people's income by helping them obtain necessary goods and services such as housing, health care, food, and child care; and raise poor people's income directly by providing government cash assistance.[29]

Higher-Paying Jobs

Impoverished inner cities and rural communities have endured a decades-long process of capital flight as manufacturing and service jobs have fled to the suburbs and abroad. That process needs to be reversed if jobs are to return. Yet private, for-profit banks have shown little interest in committing funds to community-based economic development efforts. To increase poor people's access to higher-paying jobs, President Clinton offers a national program of enterprise zones that would bribe businesses to locate in impoverished areas. Even advocates of these programs admit, as a General Accounting Office study demonstrates, that businesses are far more motivated by access to labor and infrastructure than they are by tax incentives.[30]

An alternative is to create a massive flow of funds to impoverished areas for community economic development. A national investment bank, with the power to raise funds through government-guaranteed and tax-exempt bond issues, could channel funds from public pensions and from the growing socially responsible investment movement. It could serve as a lender of first resort to companies willing to locate or expand in areas of urgent national need. Funds could be used for housing and for small business development, with preference given to locally owned companies, women, racial-ethnic minorities, nonprofits, and worker-owned businesses. With adequate financing and with technical assistance, these companies could prosper and provide needed jobs and retail outlets in impoverished communities.

Funds from the national investment bank could be supplemented by a program of direct public investment that could also provide public-service employment. In 1977, one in ten unemployed people was given a job through the public sector. Today, public-service employment programs are virtually extinct. A public works program could provide on-the-job training and build résumés for individual workers at the same time that it provides needed public services to communities.

Creating good jobs will also require labor law reform that would roll back the vicious union-busting of the Reagan-Bush years. The rise of mass unionism in the 1930s was, after all, one of the best anti-poverty programs ever, enabling generations of blue-collar workers to attain a middle-class lifestyle. Another key reform would be to raise and then index the minimum wage so that the wage floor remains intact at its original level of 50 percent of the median hourly wage in manufacturing. Comparable-worth policies and vigorous affirmative action would ensure a fair and equal prosperity. Mandated pro-rated benefits and expanded eligibility for unemployment insurance would begin to address the needs of contingent, part-time, and part-year workers.

If we are to increase people's access to higher-paying jobs, we also need to address the national scandal of educational inequalities so movingly described in Jonathan Kozol's recent book *Savage Inequalities*. Experiments in teacher and community control of schools, such as those in East Harlem and Chicago, can only succeed if the school districts have adequate funding, including state and federal supplements to local financing.

During the Reagan-Bush years, local private industry councils took over from the federal government the task of job training—at lower levels of funding—and then contracted out the actual training to a hodgepodge of proprietary schools, private firms, community-based organizations, and local schools. The evidence so far suggests that this Job Training Partnership Act (JTPA), to guarantee success, concentrated on serving the most able clients while ignoring those most in need of training. Reform of JTPA and expanded funding for other training programs like the Job Corps, along with exploration of new directions such as youth apprenticeship programs, are all needed to prepare people for higher-paying, higher-skilled work. At the same time, we need to recognize that job training can do little to increase earnings in the absence of vigorous job-creation policies aimed at high-wage sectors of the economy.

Public Needs

In a mixed economy such as ours, housing, health care, food, and child care are provided jointly through the private sector (both for-profit and nonprofit producers) and the public sector. The Reagan-Bush years witnessed a substantial rollback of public-sector provision of many such necessary goods and services, particularly public housing and Medicaid. Private nonprofits such as church-based voluntary agencies have struggled to make up for federal cuts, but clearly no real anti-poverty program can rely on "a thousand points of light." We need to think of government as providing more than a safety net in these sectors; government must instead lay a foundation, guaranteeing access to these goods and services for all. People in community-based organizations that have been picking up the slack for the past thirteen years know what their needs are. They know how to deliver goods and services in an integrated manner that involves recipients as participants and that generates mechanisms of accountability for providers. Their problem is, fundamentally, one of scale, and only the federal government has the required resources.

"Clearly no real anti-poverty program can rely on 'a thousand points of light.'"

That the private market will not build adequate housing for low-income people should by now be clear to anyone who lives in our cities or drives the back roads of our rural areas. In 1987, housing analyst Michael Stone estimated that fully one-third of the nation is "shelter poor," paying so much for housing expenses that they do not have enough money left over to purchase nonhousing essentials.[31] The nonprofit sector has jumped into this breach, building and renovating thousands of units of low-income housing. But the demand is in the millions. We need to support new initiatives by community organizations, land trusts, limited-equity cooperatives, and other experiments in social ownership of housing. We need to build new scattered-site and mixed-income housing in cooperation with nonprofits, and rehabilitate and renovate the rapidly decaying public housing stock.

Approximately 37 million people lack health insurance, many of them working part-time or part-year. It is obvious to all except the health insurance industry that a universal health-care system must eliminate the link between employment and health insurance, as Canada has done. In addition, current government programs that provide food and child care, such as the Act for Better Child Care and WIC, are woefully underfunded, and need immediate increases in funding. Many such programs, which enjoy bipartisan support, fail to reach everyone who qualifies. Increases in funding to promote 100 percent participation of those eligible are cost-effective and make real our rhetorical commitment to children.

Increasing Government Cash Assistance

Government can provide cash assistance to the working poor the same way it has provided it to the rich: through tax breaks. At present, of course, far more is provided to the affluent through, for example, the mortgage interest deduction, than to the poor. While passage of the Clinton EITC plan is an enormous step forward, even greater increases are needed for low- and moderate-income taxpayers.

Government must also provide income to the unemployed, those too ill to work, those who have chosen to retire, and those already occupied with the work of childrearing. Much of this cash assistance currently comes from state governments, but in recent years overburdened states have turned on poor people to balance their budgets. In 1991 alone, the Center on Budget and Policy Priorities reports, state governments froze or cut AFDC benefits in forty states and made cuts in general assistance programs affecting nearly half-a-million people.

Only the federal government has the capacity to shelter low-income people from such cyclical downturns in state budgets through a guaranteed annual income for those who cannot earn enough otherwise. A true anti-poverty program would expand SSI, the Supplemental Security Income program for elders and the disabled, to include those now covered under state assistance programs. Unemployment insurance reform could be folded into this federal income guarantee. Child-support assurance—a plan that has been proposed in the United States and is modeled on Sweden's—would provide a flat grant to any child in a single-parent family, regardless of whether the noncustodial parent was paying child support. One such proposal provides for a grant of $2,000 for one child, $3,000 for two children, and $3,500 for three children (the Clinton Welfare Reform Working Group has indicated an interest in exploring child-support assurance).[32] Of course, if all the programs discussed above were implemented, the number of people requiring cash assistance would be substantially lower.

During the past decade, the anti-poverty debate has shrunk to a racist and sexist discussion of the effects of welfare on families and the work ethic. Reforms aimed at pushing women into the work force—with a combination of carrots and sticks—have been attempted but only half-heartedly funded. Real welfare reform would recognize that single parents already have jobs raising children and that single-parent families face enormous barriers in a labor market in which the quality and the rewards of work are structured by race, ethnicity, and gender. Paid work alone is not an anti-poverty program for people whose best job offer is likely to be in a fast-food restaurant or a nursing-home kitchen. Certainly, poor women supporting families need education, job training, child care, and health care. But just imagine how the lives of poor women would change if we scrapped AFDC for a universal system of child allowances, paid parental leave, government-sponsored child care, and government-guaranteed child support.

How Do We Pay for It?

For some reason, proponents of anti-poverty plans are always obliged to explain how they would pay for their plans. Rarely is it acknowledged that we already pay for poverty: in output lost to unemployment, in infant mortality and shortened life expectancy, in crime and prison construction, and in the daily diminution of our capacity for human solidarity.

We do have enough money, if we could but divert it from the military contractors and the wealthy taxpayers. Like Willie Sutton, we must go where the money is: estimates of potential savings from military cutbacks range from $250 billion to $400 billion over the next five years. Despite the Pentagon's desperate search for new enemies, surely no one doubts that it is time for deep cuts in military spending. But plans for cuts cannot proceed unless we develop rational conversion plans to assist communities where the job loss is likely to be substantial.

Restoration of a progressive tax system would also raise some of the revenues we squander on the wealthy. We should reduce mortgage interest deductions for the wealthy, raise the top rate paid by the wealthiest taxpayers, increase luxury taxes, close estate- and gift-tax loopholes, create a securities transfer tax to reduce short-term and speculative activity, and close corporate tax loopholes, particularly those enjoyed by multinational corporations.

None of these proposals is new. Some of them surfaced in Jesse Jackson's 1988 presidential campaign. Others have been translated into legislative language, but languish in a Congress too timid and too craven to take action. All exist in detailed form in papers published by countless policy analysts in universities, community organizations, and think tanks across the country. Many in the Clinton administration are intimately familiar with these plans; some officials have even participated in writing them. Versions of these proposals are being tested in community-based organizations and labor unions across the country, as poor people build on their own experiences and their own resources to rescue their communities.

Perhaps in the years to come, President Clinton and the policy analysts who serve the administration will find the civic courage and the political skill to put forward meaningful proposals, drawn from the grassroots experiences of poor communities, that are commensurate with the scale of the human tragedy of poverty in the United States.

RACE

Ensuring a True Multiculturalism

GERALD HORNE

On September 10, 1992, Bill Clinton was making a routine appearance at the National Baptist Convention. The Democratic candidate for president stood on the dais next to noted black politician Jesse Jackson. An experienced campaigner and master of the photo opportunity, the "Country Preacher" moved to raise Clinton's hand over their heads in a time-tested expression of unity and victory. It was the perfect opportunity for the presidential candidate to solidify his commitment to black America.

But Clinton resisted Jackson's overture, apparently concerned that such a photograph appearing in the press would reinforce the perception that he was an "Old Democrat" captive to "special interests." This picture of Clinton and Jackson, their hands locked in struggle, instead illustrated the central problem with the candidate's—and later the president's—policy on race.

As the Democratic hopeful, Bill Clinton certainly did not want to lose what has come to be a traditional party constituency. To that end, he was willing to make certain gestures toward fulfilling the demands of minorities. Ultimately, however, both during the campaign and after, Bill Clinton has been eager to rid the Democratic Party of its colored image and has been willing to take swipes at African-Americans and others to demonstrate his mainstream credentials. On issues where considerations of race are simply unavoidable, he has sought to portray critical deci-

sions—concerning appointments, economic reform, and foreign policy—as race-neutral.

This Clinton strategy comes at a time when race has been anything
but neutral. For twelve years, the Reagan-Bush administrations worked
to overturn many of the gains of the civil rights era and used the "race
card" to distract attention from their reverse Robin Hood policies. The
results of these policies are unfortunately all too clear. Income distribution among blacks remains highly skewed compared to whites. Unemployment rates for African-Americans are nearly twice the national average. Incarceration and the death penalty continue to affect African-
Americans disproportionately. The life expectancy in Harlem is worse
than in Bangladesh.[1] Howard Beach, a crumbling Detroit, and a burning
Los Angeles symbolize that the urban crisis is simultaneously a black
crisis.

Meanwhile, Republican demagoguery has transformed critically important policies of affirmative action into political weapons to convince
the Euro-American working and middle class that minority advancement directly causes a decline in their standard of living. This playing of
the "race card" pitted victimized communities against one another
while wealth flowed elsewhere during the 1980s.

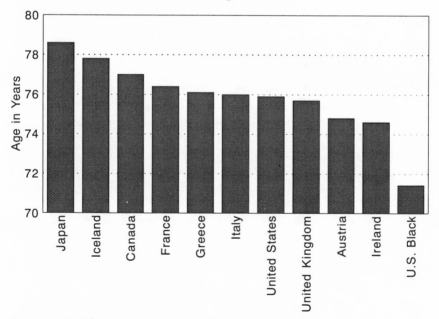

Figure 12.1   Life Expectancy at Birth in Years, 1990

Source: Adapted from Andrew Shapiro, *We're Number One* (New York: Vintage,
1992), p. 5.

Instead of addressing these problems directly and honestly, Clinton the candidate seemed concerned only with scoring political points. When it seemed that the momentum of his 1992 campaign was flagging in the wake of rumors about Gennifer Flowers and his alleged inability to stand up to peoples of color, Clinton rushed to Arkansas to preside over the execution of Ricky Rector, a brain-damaged African-American man. When questions were raised anew months later about his supposed lack of toughness, he gratuitously attacked Sister Souljah before a Jackson-initiated gathering. And throughout his campaign he promised to force "welfare mothers" to work at low-wage jobs. In the peculiar parlance of U.S. politics, such rhetoric was designed to reassure white America that its tax dollars would be no longer wasted on "lazy" blacks.

Simultaneously, Clinton made a special effort to avoid race whenever possible. As sociologist Andrew Hacker has pointed out, the Clinton-Gore volume *Putting People First* "hardly ever mentions race, even obliquely. A chapter entitled 'Cities' neither uses the term 'inner-city' nor mentions residential or school segregation."[2] During his campaign, Clinton brought few blacks into his inner circle and made few appearances before black groups. Hacker notes that the Democratic candidate "made attracting white voters his first priority" and that "for all practical purposes, the 1992 contest was staged before an all-white electorate."[3] The Democratic Party seemed all too willing to go along with this strategy. At its 1992 National Convention, for instance, there were 200 fewer black delegates than in 1988—a vivid picture of how the party wanted to present itself to the television cameras.

Despite these distancing tactics, Clinton received 82 percent of the black vote (compared with only 39 percent of the white vote) and would have lost key states (Illinois, Michigan, Ohio, and New Jersey) with just a little less African-American support.[4] Hispanics voted for Clinton in only slightly fewer numbers: 61 percent versus 25 percent for Bush and 14 percent for Perot.[5] As he brings his controversial racial strategy to the White House, Clinton offends these constituencies only at considerable risk.

True, the Clinton administration is in many ways a decided improvement over the wasteland of the Reagan-Bush years. His appointments ensure that the highest realms of government reflect greater diversity. The Congressional Black Caucus has little trouble scheduling a meeting with the president. And the selective bashing of minorities is an improvement, albeit a sad one, over the constant bashings administered by both Reagan and Bush.

But on the critical issues—from appointments and economic reform to foreign policy—the Clinton administration's strategy on race has produced a superficial multiculturalism while leaving unaddressed the significant economic and political factors that keep so many of America's minorities locked in poverty and despair.

Appointments and Disappointments

Bill Clinton pledged to have his cabinet and, indeed, all his appointments to higher office "look like America." Just as "public investment to grow the economy" was a substitute for "tax and spend," so did "looking like America" stand in place for the increasingly reviled "affirmative action." To his credit, Clinton did produce a cabinet remarkable for its racial and ethnic diversity (no mean feat considering the perennial inability of the U.S. progressive movement to diversify its own ranks).

"To his credit, Clinton did produce a cabinet remarkable for its racial and ethnic diversity."

The administration's rainbow of hues is not, however, matched by a rainbow of views. Clinton's diverse appointments reflect a very narrow stratum of political opinion, particularly with respect to economic power. For instance, Commerce Secretary Ron Brown and Energy Secretary Hazel O'Leary may be black, but their recent records have not been distinguished by a particular concern for the oppressed. Brown, the consummate Washington power broker cum attorney, previously earned a handsome salary lobbying for the likes of "Baby Doc" Duvalier, the discredited former Haitian dictator. O'Leary earned her spurs as an executive for energy monopolies known for gouging consumers and treating environmental regulations with contempt.

Other appointments have not been much better. Secretary of Agriculture Mike Espy, while representing one of the nation's poorest districts in Congress, was one of the few members of the Congressional Black Caucus with kind words for the Democratic Leadership Council (the "Democrats of the Leisure Class," as Jesse Jackson likes to call the DLC). Espy has further demonstrated his conservativism by appearing in advertisements for the National Rifle Association and cozying up to Mississippi agribusiness and wetlands developers.[6]

Former big city mayors Henry Cisneros of San Antonio (now secretary of housing and urban development) and Federico Peña of Denver (now secretary of transportation) were both reviled in their home-towns for squandering capital—political, public, and otherwise—on boondoggles while hunger and homelessness proliferated. Peña pushed vigorously for a major new airport that is larger than the island of Manhattan while Cisneros laid the groundwork for a massive new football stadium, the infelicitously named "Alamo-dome," that has yet to find a professional football team to grace its gridiron. In office, Cisneros has at least made some sensible comments. "Race," he told the *New York Times*, "is at the core of the problems which confront America's urban areas. ... That is not a message that resonates well with some of the New Democrats."[7] But it is not clear whether Cisneros will actually translate this insight into concrete policies.

In any case, the high profile appointments of these former mayors obscure the fact that there are relatively few Latinos in the administration. Indeed, according to the *Washington Post*, Clinton appointed fewer Latinos to high-level positions than did George Bush.[8]

It is certainly a worthwhile goal to have those who "look like America" occupy high-level posts. But as Bush's appointment of Clarence Thomas to the Supreme Court should have suggested, looks are not enough. The Clinton administration—and its successors—must recognize that a diversity of ideas is necessary. With its appointments, the administration has deliberately chopped off one side of the political spectrum.

Witness the experience of Johnnetta Cole, the president of Spelman College in Atlanta. Rumored to be the initial choice for secretary of education, Cole was subjected to a vicious campaign of red-baiting spearheaded by the *Washington Post*, the *New York Times*, and *Forward*. Her name quickly disappeared from the short list as conservatives applied their own brand of "political correctness" to the appointments process. Washington lost not only an accomplished advocate for better education but a distinctly progressive voice as well. Moreover, because African-Americans tend to be more progressive than most other sectors of the electorate, Johnnetta Cole would have represented her community more faithfully than Hazel O'Leary.

The application of a political litmus test to minority appointments could be even better seen with the Lani Guinier nomination. In spring 1993, the Clinton administration nominated Guinier for the position of assistant attorney general, a choice that seemed logical, proper, and historically justifiable. After all, the post involves enforcement of the Voting Rights Act, legislation that Guinier knows intimately as a scholar.

Guinier and her supporters did not altogether envision the right-wing campaign to derail her nomination. Leading the charge against Guinier was Clint Bolick, a Reagan retread, who assailed her in the *Wall Street Journal* as a "quota queen."[9] This racist and sexist phrase, also picked up by *Newsweek*, was a play on one of Ronald Reagan's favorite expressions, "welfare queen." With two words, a respected legal scholar suddenly became linked both to the presumed looting of the public coffers by black women on welfare and to affirmative action plans that give jobs to "unqualified" minorities.

Guinier was accused of seeking to empower African-Americans at the expense of the nation's majority. In her zeal to protect minority rights, we were told, she was prepared to trample the will of the majority. Ironically, this charge came after the successful filibuster by the GOP minority in the Senate—an unrepresentative body to begin with—to stymie the Clinton administration's economic stimulus package. Moreover, some of the very same forces that howled about Guinier and her alleged fascination for "quotas" had successfully argued for a parliamentary quota for the white minority in what eventually became Zimbabwe (and will likely be arguing as well for special protection of minority rights in South Africa as that nation readies itself for majority rule).

Finally, Guinier's views on ensuring minority representation, including such proposals as cumulative voting and super majorities, are neither theoretical nor nonsensical. In an article published in the *New York Times* only after Clinton's withdrawal of Guinier's nomination, Peter Applebome observed that "rather than bizarre, exotic blooms, such plans have a long electoral history ... [and have been] used successfully and with minimal controversy in many municipalities and legislative districts, particularly in the South."[10] Guinier's critics willfully distorted her positions to make them appear to be outside the legal mainstream.

This double-barreled assault could have been countered in the op-ed pages and the talk shows. But the Clinton administration, the progressive legal community, the Congressional Black Caucus, and other relevant parties declared a unilateral cease-fire during the battering of Guinier's record. By the time many became aware that her nomination was in jeopardy, it was too late. Instead of vigorously fighting for his nominee—as Bush had done for Clarence Thomas—Clinton capitulated in the face of a right-wing challenge on the question of civil rights. To boost his sagging popularity among conservative elites, Clinton revived his campaign strategy and got tough with "special interests."

As a result, the nation was deprived of a discourse on the meaning of voting, democracy, and minority rights. It was precisely this dialogue that Clinton feared most. After all, such a discourse might have reopened the issue of the Democratic Party's alignment with minority interests and adherence to affirmative action as a principle. For a president and a party desperate to appear race-neutral, a debate on voting rights was politically problematic, regardless of its educational value.

Not only was an opportunity missed to stimulate public debate but, ultimately, the Clinton administration may have jeopardized the crowning achievement of the civil rights movement—the Voting Rights Act itself. For example, the *Wall Street Journal* denounced Guinier for seeking to apply the Act to racially discriminatory electoral structures used to elect judges.[11] The *Journal's* argument was not, however, with Guinier but with the Act that mandates such an application. Shortly after the scuttling of the Guinier nomination, the Supreme Court ruled that a district in North Carolina, designed to create a black majority, constituted racial gerrymandering. Yet this principle of redistricting has been an accepted legacy of the civil rights era. In fact, thirteen of the sixteen blacks elected to Congress in 1992 are in Washington today because of this measure.[12] By allowing Guinier's proposals for improving representative democracy to appear otherworldly, the Clinton administration created a climate in which civil rights mainstays are thrown into question.

Clinton's strategy of keeping his distance from racial issues not only endangers minorities in need of civil rights protection but also strengthens the hands of conservative politicians. Playing the "race card"—as in the Guinier case—provides easy victories for the right wing in their overall fight to halt social progress. Not surprisingly, the ditching of Guinier was preceded by the appointment of long-time Republican press manipulator David Gergen as presidential counselor. The unchallenged right-wing distortions of the Voting Rights Act were followed quickly by Clinton's decision not to seek an increase in the minimum wage.

During the Reagan-Bush era, the Republicans played the race card to distract attention from the economic impoverishment of the country. Clinton's refusal to address racial matters may in fact handicap the administration in its attempt to bring America out of recession.

Dollars and Sense

As a candidate, Bill Clinton promised to focus on the economy like a "laser beam." In office, he indeed concentrated on passing his budget through Congress in the hope of reviving the economy as quickly as possible. Certainly minorities have much to gain if the economy improves. Yet there is reason to question whether Clinton's particular reforms have much to offer minorities, who are disproportionately poor and working class.

Regardless of Clinton's intentions, the political climate on Capitol Hill militates against redirecting funds from the rich to the poor. A broad political consensus ensures that defunding programs that benefit the poor is politically acceptable, while other policies such as taxing the rich and slashing the military budget meet with immediate political opposition.

By presenting only modest defense cuts and tax increases for the wealthy, the Clinton administration demonstrated that it did not intend to undermine this consensus. Clinton has further acceded to the de-

Income Bracket

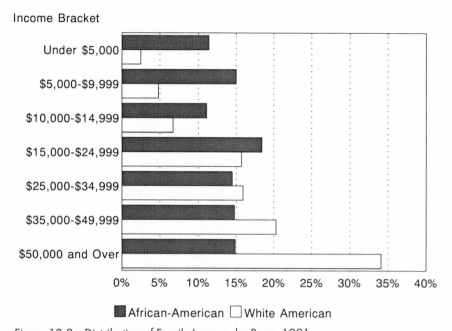

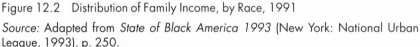

Figure 12.2   Distribution of Family Income, by Race, 1991

Source: Adapted from *State of Black America 1993* (New York: National Urban League, 1993), p. 250.

mands of conservative Democrats to slash entitlement programs and reduce his stimulus package to a negligible amount. Bernard Anderson, the well-known black economist, stated in *Black Enterprise* that he did not see anything in Clinton's policies "that gives us confidence that black voters will also be beneficiaries." The magazine went on to argue, "Indeed, no one, including Clinton and U.S. Commerce Secretary Ron Brown has been able to clearly state how the Administration's policies will address inequities in education and job training, employment and business development facing African-Americans."[13]

It is understandable why this authoritative journal for black business would be so pessimistic. In 1992, 1.96 million black adults did not have jobs. Last year the black unemployment rate was 14.1 percent or 1.91 times the rate for workers generally and 2.17 times the rate for Euro-American workers.[14] In 1993, these figures are not expected to change significantly. The situation for other minorities—Puerto Ricans and Dominicans in New York City, Mexican-Americans and Salvadorans in Los Angeles, or Native Americans in Minneapolis—is even worse.

These numbing figures persist in part because of the erosion of the manufacturing sector, which has employed so many minorities. Furthermore, the public sector, which has also employed a disproportionate number of minorities, is still reeling from the privatization of public-sector services and the downsizing of government. Whatever job growth that does take place in this economy may not benefit minorities, for many of these new jobs are outside urban areas or are inaccessible by mass transit.

It is unlikely that Clinton's plans to spur the growth of small business will make a difference. In 1987, the Commerce Department reported that there were 1.2 million minority companies, a 64 percent increase from 1982. Yet, despite making up 17 percent of the population, minorities still own only 9 percent of businesses and generate an infinitesimal share of the receipts—only 3.9 percent.[15] Hence, Clinton's effort to boost small business will not put a sizable dent in the deteriorating economic prospects for minorities in general.

If Clinton were to adopt a strong pro-union policy, he would better aid minorities, who are more represented in organized labor than in the business community.[16] With all of its faults, the trade union movement was and still is indispensable to the success of the civil rights movement. Minority workers in unions are much better off than minority workers who are not in unions. They have higher salaries, better working conditions, and greater job security. Clinton, who was elected with the assistance of organized labor, has been expected to reverse the anti-union policies of the Reagan-Bush years. He has promised to strengthen worker protection clauses in the North American Free Trade Agreement and to sign into law a ban on replacements for striking workers.

On the other hand, Clinton's proposed "new partnership" between labor and management has been cast primarily as a business strategy. Secretary of Labor Robert Reich has even proposed amending the 1935 Wagner Act to facilitate "employee involvement" in the twenty-first-century American workplace, a tactic that many unionists see as just a cover for the creation of company unions.[17] Other programs such as the National Service can be interpreted as end-runs around organized labor. By placing students and youth in public-sector positions, the national service program would replace high-wage unionized positions with temporary low-wage labor. While students may benefit from such a program, working-class minorities in either the twenty-first-century workplace or the public sector probably will not.

Clinton's "race-less" approach to the economy may prove strategically counterproductive. In his haste to avoid being labeled a "captive" of "special interests"—minorities and labor—Clinton has couched his proposals so as not to alienate conservative white elite opinion. This lack of presidential boldness jeopardizes the White House program by not activating, perhaps even demobilizing, those most likely to rally to his support and by capitulating to the elites most likely to resist his initiatives.

"Clinton's 'race-less' approach to the economy may prove strategically counterproductive."

Indeed, Clinton's effort to revive the economy may fail precisely because of his inability to grasp these race-class issues. In the 1930s, Franklin Delano Roosevelt recognized that dragging the U.S. economy out of the morass of the Great Depression required putting more money into the hands of more people. He therefore established government-work programs and enabled unions to organize more easily and demand better working conditions and wages. Since the 1930s, the U.S. population has become darker in hue and will be even more so in years to come. Fighting recession in the 1990s therefore requires redistribution programs that target minorities—through affirmative action programs—to boost lagging purchasing power in depressed urban and rural areas. But such targeted programs conflict with Clinton's determination to submerge the race question and to preempt the GOP's continuing effort to play the "race card."

As the economy continues to deteriorate and civic protest escalates in response, the administration may lean more and more toward treating the symptoms with a truncheon. Clinton's "get tough" mentality was already evident in his campaign calls for 100,000 new police officers and a National Police Corps comprised of unemployed veterans and former military personnel.[18] The combination of economic deterioration and unchecked police brutality has already sparked conflagrations in Los Angeles, Miami, and a number of other cities. Clinton has so far refused to target the most vulnerable urban areas with economic aid. By playing into a garrison mentality with this tough-on-crime rhetoric, the president may simply be adding fuel to the fire.

Race for the World

Bill Clinton has not shrunk from applying his "get tough" approach to foreign affairs, bashing colored folk abroad with as much selective forcefulness as he has at home. Just as he wanted to demonstrate his mainstream credentials by executing Ricky Rector, abandoning Lani Guinier, and backing down on the minimum-wage increase, Clinton has thrown his weight around on the international scene—at the expense of Iraqis, Haitians, and Japanese—to prove that a Democratic president can carry as big a stick as a Republican.

True, the administration has scored certain successes. After the patient efforts of UN mediator Dante Caputo, a negotiated settlement has been achieved that should return Jean-Bertrand Aristide to Haiti. In another heralded move, the Clinton administration finally recognized the Angolan government of Jose dos Santos, reversing a long-standing and quite ignoble Reagan-Bush policy.

Even these victories, however, have been partial. Consider, for instance, the Haitian situation. Since a military coup ousted the democratically elected government in Haiti in September 1991, 40,000 people have fled the small Caribbean country. Scores of refugees, many infected with the HIV virus, were held at the U.S. naval base at Guantánamo Bay, Cuba. Immigration officials who interviewed these refugees said that they had a well-founded fear of persecution, thus providing grounds for political asylum. But instead of being brought to the United States for further immigration hearings, they were kept in a shantytown encircled by a razor wire fence—without legal representation or adequate medical care.

During the 1992 presidential campaign, Clinton repeatedly promised to close this detention camp. Once in office, however, he continued the Bush administration policy of barring the Haitians. Angry protests and constant heckling subsequently accompanied Clinton's public appearances. Students organized hunger strikes at a number of college campuses. In February, Jesse Jackson visited the refugees at Guantánamo and began his own ten-day hunger strike in solidarity.

Ultimately it was a Bush appointee, federal district judge Sterling Johnson, who took the Clinton administration to task. Government policy, Johnson argued, "deviated" from its own stated principles and the Haitians should therefore be released from detention.[19] Although the Guantánamo facility has since been dismantled, the Supreme Court upheld the Clinton administration's continuation of Bush policy on repatriating the refugees. Only the threat of more refugees in the wings pushed Clinton toward pursuing a plan that restores Aristide to power. This negotiated agreement, signed in July, is controversial in its own right. The plan allows the embargo to be lifted and aid to be resumed before Aristide actually returns to the country. Unhappy with these provisions, Aristide's representatives reportedly were bullied into signing by U.S. special envoy Lawrence Pezzullo.[20]

On policy toward Africa, the Clinton team likewise promised new directions. The recognition of the Angolan government of Jose dos Santos, under siege by the previously U.S.-backed UNITA guerrilla forces, is one such indicator of the new policy. But the administration has done nothing to help rebuild Angola, a nation with one of the highest number of amputees in the world as a result of land mines and other explosives. White House policy toward South Africa has also been disappointing. Given the extent of black support for the Democratic Party, many expected that the administration would pressure Pretoria to move more forthrightly to free and fair elections, now scheduled for 1994. But the administration instead adopted a conservative wait-and-see attitude.

Elsewhere in Africa, Clinton has not been so reticent. The president, for instance, went beyond his predecessor's policies by signing off on air strikes against Somalia. Though these strikes were presumably in retaliation for factional attacks on UN peacekeepers, the question still remains if this escalation in hostilities will ease the famine or otherwise improve conditions for the Somali people. Moreover, U.S. attempts to assassinate Somali faction leader Mohamed Farah Aidid by bombing his headquarters—a death sentence verdict without a trial—does not reflect well on the United States as the purveyor of law and order for the region.

In the *Los Angeles Times*, Randall Robinson, leader of the influential lobbying group Trans-Africa, criticized administration policy toward the region:

> The Administration took far too long to recognize Angola. It has no policy to date of any consequence on Zaire. Mr. Mobutu Sese Soko stands between the people of Zaire and a democratic outcome. He refuses to leave, and the Clinton administration has declined to respond to his refusal to step down. We've got to put teeth in that policy. We haven't signaled presidents like Frederick Chiluba in Zambia our support by inviting them to visit the Oval Office.[21]

Clinton's appointments may shed light on why the administration's Africa policy has thus far been so disappointing. At the State Department, Deputy Secretary Clifton Wharton, one of the most senior African-Americans in the administration, opposed the divestment of stocks in companies involved in South Africa in his prior position as head of the teachers' pension fund, TIAA-CREF. Frank Wisner and Charles Freeman, in high-level posts at the Defense Department, played prominent roles as State Department officials in formulating the odious policy of "constructive engagement" during the Reagan-Bush years. The Defense Department's veteran Africa specialist, James Woods, has been helping his employers justify the still bloated Pentagon budgets of the post–Cold War era by looking for new ways for the United States to maintain a presence in the region. As chief economist at the World Bank, Treasury Department appointee Lawrence Summers was notorious for making a "cost-benefit" analysis to justify using Africa as a dumping ground for U.S. toxic wastes.[22] The continuity of Africa policy from Bush to Clinton is partially attributable to the continuity in the cast of characters formulating and implementing policy.

In other areas of the world, the administration has been groping for an appropriate enemy to replace the Soviet Union. The specter of Arab terrorists, the June bombing of Baghdad, and the tightened embargo of Cuba all indicate that the administration is comfortable with demonizing people of color. Particularly troubling from the domestic point of view has been the escalation of tensions with Japan. The Clinton administration, while talking incessantly about the economy, has capitalized on a public perception of Japan as the new enemy of choice to replace the Soviet Union. Just as presidents in the past were expected to stand up to Moscow—the chief challenge to U.S. superpower pretensions—now it seems that the occupant of the White House is expected to stand up to Tokyo.

In a disturbing domestic parallel, bias crimes against Asian-Americans have also gone up significantly in recent years: Vincent Chin, a Chinese-American murdered by an unemployed white autoworker who blamed his declining economic status on Japanese imports; Yoshi Hattori, a Japanese exchange student shot in the chest by a white man after ringing the wrong doorbell in Baton Rouge on Halloween 1992; the apparent targeting of Korean-American merchants during the 1992 disturbances in Los Angeles. This trend can even be seen in the cinema as the new challenge from Asia is being refracted through black eyes in such films as *Rising Sun* and *Menace II Society.*

In his efforts to avoid difficult race matters, Clinton has remained largely silent on these disturbing links between enemy imaging abroad and an upsurge in domestic racism. In Germany, Chancellor Helmut Kohl similarly refused to lead a campaign against anti-foreigner attacks following his country's unification in 1990. If Clinton does not speak out more forcefully, he runs the risk of a similar outbreak of ugly racism in the United States.

Applying the Street Heat

After one year in office, Bill Clinton has demonstrated that he will push for progressive change only if pressured to do so. Such "street heat"— demonstrations, orchestrated phone calls, mailgrams, e-mail messages, petitions, rallies, and mass actions—will make Clinton think twice about bashing minorities or hiding behind bland, race-neutral positions.

Street heat is not enough, however. As long as peoples of color have no viable political alternative to the Democratic Party, they will continue to be taken for granted. Thus, encouragement and support must be given to budding political initiatives such as the New Party, the 21st Century

Party initiated by the National Organization for Women, the Greens, local initiatives like the Majority Coalition in New York City and the Peace and Freedom Party in California, and the labor party proposed by Tony Mazzochi of the Oil, Chemical, and Atomic Workers.

For a detailed program of what should be done on the national level, one starting point is the alternative budget of the Congressional Black Caucus (CBC). In 1993, a newly enlarged CBC (with 39 members, including one senator and many high-ranking committee people) put forward its annual budget and, as usual, their reasonable proposals were ignored by the mainstream press. The budget included $200 billion over five years to house poor and moderate income families, $6 billion for 2 million disadvantaged students, and a shorter waiting period for drug treatment programs. Congresswoman Maxine Waters of south-central Los Angeles has pushed for $250 million to help unemployed young people between the ages of seventeen and thirty find a place in the work force. She has asked for $100 in weekly stipends for students attending basic education or vocational courses and also has tapped funds for summer jobs.

On the revenue side, the CBC rejects Clinton's proposals for new energy and Social Security taxes because of their cost to those on low incomes. Instead, the CBC alternative budget seeks to raise taxes on large corporations and profits from investments. Its budget also eliminates deductions for both first homes—to a mortgage ceiling of $300,000—and second homes. And it requires substantially reduced spending on the military.

"A rising tide does not necessarily lift all boats;
that is especially true for those boats
stuck at the bottom or for those
without boats altogether."

The situation for minority workers and minority business will not improve by itself. The plight of minorities will not be alleviated without targeted and conscious affirmative action. A rising tide does not necessarily lift all boats; that is especially true for those boats stuck at the bottom or for those without boats altogether. However, in the present political environment, affirmative action has become a dirty word. We are told that affirmative action is, in fact, "reverse discrimination" against Euro-

Americans. We are told that affirmative action only benefits a black elite, even though this policy has been most effective and prominent in such public arenas as firefighting and police forces.

The president must use the White House as a "bully pulpit" to proclaim that the nation cannot advance unless those at the bottom are given special assistance—and those at the bottom are disproportionately persons of color. As such, affirmative action is not charity. It is another form of stimulus to revive the economy. To assume that minorities will benefit from "universal" measures is misguided. Programs such as the Women's Self-Employment Project in Chicago—which provides loans to and targets low-income Latinas and African-American women—need federal backing and should be replicated nationally.

The links between foreign and domestic policies are clear. If the deteriorating conditions in east Los Angeles and Harlem are to be alleviated, funds will inevitably have to be taken from the Pentagon and the ability of the United States to wage war abroad will have to be circumscribed. The failure to grasp the connection between domestic and international policies has been one of the signal weaknesses of civil rights organizations like the NAACP and the National Urban League (NUL). Every year the NUL calls for a "Marshall Plan" for the cities—massive spending on urban education, job creation, and the like—without linking this eminently desirable proposal to a dramatic downsizing of the Pentagon budget and a radically altered U.S. foreign policy.

On foreign policy, the Clinton administration should keep the pressure on the South African government until free and fair elections are held. The administration should work to ensure that South Africa remains unitary and not a patchwork of white- and black-majority regions. An overall approach to that region should involve direct U.S. assistance—and reparations—to rebuild Angola, which has been decimated by U.S.-sponsored guerrillas. Aid to sub-Saharan Africa in general should be increased dramatically, particularly in such areas as education, health, and infrastructure development; the same holds true for the Caribbean and Haiti.

Debt relief for areas of Africa, Asia, and Latin America is crucial. Economic development cannot take place as long as the albatross of interest payments weighs down these countries. Reducing the debt burden should not be seen as charity but rather as part of global economic recovery.

The administration should speak out on bias against Asian-Americans and Arab-Americans. That Asian and Arab nations are coming to replace the Soviet Union as the major lightning rods for U.S. fears and frustrations carries dire consequences for domestic race relations. If the White House does not become a "bully pulpit" for anti-racist leadership, the

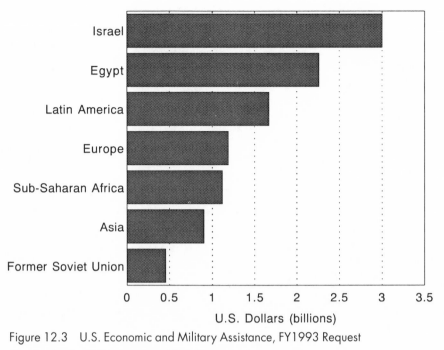

Figure 12.3   U.S. Economic and Military Assistance, FY1993 Request

Source: Agency for International Development.

raging ethnic conflict that now grips many areas of the world could be replicated here.

On the question of appointments, the administration should not only oust the holdovers from the Reagan-Bush years, such as Wisner and Woods, but should also strive for a diversity of views to complement the diversity of looks. PC warriors opposed highly qualified nominees such as Lani Guinier and Johnnetta Cole because of their views. Such litmus tests jeopardize any faintly progressive Clinton initiative as well as do a disservice to minorities, whose dire plight often leads them to diverge from an often misguided mainstream consensus.

These prescriptions are predicated on the notion that ignoring race and exploiting race are both highly dangerous gambits. The nation deserves better. Minorities and their allies will stand for no less.

GENDER

Guaranteeing Real Equality

JULIANNE MALVEAUX

Alexis Herman, now the White House public liaison, tells a revealing but all too commonplace story from her days as the chief operating officer at the 1992 Democratic National Convention. When she went to meet with a group from New York, a staffer gave her the brush-off: the assembled group was "waiting for Mr. Herman." She sat quietly and waited as others filed in and took their seats, all directed to "wait for Mr. Herman." Finally she decided to put the older white man who was directing traffic out of his misery by letting him know that *Ms.* Alexis Herman was indeed there.

To paraphrase the advertising jingle, women have come a long way, baby, but they still have a long way to go. Women's progress? Oscillation is perhaps a more accurate description. For every gain, there seems to be a corresponding setback. For every advertisement that trumpets women "in control," there is a film like *Pretty Woman* or *Indecent Exposure* that exploits retrograde rescue and seduction fantasies.

Although women enjoy a degree of freedom unimagined only two generations ago, a continuing and systematic inequality still distorts our society. Child care remains a scarce resource. Health research does not reflect women's concerns. Violence against women remains endemic.

Sexual discrimination persists from the highest levels of government to the lowest paid position in the workplace.

In 1992, the "year of the woman," the situation was supposed to change. After the embarrassment of the Clarence Thomas confirmation hearings, women's organizations declared that they were no longer going to tolerate the status quo. And indeed, after concerted political organizing, a group of new female politicians descended upon Washington. The number of women in the U.S. Senate, for instance, increased by 300 percent in 1992. But these six women still constitute a small minority (and one so unprecedented that it has required a new Senate bathroom). To compound this sense of oscillating status, many of the women elected because of the "Anita Hill effect" were mute when the conservative media skewered the respected law professor Lani Guinier, Clinton's choice for assistant attorney general. At least one of the "Hill" senators, Dianne Feinstein (D-CA), reportedly lobbied behind the scenes to have the Guinier nomination withdrawn.

In part capitalizing on the "year of the woman," Bill Clinton was swept into the White House with 45 percent of the female vote. His administration has promised much. The credentials of its leading players are solid—Arkansas Governor Clinton was, for example, named a "good guy" by the National Women's Political Caucus in 1988. The First Lady, Hillary Rodham Clinton, has a well-documented interest in women's equity and children's rights. The administration certainly benefits from comparisons with its recent predecessors. By doing absolutely nothing, the Clinton White House would still be an improvement over the previous twelve years.

"By doing absolutely nothing, the Clinton White House would still be an improvement over the previous twelve years."

On a number of issues, the new administration has indeed been a positive force. Its successes, however, have been partial. Clinton's appointments, for instance, have been an improvement over the past, with women placed in many nontraditional jobs. But critical appointments have been bungled, with the implicit message that women are to be judged by a different standard than men. The approach to family policy has been an improvement, but primarily for families with workers in large corporations—a shrinking number. The 1993 budget, especially its earned income tax credit, represents an attempt to improve the lot of the disadvantaged. But the administration's reluctance to push for the minimum-wage increase is a grave disappointment. Innovative ideas, like the volunteer corps for students, have been structured with little concern for their impact on women or students of color.

Political calculations have, for the most part, been driving Clinton policy, and politics decree that the administration court mostly white, mostly middle-class, women voters. Insofar as the women's movement represents such a constituency, the Clinton administration will play ball with feminists. But issues of concern to other sectors of the movement are too provocative for an administration determined not to rock the boat. Despite attractive rhetoric on gender questions, the administration has demonstrated little willingness to expend political capital on principle.

The Era of Backlash

It can only be hoped that historians will look back at the Reagan-Bush era as a singular discontinuity. A trend of improvements for women, begun in the early 1970s, was reversed in the 1980s. In the workplace, the home, and in the highest reaches of government, women saw hard-earned gains eroded.

In the judiciary, for instance, women's appointments dropped from 15 percent under Carter to 8 percent under Reagan. Reagan also discontinued both the Coalition on Women's Appointments and the Working Group on Women.[1] Several federal offices that monitored affirmative action gains for women—for example, the Equal Employment Opportunity Commission and the Office of Federal Contract Compliance—were gutted under Reagan.[2] The administration virtually disassembled the office implementing the Women's Educational Equity Act that was designed to combat sex discrimination in schools. In a characteristic gesture, the administration fired or reassigned the female employees but retained all the male employees.[3]

Important pieces of legislation were introduced during this period, but they either languished in Congress or suffered a presidential veto. The Family and Medical Leave Act appeared in 1985 only to be twice vetoed by Bush. The Violence Against Women Act, the Women's Health Equity Act, and other pieces of legislation were introduced but not acted on in the 1988–1992 period, while bills concerning child-support enforcement, job discrimination, and economic equity also got bogged down in congressional committee quagmires.

This political climate, fostered by a set of administrations openly hostile to feminism, encouraged a backlash against women's gains in society at large. Conservative politicians, fundamentalist preachers, and traditionalist image-makers blamed feminism for everything from increasing crime rates to an erosion of national values. Often overlooked, however, is the economic dimension to this backlash. Economic restructuring in the 1980–1992 period—a movement away from manufacturing to service jobs, a decline in average real wages, spreading poverty[4]—placed an especially heavy burden on women's shoulders. While they had lower unemployment rates than men, women were more likely to be found in the lowest paid occupations. Female workers frequently found themselves in part-time positions, and many would have held full-time jobs if such were available.

Backlash, in other words, was not just directed against middle-class white women. There are the classic examples journalist Susan Faludi cites: the misogynist movie *Fatal Attraction*, the retro frills of the fashion industry, the anti-feminism of popular psychology.[5] But there is also the tragic Imperial Foods fire in Hamlet, North Carolina, in 1991. The federal government had not inspected the site for health and safety violations in nearly a decade. Most of the women who plucked chickens by hand for Imperial Foods earned about $4.25 an hour. Of the twenty-five people who perished in the fire, the majority were women of color.

"Despite the much touted 'economic recovery' from 1983–1989, poverty grew during this period, especially for women."

Despite the much touted "economic recovery" from 1983–1989, poverty grew during this period, especially for women. At the same time, federal leadership betrayed increasing hostility toward the poor. The real value of Aid to Families with Dependent Children (AFDC) benefits fell steadily over the past decade. Welfare—and particularly the "welfare mother" stereotypically portrayed as young and black—was scapegoated as the basis of many of our nation's economic problems. The feminist community's failure to make public assistance an organizing focus only facilitated the Reagan-Bush administrations' onslaught against the poor and against women.

Women's issues were often not so much ignored in the Reagan-Bush years as couched in "market" terms. The Women's Bureau in the Bush administration spent most of its energy on "glass ceiling" issues—the impediments to women's advancement in the white-collar workplace—which affect, at most, 20 percent of the female labor force. Bush pointed to an increase in small business ownership among women as a positive outcome of economic recovery. Yet fewer than 3 percent of all women own businesses. Moreover, small businesses frequently fare poorly on other women's issues: they are less likely to offer health insurance or other benefits and are more likely to pay lower wages.

Issues of reproductive freedom were among the most controversial issues in the Reagan-Bush years, a period that can best be described as a twelve-year assault on *Roe v. Wade*. Implicit federal support of "pro-life" forces encouraged the blockade of family-planning clinics. The "gag rule" on doctors and nurses in government-funded family-planning clinics restricted women's access to abortion information. A ban on fetal tissue research similarly limited women's constitutional right to reproductive freedom. The Hyde Amendment prohibited payment for abortions with federal funds, discriminating particularly against poor women.

While reproductive choice is among the most important issues for women, a Ms. Foundation poll indicates that women rank issues of economic security such as equal pay, flexible schedules, and health care as their top priorities.[6] These issues are less likely to garner headlines than more controversial questions like abortion and sexual harassment. Indeed, by focusing on the latter issues, the Bush administration was able to deflect concern about key economic issues. The fact that then-candidate Clinton addressed these issues in his platform document *Putting People First* perhaps explains the gender gap that ensured his presidential victory.

Beancounting

The Clinton candidacy generated enormous optimism among progressive women. Unlike the previous two presidents, Clinton clearly understood the issues. In *Putting People First*, he wrote, "Never before have American women had so many options—or been asked to make such difficult choices. It's time not only to make women full partners in government, but also to make government work for women."[7]

Two Clinton statements illustrate the conflicting approaches he took to women's issues prior to taking office. On the one hand, while campaigning and in accepting his nomination, Clinton described himself as the son of a working woman, spouse of a working mother, and father of a daughter who would enter the workplace. Women thought he "got it" when he made these statements, that he understood the intersection between household and workplace. Moreover, the Clinton-Gore platform specifically promised to safeguard a woman's right to choose; protect women's rights in the workplace; support pro-family and pro-children policies; ensure affordable, quality health care; and crack down on violence against women. This platform compared starkly with that of the Republicans, which was at best indifferent to women's concerns.

After criticism that not enough women had been appointed to the Cabinet, however, a tight-lipped and angry president-elect denounced women's groups as "bean counters" in December 1992. The outburst was minor in comparison with a series of tense presidential statements to the press in the early months of the administration—statements that mellowed in the détente following the appointment of David Gergen as presidential counselor in June 1993. The "bean counting" remark suggests that a president who "gets" part of the women's equity agenda does not really get all of it.

Yet how do we measure women's progress in the labor market without counting? If women are the majority of the population and a president says his administration will "look like America," shouldn't women be half of all appointees at every level? Does such insistence suggest reliance on quotas (which Clinton opposes), or does it suggest simple fairness and a persistence in looking at the institutional factors that generate unequal outcomes for women?

Rhetorically, then, Clinton is caught between real understanding and obtuse petulance. Such schizophrenia is reflected in his policies on gender. Perhaps more than in any other policy arena, the president has done a fair job in keeping his promises. At the same time, the Clinton record has been marred by the mishandling of some appointments, notably that of University of Pennsylvania law professor Lani Guinier, and has been hampered by pragmatic politics, the priority status accorded the budget, and an inability to deal with and address institutional aspects of gender discrimination. It is not clear, however, whether the administration ever intended to deal with the deeper roots of inequity in American society, despite its lofty rhetoric.

Appointments

Appearances send signals both direct and subliminal, and photo opportunities tell a story about who has power, who has access, and who surrounds the president. But appointments only represent the tip of the policy iceberg. A Cabinet member may be a figurehead with little power, and some staff members wield more power or influence than members of the Cabinet.

Because expectations of Bill Clinton were so high, his Cabinet appointments were each thoroughly scrutinized on the basis of race, gender, and affiliation (for instance, to civil rights groups and women's organizations). By and large, Clinton has been sensitive to these concerns while making appointments. Indeed, some have argued that he has been too sensitive. Six months after he took office, so many senior posi-

Table 13.1 Administration Appointments as of August 1993

	Total	Women	Women (%)
Presidential Appointees	611	199	32.6%
Senior Executive Service	362	140	38.7%
Schedule C	990	565	57.1%
Total	1,963	904	46.1%

Source: Office of Presidential Personnel

tions remained vacant that some critics described 1600 Pennsylvania Avenue as the "home alone" White House.

So far, the Clinton appointments are an improvement over the Bush record. While about 20 percent of Bush appointees were women, nearly a third of the new presidential appointments are women. When the total number is considered, more than 45 percent of the Schedule C (civil service–exempt political appointments), Senior Executive Service, and presidential appointments are women.

In addition, the nature of the female appointments is significant. Laura Tyson is the first woman to chair the Council of Economic Advisers. Janet Reno is the first woman to serve as Attorney General. Women appointees serve in nontraditional jobs, such as secretary of energy (Hazel O'Leary), director of the African Development Bank (Alice Deer), deputy director of the Office of Management and Budget (Alice Rivlin), and general counsel for the Department of Defense (Jamie Garelick). In the Justice Department, by August 1993, an unprecedented six of fourteen appointees to U.S. attorney were women. Women of color are represented among these appointees, as are attorneys with experience in public defenders' offices, indicating a sensitivity to the legal rights of the poor.

At the White House staff level, women have also been appointed to positions of influence and power. Six women, including Public Liaison Alexis Herman and Domestic Policy Adviser Carol Rusco, hold the title "Assistant to the President," which carries unofficial Cabinet status. Dee Dee Myers is the first woman press secretary, and women are represented at senior levels in virtually every White House office.

Women who have been activists and advocates of women's issues have joined the Clinton team. These include former University of Wisconsin Provost Donna Shalala (now secretary of the Department of Health and Human Services) and Karen Nussbaum, the former director of the working women's organization 9 to 5 (and now director of the Women's Bureau). Further, the appointment of Ruth Bader Ginsburg to the Supreme Court proves that a career commitment to equal rights for women is not a disqualifier for high office.

Despite this laudable record of appointing women, the administration fumbled several critical nominations, revealing a degree of insensitivity to certain women's issues. The withdrawn nomination of Zoe Baird was partly a function of poor preparation on the part of Clinton staff, but partly a function of indifference by Clinton staffers to the hardships of private-household workers.

The Guinier case, addressed at greater length elsewhere in this volume, was also sobering. The president's claim that he had not read Guinier's work was disingenuous. His vehement protest against "social engineering" and "guaranteeing outcomes" was specifically directed to issues of race, but implied that he felt there were limits to government involvement to ensure gender equity as well.

The Clinton White House seems to have learned a lesson from the Guinier experience. The handling of Surgeon General–designate Dr. Joycelyn Elders's nomination, for example, was quite adroit. The White House staff issued briefings, arranged meetings with key senators, and stuck by Dr. Elders despite her controversial positions on sex education that attracted early opposition from congressional conservatives and their constituents on the far right.

In some cases, paradoxically, the appointment of "good" progressives has also generated the unfortunate side effect of muting dissent on the left. Progressive policy analysts are now more likely to hold off on legitimate criticisms in order to give the administration a "fair" chance. With the left relatively quiet and the right demonstrably vocal, the Clinton administration is not likely to veer leftward from its anchored position in the center—even if it were inclined to do so.

Choice and the Family

Two days after he took office and twenty years after abortion was legalized, Clinton issued five abortion-related directives. He lifted the "gag rule" for nonphysician personnel at federally funded Title X clinics, removed the moratorium on fetal tissue research, agreed to allow privately funded abortions in military hospitals, permitted federal funds to be used in international programs involving abortion-related activities, and overturned the ban on importing the French abortion pill RU486.

These actions reversed twelve years' worth of abortion restrictions. But they did not have the effect of "trickling down" to poor women. In other words, the sudden availability of RU486, while important, means little to the woman who cannot find a clinic in her county or to the woman whose reproductive choice is restricted by the Hyde Amendment. Given how close the votes are on economic issues, the president did not seem to have the political chits to cash in to guarantee a repeal of

Hyde. Only in the District of Columbia budget was money for publicly funded abortions retained.

Abortion coverage could figure prominently in the president's eagerly awaited health-care reform. Here again, Clinton's aversion to controversy will clash with his rhetoric about choice. Many supporters of national health insurance, such as the Catholic Conference of Bishops, will not want abortion covered under a new health-care plan. If "compromise" means that states will decide whether to include abortion in health plans—and many states do not today—health-care reform offers little to poor women in terms of reproductive choice.

On the family front, Clinton's most notable success has been his signing of the Family and Medical Leave Act. But this move, accompanied by considerable fanfare, was only a partial victory for women: the legislation had been substantially watered down from the original 1985 proposal. The earlier version would have provided almost all employees eighteen weeks of unpaid leave for the birth, adoption, or illness of a child, along with twenty-six weeks for individual illness. The bill would have required employers to maintain health benefits during the leave, and would have established a study group to look into ways of providing salary replacement for those taking time off. After two years of hearings and favorable response, the bill was not voted on.

In the years since 1985, the bill has been modified to exclude those working for small businesses (in 1987, small business meant firms with less than fifteen employees; by 1992, the category was expanded to include firms with fewer than fifty employees). In addition, the length of unpaid leave has been reduced from eighteen to twelve weeks. New and part-time employees are now excluded from coverage. Because of these exclusions, only half of the labor force is covered by the family leave act, a major failing that seriously undermines its progressive intent. In addition, because the leave is unpaid, those who cannot afford to take time off are not likely to have access to this "social" benefit, and will instead manage double and triple shifts or leave their jobs altogether.

Although the bill has been redesigned in their favor, small businesses have still objected to the Family and Medical Leave Act, which went into effect in August 1993. Other critics have argued that the legislation will discourage hiring or will encourage businesses to favor temporary and part-time workers over permanent workers. These concerns are not easily dismissed. Perhaps, then, the workplace is not the appropriate medium for social policy. In other words, linking family and medical leave, health insurance, and other benefits to employment status often has the effect of making benefits unavailable to those whose employment is precarious. It also reinforces a dual-benefit structure in society that includes those who have "good jobs" while excluding those who do not.

Equity Economics

In the thirty years since the passage of the Equal Pay Act, the gap in salaries between full-time working women and full-time working men narrowed by about a third. In 1963, women earned 59 cents for every dollar men earned; by 1993, that number had risen to 71 cents. The pay gap is neither the most comprehensive nor the most qualitative measure of women's status in society. But it does gauge the nature of women's economic progress. Although women have not reached economic parity with men, there has been some improvement, albeit one that has privileged white women. Full-time African-American women workers still earn 65 cents for every dollar white men earn, and full-time Hispanic women make about 57 cents for every dollar.[8]

Pay gaps persist in part because women are concentrated in low-wage employment, in part because men's work and women's work is not comparably valued. The movement for pay equity, stalled during the Reagan-Bush years, has gained momentum under Clinton. But there still have been no official pronouncements from the president, the sec-

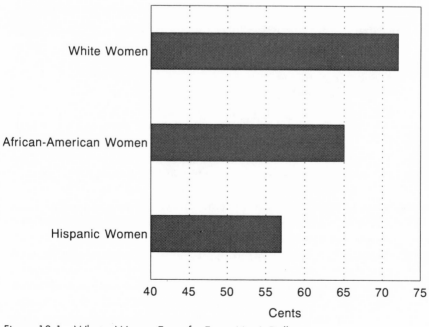

Figure 13.1   What a Woman Earns for Every Man's Dollar

Source: U.S. Bureau of the Census, Current Population Reports.

retary of labor, or the director of the Women's Bureau about any federal pay-equity initiatives.

Families are dependent on women's work for their well-being. Indeed, the *only* type of family that experienced income growth from 1979 to 1989 was married couples with a wife in the paid labor force.[9] Thus, fair pay for women's work affects not only women but family survival as well.

"Fair pay for women's work affects not only women but family survival as well."

Some 68 million Americans earn less than $10,000 per year; two-thirds of these workers are women. Almost 6 million workers earn the minimum wage. Again, two-thirds are women; about one-third or 2 million workers support families.[10] Clinton partly addressed the interests of the working poor, most of whom are women, by including the Earned Income Tax Credit (EITC) in his budget package. Designed to help low-income, full-time working people with children, the EITC is based on the premise that no one who works forty hours a week or more should live in poverty. The credit, which will be provided to the working poor whether they owe taxes or not, will make up the difference between full-time work and the poverty line.

While a step in the right direction, the EITC excludes those poor who are employed part-time. Since part-time and temporary employment is a growing feature of our downsizing economy, it is likely that many low-income people will find themselves in poverty despite the EITC. Thus, many single women heads of household, large numbers of whom either combine part-time jobs or work part-time because neither full-time work nor affordable child care is available, will be left out in the cold. If EITC is to help working families with children, the role of affordable child care in facilitating labor force involvement must be recognized.

Given growing part-time employment, it is also disappointing that the administration has backed off from an earlier commitment to increase the minimum wage. From 1981 to 1990, the minimum wage was stuck at $3.35 an hour. It has since risen to $3.80 and today stands at $4.25. Minimum-wage earners are private household workers, home health-care providers, food handlers, and maintenance workers. They park cars, pump gas, and watch children. The gap left by the EITC's requirement of full-time work could be partly filled by an increased minimum wage. As with many matters, however, the administration has not yet demonstrated the political will to pursue this fundamental issue of fairness.

Clinton has pledged to "end welfare as we know it," and while welfare reform is a laudable goal, his two-year "up or out" proposal seems harsh. It would disproportionately affect single mothers, many of whom need welfare supplements to avoid starvation and homelessness—for themselves and their families. Clinton's attempt to give welfare reform federal priority status on a par with health-care reform reinforces the misapprehension that public assistance is more of a budget drain than other federal expenditures such as the military. While few would argue that the current public assistance system should be maintained as is, it is inconceivable to hold those at the very economic bottom to a labor market standard equivalent to more highly skilled workers.

As the Department of Labor designs job-creation programs, those who care about fair pay and gender equity will need to be especially vigilant. If these programs duplicate the public works programs of the past, there will be a heavy male bias in employment and training. Public works programs tend to train workers in the crafts, construction, and highway maintenance. Since women hold fewer than 2 percent of those jobs, status quo job-creation programs will do little to change the inequity. The same holds true for Clinton's proposed student service corps. Should young women be directed to early childhood education and young men to environmental conservation? Unless those shaping the program and making assignments are prepared to consider gender equity as part of their mission, such an outcome is likely.

An equitable economic policy necessarily extends to the foreign policy realm. Foreign policy issues are not often perceived as women's issues. Throughout the developing world, however, mandated structural adjustment policies by international monetary agencies negatively affect those most heavily represented in the agrarian sector—namely, women and children. "The repercussions of structural adjustment," writes one analyst of African development, "have been exacerbated by women's subordination within the household, by continuing constraints on peasant productivity, and by mass unemployment."[11] U.S. leadership in alleviating these conditions has been conspicuously absent.

A world conference on women is scheduled for 1995. What role will the Clinton State Department play? To date, no one in the State Department has been charged with preparing for the conference. While Clinton did not promise to pay attention to the status of women in world development, he nevertheless has an opportunity to shape a foreign policy that extends beyond the old-boy network of international policymakers and looks at the role that the developing world plays in our own economic survival.

Putting Which People First?

The Clinton administration has implemented policies that improve the lives of some women, and not others. Generally, those who have been ignored are poor women and women of color. Clinton has moved boldly in the appointments arena, but slowly and cautiously in formulating public policy that deals with issues of fundamental equality. Thus the administration has legislated family and medical leave, but only for half the population. It has attempted to raise wages for the working poor, but only for those who work full-time. It has lifted the ban on RU486 knowing full well that this has little impact on poor women's access to health care.

What should the president do instead? He must tackle issues of labor market restructuring from the bottom up. Welfare reform therefore can only come after policies are implemented that increase the availability of child-care services and that increase the minimum wage. On job creation, he must concentrate on the truly difficult constituencies—the "unemployed core." And he must embrace bean-counting, not put it at arm's length. Measurement is not evil. It is a way to evaluate progress. Public policy has racial and gender implications: we need to know, for example, how many women will be included in a student service program and we need to know what kind of work they will do. Such considerations, rather than detracting from the content of programs, enhance their potential for success and ensure that *all* people will have access to the available opportunities.

In the first year of the Clinton administration, the inclusive rhetoric of "putting people first" collided with social structures that manifestly put people last. Worse, these structures put some people last more frequently than others. Too much of the "good life" in our society is built on women's unpaid work and on the existence of an unorganized, low-wage labor force in the service sector that provides low-cost perquisites for others. Dismantling these unfair structures will have very real consequences. Increasing the minimum wage, for example, will mean that working women who depend on household workers will have to shoulder an added expense. Paying food-service workers more money may mean that the cost of food will go up. How much equality are people prepared to advocate when it affects them so personally?

Rather than requiring these sacrifices, the Clinton White House has found it a lot easier to focus on incrementalism and to celebrate the personal stories of the many in the administration who have had to overcome obstacles to reach their positions. This Reagan-style individualism figured as an important subtext in the appointments process—this nominee was poor, that one an immigrant, yet another a sharecropper's son. That individuals overcome obstacles is laudable, but it does not speak to the condition of people at the bottom. Indeed, an overemphasis on individual achievement suggests that those at the bottom can achieve if only they, too, have the backbone. Such Horatio Alger-ism misrepresents the serious structural impediments that prevent women, people of color, and the poor—whatever their talents—from moving ahead in life.

Public policy that supports and moves U.S. society toward equality should focus on conditions like fair wages, affordable health care, and available child care that would enable full participation in our society and economy. The Clinton administration has tackled the comparatively easy gender questions but avoided the truly challenging ones. It has at least restored many of the gains lost during the 1980s. But it will have to work harder, and adhere more closely to stated principles, in order to bring American society truly into the 1990s.

Building Authority, Responsibility, and Capacity

DAVID MORRIS

President Clinton urges Americans to ask not "What's in it for me?" but rather "What's in it for us?" He appeals to his audiences to develop "a new spirit of community, a sense that we're all in this together."

The president's words are compelling, but he is speaking to a nation taught for several generations not to think in terms of "us." A nation of immigrants has little shared history or culture. Instead, the United States has emphasized the individual, not the group. We take it for granted that public is bad and private is good, that collective is bad and personal good, that cooperation is bad and competition good. We cherish the slogans "Don't tread on me" and "Live free or die." We are taught from the cradle that whenever "we" becomes as important as "me," whenever the social becomes as important as the individual, we are heading down a slippery slope toward tyranny and misery.

This harsh American emphasis on individualism has always been tempered by the historical presence of extended families, of ethnic neighborhoods, of family farms, of small towns—places where people know when you're born and care when you die. But in the last generation we have moved more often and increasingly farther from our places of birth. Less rooted, we are less involved in our immediate communities. Neighborhood gathering places—cafes, grocery stores, even libraries and churches—are rapidly disappearing. Over 70 percent of us do not even know the people next door.[1]

Little by little, we have lost our sense of mutual aid and cooperation. Two-thirds of us give no time to community activities. Fewer than half of all adult Americans now regard the idea of sacrifice for others as a positive moral virtue.[2] Both inside and outside the workplace we are increasingly disconnected, looking out for number one, voting only our narrow self-interest. "Virtual" communities and "virtual" corporations, where physical proximity is replaced by electronic "visits," are substituting for tangible community involvement and contact. Meanwhile, the scale of public and private institutions continues to grow. Decisions are made in an unintelligible and inaccessible process remote from the people and places that will feel their impact.

Some view this decline in the importance of territorial communities as an inevitable consequence of modernity: localism will naturally have diminished importance in an age of globalism. But this theory of the inevitable decline of community implies that public policy has been neutral on the issue. It has not.

For half a century Democratic and Republican administrations have consistently pursued policies that disabled rather than enabled compact, strong, and productive communities. Urban renewal programs literally bulldozed hundreds of inner-city neighborhoods. Federal housing programs subsidized suburban sprawl. Highway programs built roads at the expense of mass transit. In the past decade federal tax and regulatory policies encouraged leveraged buyouts and hostile takeovers that shuffled hundreds of billions of dollars in corporate assets and forced tens of thousands of workers to abandon their communities in search of jobs. The government has consistently supported centralizing rather than decentralizing technologies: nuclear power rather than solar energy, garbage incinerators rather than recycling, tomato harvesters rather than diversified crop farming.

"Does Bill Clinton offer a new beginning for American communities? Campaign promises and early initiatives justify a cautious yes."

Does Bill Clinton offer a new beginning for American communities? Campaign promises and early initiatives justify a cautious yes. The president has, for instance, supported small manufacturing, community development banks, and a large degree of decentralized authority. But will these initiatives be at the margins of public policy or at its center? And what role can federal authority ultimately play in strengthening regions so distant, geographically and conceptually, from the Beltway? The Clinton administration's success in these areas will depend in large part on its commitment to a trio of principles—authority, responsibility, and capacity (ARC)—and its acceptance of the dictum that small is not only beautiful but eminently sensible as well.

The ARC of Community

Praise for community comes from both sides of the political spectrum. Conservatives like Michael Novak have long applauded the virtues of family, voluntary associations, and a vibrant civil society. Likewise, liberals like Amitai Etzioni have emphasized the central role of kinship groups and tightly knit communities in fostering basic moral values such as mutual respect and nonviolence.

Communitarian liberals and social conservatives stress the importance of obligations as well as rights. The list of our responsibilities to one another is long and varied: voluntary organ donation, regular voting, a willingness to pay taxes, and so forth. Such personal responsibility to the general welfare is an important component of strong communities.

But in and of itself responsibility is not sufficient. Hundreds of communities that have exhibited the kinds of values that Novak and Etzioni embrace have been unable to defend themselves from powerful external forces. Middle-class neighborhoods in the Bronx were destroyed when the Port Authority of New York imposed the Cross Bronx Expressway on them. In the 1970s, the close-knit Polish neighborhood of Poletown in Detroit was levelled to make way for a new automobile plant that never opened. As Alexis de Tocqueville wisely noted more than 150 years ago, "Without power and independence, a town may contain good subjects, but it can contain no active citizens."

Aside from responsibility, strong communities need sufficient authority to make the rules that can ensure their future. In the late 1970s, for instance, Vermont enacted a land-use law that included, along with the ubiquitous environmental impact statement, an economic impact statement as well. On the basis of this economic assessment, the state denied a building permit for a regional mall because it would have destroyed the downtown business sector of nearby Burlington. The citizens of Vermont and Burlington properly exercised the right to defend their neighbors' businesses and jobs against absentee-owned regional superstores whose work force consists largely of temporary, part-time employees.

Governments often view communities as obstructionist, unwilling to accept even necessary development. Government officials have even invented an acronym—NIMBY or "Not In My Backyard"—to describe this phenomenon. Yet in many cases citizens' opposition is less a knee-jerk, innate obstructionism than a reflection of their lack of participation in the project conception and design.

For years Georgia state officials had tried to impose large landfills on small rural communities. For five years, this siting process was paralyzed by local opposition. Finally, Georgia allowed its citizens to design their own policies. After nearly ninety public meetings over four months the citizens of Atkinson County resolved to accept a landfill, choosing one that could handle only their own wastes and not those of other communities. Significant local authority can beget personal responsibility.

Yet responsibility and authority are both inadequate without the power and self-confidence that comes from owning productive capacity. Today we have lost most of the skills of self-reliance and no longer own the productive capacity needed to balance central economic and political authority. Over 85 percent of us work for someone else, and for most of us that someone else does not live nearby.

Communities with widespread local ownership tend to be more vibrant and stable. Citizens participate more in local affairs. Local owners have a stake in the community. Their kids go to local schools. The world's largest producer of automated nailing systems for wooden pallets—Viking Inc. of Fridley, Minnesota—is owned by its 120 workers. Vice President Dean Bodem acknowledges that the company would have left the state if it had not been employee-owned. "Because the employees own the company, it really ties us to Minnesota. If someone else would have bought this company, there's a high probability they would have moved it."[3] Viking's worker-owners know that their business generates the revenues used, in part, to educate their children.

Contrast this with the situation in northwest Indiana. The Calumet Project for Industrial Jobs evaluated seventeen plant closings from the 1980s and concluded that eleven could probably have been stopped via early intervention. All of the plants were absentee-owned. Most had recently changed hands. Plant closings, job loss, social disruption: such are the hazards of giving external authorities control over a community's life and work.

Social conservatives and communitarian liberals alike are apt to recite the proverb, "Give a man a fish and he will be without hunger for a day. Teach a man to fish and he will never be hungry." Yet the ability to fish will not keep someone from starving if he or she has no access to a net or a boat. Even a boat is insufficient if the community lacks the authority to prevent overfishing or stop the pollution that can destroy the fish's spawning grounds. And all of these additional considerations are immaterial if the person fishing bears no greater responsibility to the community at large—for safeguarding the environment, providing social services, and enabling the individual to pursue his or her own livelihood.

Authority, responsibility, capacity—these, then, are the cornerstones of sustainable communities. While both liberals and conservatives see the importance of personal responsibility, neither believes strongly in delegating authority or in public policies that promote locally owned productive capacity. In this respect liberals and conservatives alike subscribe to the Darwinian model of economic evolution in which large-scale institutions appear as an inevitable stage in economic history.

There is no label for those who believe in strong territorial communities. "Anarchist" would be historically appropriate. But the word has long since lost its original connotation as a belief in personal responsibility and humanly scaled institutions, and has come to mean instead a lack of structure and discipline. Historically the term "progressive" described a movement committed to public ownership and direct democracy. The challenge to modern-day progressives is to integrate a concern for communities and a support for humanly scaled technologies and organizations into their platforms.

Scale

"The real voyage of discovery," Marcel Proust observed, "lies not in seeking new lands but in seeing with new eyes." We need to see our communities not only as places of residence, recreation, and retail but also as places that nurture active citizens who make the rules that govern their lives and who have the skills and productive capacity to generate real wealth. Local economies must be more than branch plants of planetary corporations. Local government must be more than simply a body that reacts to higher levels of government.

This process of seeing with new eyes requires challenging the conventional wisdom that bigger is better, that separating the producer from the consumer, the banker from the depositor, the worker from the owner is an inevitable outcome of modern economic development. Surprisingly little evidence supports this conventional wisdom. In every sector of the economy the evidence yields the same conclusion: small is the scale of efficient, dynamic, democratic, and environmentally benign societies.

In education, for instance, one recent, exhaustive study on school size found that small schools have less absenteeism, lower dropout rates, fewer disciplinary problems, and higher teacher satisfaction than big schools. Commenting on this study by University of Chicago education professor Anthony Bryk, the *New York Times* notes that "now many researchers and educators alike see big urban high schools—those with 2,000 to 5,000 students—as Dickensian workhouses, breeding violence, dropouts, academic failure and alienation." By contrast, schools with 400 students or less have "fewer behavioral problems, better attendance and graduation rates, and sometimes higher grades and test scores. At a time when more children have less support from their families, students in small schools can form close relationships with teachers."[4] Acting on these insights, Chicago, Philadelphia, New York, and other cities have begun subdividing existing school buildings into several autonomous schools.

The same scale of institution that best cares for our children best cares for our money. "[O]nce a bank is larger than $400 million in deposits, economies of scale appear to be exhausted," acknowledges Robert Parry, president of the San Francisco Federal Reserve Bank.[5] In 1990, 11,194 of the 12,165 banks in the United States had assets under $300 million.[6] The Southern Finance Project compared banks that focused on their surrounding community to those lending all over the country. Banks that restricted lending to local borrowers were more than twice as profitable as those whose loans were geographically dispersed. Those that stayed close to home actually reduced overhead costs and suffered significantly fewer bad loans.

In manufacturing, too, small scale pertains. From 1979 to 1989 small and medium-sized businesses created more than 20 million new jobs while the 500 largest U.S. companies lost almost 4 million jobs.[7] Small manufacturers constitute over 98 percent of the 360,000 U.S. manufacturing enterprises. Two-thirds of these have fewer than twenty employees.

Some companies are taking a cue from school reformers and are subdividing factories into autonomous units. The Baltimore cardboard box plant of the Chesapeake Packaging Company, under the direction of plant manager Bob Argabright, divided the building into eight separate "companies." Each has responsibility for budgets, production, and quality levels. Each does its own hiring and deals with external and internal customers. When Argabright took over in 1988 the plant was losing money. Within a year it had turned a profit. By 1992 profits had increased more than five-fold.[8]

Compactness can also encourage creativity. Dr. Thomas J. Allen, director of the International Center for Research on the Management of Technology, has found that more than 80 percent of an engineer's ideas come from face-to-face contact with colleagues and that engineers will not walk more than about 100 feet from their own desks to exchange thoughts with anyone. Thus, Corning Glass Works' William C. Decker

Engineering Building is equipped with twelve separate discussion areas, each with coffee machine and wall-sized blackboards. To facilitate interaction, the building's three floors are connected by seven sets of open stairs, two escalators, a double bank of elevators, and several ramps.[9]

Even in the information age, geography and proximity matter. Indeed, more and more observers see a future in which nations break down into smaller units that then become the primary engines of a global economy. The globalization of economies and the regionalization of politics may go hand in hand. Thus, even as Europe moves toward a single internal market, regions have begun to exercise more autonomy, whether areas within countries such as the Basque or Catalan regions of Spain or areas that cut across countries such as the Alpine-Adriatic community. Closer to home, several western Canadian provinces and northwestern U.S. states have recently signed an economic compact for a new transnational "country" called Cascadia.

Several commentators predict the emergence over the next decade or two of 50–100 large "city states"—regions in which a major world-class city generates much of the economic activity. Economic development specialists such as Michael Porter of the Harvard Business School now emphasize the importance of geographic proximity for innovation. Porter points out that a 100-square-mile area in northern Italy is the world's leading footwear producer. Some 300 firms manufacture cutlery in one German town, Solingen, making it the center for that industry. In the United States, regional industrial clusters include Detroit for auto equipment and parts; Rochester, New York, for photography and optics imaging; South Florida for health technology and computers.[10]

"Perhaps the most appealing aspect of strong communities is their popularity."

Perhaps the most appealing aspect of strong communities is their popularity. The majority of the population supports community-team policing, home-based health care, community banks, neighborhood schools. For instance, the Carnegie Foundation found that of parents surveyed more than 80 percent favored neighborhood schools.[11] Almost seven out of ten respondents to *American Banker*'s 1990 consumer survey preferred community-oriented banks; only 23 percent preferred banking with a big institution.

The Clinton Approach

At this point the evidence is still inconclusive about whether the Clinton administration will strengthen the ARC of community and make humanly scaled institutions and strong territorial communities a central theme that cuts across major policy initiatives. The initial signs are positive. The concepts of personal responsibility, decentralized authority, and local productive capacity are not alien to this administration.

For ten years Bill Clinton was governor of Arkansas, a state with a population the size of Philadelphia, Chicago, or the Twin Cities. He is therefore no stranger to the possibilities of small towns and regions organizing their resources so as to generate the greatest possible wealth. Moreover, several members of the administration have been mayors and know firsthand about the role of neighborhoods and small businesses in economic, political, and social development.

Clinton favors small manufacturing. His proposed economic stimulus package gave the biggest tax breaks to those who invest in start-up and small firms. The budget for the National Institute of Standards and Technology, which provides matching funds to help industry develop new technologies, is expected to rise from $68 million in 1993 to $758 million in 1997. By 1997 Clinton expects to help establish 100 manufacturing extension centers connected to a nationwide, integrated fiber-optic network that will encourage a new range of products and services. Clinton also proposes a major apprenticeship program, patterned after Japan's or Germany's, to link high schools and local businesses as a way to upgrade the educational system and improve the skills and prospects of the majority of American high school graduates who do not go on to college.

Clinton knows that strong communities need access to capital. He proposes an initial federal appropriation of $382 million over four years to support more than 100 community development funds. The administration understands both the need to strengthen the 1977 Community Reinvestment Act and to extend its reach to the rapidly growing non-bank financial sector.[12] At the Department of Housing and Urban Development, Secretary Henry Cisneros and Assistant Secretary Andrew Cuomo can be expected to rely much more heavily on neighborhood organizations and nonprofit housing corporations as service providers.

Nevertheless, important questions remain. How much authority is this federal government willing to delegate to local communities? Will local ownership or decentralized production technologies become central elements in its strategic plans?

Democratizing the Economy

The administration believes in making workers partners with management. Yet it is unclear whether this empowerment means ownership and control. Secretary of Labor Robert Reich has argued that jobs, not ownership, should be the key objective. It does not matter to him whether a factory is owned by Toyota or General Motors so long as that factory is located in the United States. Reich may be right when he compares two global corporations like Toyota and GM, whose strategic plans are becoming increasingly similar. He is wrong, however, to compare a locally owned company, which has a stake in the community, to a multinational, whatever its country of origin.

The president's desire to build a partnership between management and labor is occurring at a time when corporations are increasingly breaking ties with their workers. The average blue-collar worker receives only seven days notice before losing his or her job, only two days when not backed by a union.[13] The UCLA Institute for Industrial Relations reports that contract workers comprise 24 percent of current corporate payrolls, with a 40 percent share expected by the end of the decade.[14] A temporary work force does not bode well for community stability.

Making workers true partners in business means making them owners. About 10,000 companies now have Employee Stock Ownership Plans (ESOPs). In about 20 percent of these companies, the workers own the majority share. But ESOPs are not the only form of ownership available. As Gar Alperovitz has pointed out, there are many kinds of customer- or worker-owned institutions in this country: 13,000 credit unions, nearly 100 cooperative banks, more than 100 cooperative insurance companies, almost 2,000 municipal utilities, and about 115 telecommunications cooperatives.[15]

In the financial sector Clinton could build a nationwide network of community banks from the debris of the bankrupt savings-and-loan (S&Ls) institutions. Tom Schlesinger, director of the Southern Finance Project (SFP) calls this "making lemonade from S&L lemons." As of spring 1993, according to SFP, the federal government owned eighty-one thrifts with more than 1,000 branches. More than 400 of these branches are located in low- and moderate-income communities in twenty-five states and 150 cities.

The Resolution Trust Corporation (RTC), formed in 1989 to oversee the closure and sale of bankrupt thrifts, has ignored the needs of communities and instead has curried favor with huge national banks. The RTC is closing dozens of branches in communities already suffering from a lack of access to capital, while this federal authority's pattern of sales has sharply increased the concentration of capital in local banking markets previously characterized by healthy levels of competition.

The RTC should be required instead to favor community-based institutions when selling deposits. One billion dollars could be diverted from the several billion dollars Clinton has proposed for expanding enterprise zones (now called empowerment zones). Given the current 6 percent equity capital requirement for banks, $1 billion could fully capitalize all 427 community banks with deposits of $12.9 billion. A targeted, aggressive network of neighborhood development banks arguably would galvanize far more beneficial community development than an equal number of enterprise zones.

President Clinton has also demonstrated his interest in sending more money back to communities and doing so with fewer strings attached. Local government is where the rubber meets the road. It is also the level of government of which the citizenry is the least cynical. A recent study from the Kettering Foundation concludes, "We have found that people's perception of having a diminished voice in national politics does not hold as true on the local level."[16]

Most local governments rely on property taxes as their primary source of income. Raising property taxes encourages middle-class homeowners and businesses to move to a neighboring jurisdiction with lower taxes. The effect is to encourage jurisdictions to compete against one another and to exacerbate the disparity of service levels between rich and poor communities. The federal government, on the other hand, relies primarily on income taxes and cannot be played off against other jurisdictions (except by big corporations who can move to offshore locations).

Localities have recently been starved of funds. Direct federal aid to local governments in real dollars fell by more than half during the 1980s, from $17.2 billion in 1980 to $7.5 billion in 1990. The federal share of city budgets fell from 18 percent in 1980 to 6.4 percent in 1990.[17] Meanwhile, state governments were putting more responsibility for services onto local governments. In 1991, for instance, California's state government shifted more than $2 billion in welfare, mental health, and medical programs from the state to the counties. "We're at the bottom of the totem pole, so we're getting everything dumped on us," says Frank Shafroth, director of policy and federal relations for the National League of Cities.[18]

The federal government should finance some of the functions now borne by communities, particularly health services. In Australia, for instance, the income tax pays for universal health coverage. The United States is the only industrialized nation that does not give its citizens, as a right of membership in the national community, access to medical care. It is our most important signal to ourselves that in America we have no commitment to one another. This lack of mutual aid in medical care

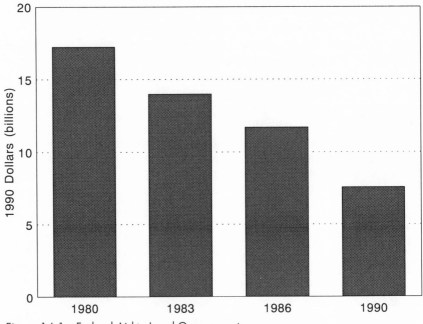

Figure 14.1   Federal Aid to Local Governments

Source: U.S. Department of Commerce, Bureau of the Census.

makes us all insecure. Universal health care may be the single most important step in rebuilding a sense of community in this country.

The federal government should dramatically expand its use of block grants. All federal money except for entitlements like Social Security and military expenditures should be returned to communities as a lump sum, with the federal government also shifting funds from richer to poorer communities. In his defeated economic stimulus package, President Clinton did dramatically expand lump-sum community development block grant spending, but he has yet to embrace block grants as the defining principle of government finance.

Federal spending now fragments communities. Cities receive money from dozens of different bureaucracies, each responding to different regulations. Transportation, housing, social services, economic development, water works funds—all of these come from a different federal pot. The result is an inefficient and sometimes internally inconsistent use of resources. It is impossible to plan comprehensively when the community is artificially broken up into dozens of bureaucratic cubbyholes.

Transferring money back to communities in this manner would not guarantee better decisions. But it would match authority to responsibility, bringing decisionmaking down to a level that enables direct participation and comprehensive planning.

Traveling and Talking

Physical transportation systems that rely on private cars and trucks are the enemies of community. By their nature they invade and fragment. Jane Jacobs describes the process in central cities:

> Traffic arteries, along with parking lots and filling stations, are powerful and insistent instruments of city destruction. To accommodate them, city streets are broken down into loose sprawls, incoherent and vacuous for anyone afoot. Downtowns and other neighborhoods that were marvels of close-grained intricacy and compact mutual support are casually disembowelled. Landmarks are crumbled or are so sundered from their contexts in city life as to become irrelevant trivialities. City character is blurred until every place becomes more like every other place, all adding up to Noplace. ...[19]

Physical transportation now claims about one-third of the land mass of cities. If national statistics are translated to the community level, every neighborhood has two or three people killed each year by cars and dozens more who suffer serious injury.

Perhaps more than any of its predecessors, the Clinton administration is filled with people who understand the enormous social, economic, and environmental costs of our transportation systems. Whether they will aggressively confront the country with this reality is unclear, especially after their bruising setback over the elegantly designed but quite modest BTU tax. One of their priority issues is to reduce vehicular generated pollution. Although interested in the type of fuel that powers the vehicle, they have to date evidenced less interest in the burdens imposed by the vehicle itself.

Americans love cars and hate welfare. Bill Clinton needs to speak to that dichotomy from the bully pulpit and explain that our private vehicles are by far the nation's biggest welfare cheats. The highway trust fund is a unique, self-perpetuating paving and construction fund financed by a dedicated tax.[20] Yet even the tens of billions of dollars each year that swell the highway trust fund cover only about half the cost of roads and a tiny fraction of the overall medical, social, environmental, police, and fire costs generated by vehicular use. By some estimates the subsidy to cars and trucks is well over $300 billion a year, thirty times more than the federal government gives in aid to cities.[21] If Americans had to pay the true costs of personal vehicles, they would not be able to afford them.

"If Americans had to pay the true costs of personal vehicles, they would not be able to afford them."

If physical transportation is the enemy of a sound economy and strong, cohesive territorial communities, electronic transportation can be their friend. It is by now commonplace to talk about how our economies have become more and more information-intensive. But we have yet to examine how this fact of technological life can help build a productive capacity and a cosmopolitanism within communities.

The future digital highways can allow our homes, neighborhood centers, and small businesses not only to visually communicate with one another over long distances but to produce and distribute services and even goods from our communities. In the 1980s we began to send a physical product, faxes, via the telephone lines. In mid-1993, IBM and Blockbuster Video signed an agreement that turned the latter's retail stores into manufacturing plants. Customers go into a booth and select music from a video screen connected to a mainframe computer. Then the music is "downloaded" to the store and "written" to a blank compact disc, much as the fax machine writes the sender's text to a piece of paper. In the near future the same process will undoubtedly be applied to books, with customers waiting a few minutes at stores for their purchases to be produced on high-speed laser printers. This concept of on-site manufacturing has widespread industrial applications. Some companies already use "rapid prototyping" technologies to build three-dimensional solid products from vats of molten plastic.

The coming of information highways allows us to look at households, retail stores, and neighborhood centers as producers of basic wealth. We can begin to envision the dual economy of a global village and a globe of villages: a planetary information web interconnecting self-reliant and self-conscious territorial communities.

Global information systems can also help overcome a key failing of territorial communities: parochialism. Indeed, this is the principal challenge and criticism of a public policy that emphasizes strong communities. But it is clear that the ability to "visit" easily with other cultures and to talk with their residents—instantaneous translation will be part of the new information systems within a decade or so—will enormously widen our perspective. The inward-looking orientation of territorial communities will be offset by the planetary perspective of its informationally based economies.

Will the Clinton administration champion a cooperatively owned, easily and cheaply accessible information system that moves productive capacity back into our homes and communities? Under the direction of Vice President Al Gore, the Clinton administration is aggressively promoting the rapid deployment of a national high-speed telecommunications infrastructure. Yet to date the role of the federal government appears limited to accelerating the construction process, not designing the infrastructure so that it revitalizes communities.

The Clinton proposal, for example, excludes at least in its first phase the quintessential community-based information institution—the public library. More than 60 percent of all Amerians visit a library at least once a year. The public library represents cooperation and community in an age of competition and globalism. An information policy that puts community first would place America's 15,000 public libraries at the head of the connection line.

Who will own the new information infrastructure? Who will be able to access it and on what terms? So far, the Clinton administration has not addressed this problem. Mitch Kapor, founder of Lotus and now head of the Electronic Frontier Foundation, champions a Jeffersonian view of information technology. He worries that the future information system could look more like the present cable television setup than the present telephone or Internet systems. His nightmare is that "we could have tremendous bandwidth into the home and individuals and groups not have any access to it but continue to be passive recipients for whatever the people who control access to that medium want to do with it."[22]

Sustainable Development: Local Capacity

Environmentally benign development is a thread that connects many Clinton initiatives. This approach to development does not, at present, have a direct community orientation, but it certainly has an indirect one. Such development implies reduced waste and the increasing substitution of renewable for nonrenewable resources. Each of these strategies, at least in theory, can help build stronger local economies.

Improving efficiency reduces our reliance on imported materials. Recycling further reduces that dependence and also generates a supply of valuable industrial materials close to the final customer. Manufacturers tend to locate near their sources of raw materials. Now many are locating near large suppliers of used materials. In the hierarchy of solid waste management, re-use is better than recycling. Because transportation costs of shipping whole products back to remote manufacturers for recycling are high, re-use further miniaturizes the economy.

When we need new materials, an environmental approach recommends that we use renewable resources. This, too, favors a shortening of the distance between producer and consumer. Minnesota, for instance, has sufficient winds to generate many times more electricity than the state consumes. A rooftop in Phoenix, Arizona covered with solar cells can generate sufficient electricity not only to heat and cool the home but to run the family's electric car. Neither Arizona nor Minnesota need be reliant on Saudi oil or Wyoming coal.

Wind and direct sunlight can provide significant quantities of energy. But they cannot supply molecules to make a physical product. For that we need to use another renewable resource: the stored solar energy in plant matter. Anything that can be made out of a hydrocarbon—chemicals, fibers, plastics, paints—can be made out of a carbohydrate and probably once was. The first plastic, invented in the 1880s, was made not from petroleum but from cotton. The first synthetic fiber was not nylon but rayon made from wood pulp.

Oil is cheap to transport, encouraging large plants distant from their raw material supplies. Plant matter is bulky and expensive to transport, encouraging modestly scaled biorefineries located near their raw material providers. In the future, cooperative biorefineries could use fast-growing trees or grasses and even single-cell algae as their raw material.

Consider the two futures implied by two Minnesota refineries. Just south of Saint Paul stands the Koch petroleum refinery. It produces about 40 percent of Minnesota's transportation fuels, 800 million gallons a year. Koch is an out-of-state corporation. Its raw materials are imported. Its facility is harmful to both its workers and its neighbors.

Compare this ecological eyesore with a biorefinery located three hours southwest of Saint Paul in Marshall, Minnesota. Minnesota Corn Processors (MCP) is owned by 2,700 corn farmers. Its plant produces corn meal, corn oil, carbon dioxide, corn syrup, ethanol, and industrial starch. Virtually all its raw materials are purchased locally. Virtually all its sales are in the region in which it is located. MCP is highly profitable, yet it satisfies only 2 percent of Minnesota's transportation needs, producing about 35 million gallons of ethanol a year.

Which raw material and organizational structure is best suited to a strong Minnesota economy? Two absentee-owned Koch-type refineries or fifty cooperatively owned MCP-type refineries?

Twenty years ago, recycling and solar energy and biochemicals were futurist dreams. Today they have become increasingly cost-effective. In 1980 it was cheaper to throw away a ton of garbage than to recycle it. In 1993, in most parts of the country, the opposite is true.[23] In 1980 the cost of electricity generated from wind turbines was about seven times the

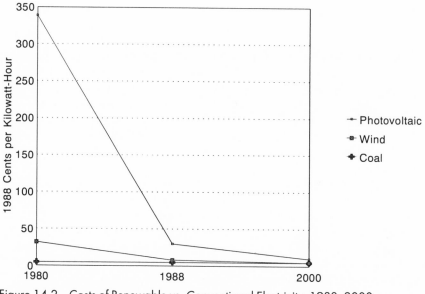

Figure 14.2   Costs of Renewable vs. Conventional Electricity, 1980–2000
Source: Worldwatch Institute.

price of conventional electricity. Today, in some parts of the country, wind-electric generators are the cheapest of all new power plants. In 1985 few consumer products were primarily derived from plants. Today such goods compete in almost every major category. Biopaints have captured 3 percent of the paint market. Vegetable oil–based inks have 8 percent of the ink market.[24]

Today recycling, solar energy, and biological products are significant businesses, even major industries. But they are still at the margins of the economy. The task of the new administration is to make them central to the next economy and to do so in a way that fosters community.

The federal government can facilitate this process by, for example, mandating that products contain minimum amounts of recycled content. A dozen states already have such legislation applied to newspapers, telephone books, fiberglass insulation and glass, and plastic containers. A federal law would overnight create huge markets for recycled materials and make manufacturers responsible for their products even after disposal.

Federal procurement could also accelerate the introduction of decentralized devices like solar cells and fuel cells. On the spending side of the equation, the federal government should put R&D funds for renewable resource–based technologies at the top of its agenda.

The Local Is Global

It is not enough for the Clinton administration to promote strong communities with national programs. In an increasingly planetary economy, strong communities must be nurtured and protected by international policies too. As Robert Kuttner has noted, "[I]n the newly turbulent global economy, a social contract in one company is as elusive as 'socialism in one country.' Even a manager with the best will in the world—and the best union—cannot guarantee that the company will be in business next decade, or even next year, to reciprocate the workers' loyalty. The larger social contract is the responsibility of government."[25]

Free-trade agreements, our courts have ruled, supercede state and federal laws. What is the potential impact and reach of existing trade agreements? Consider a recent European Commission (EC) report.[26] Responding to a barrage of U.S. criticism concerning European trade barriers, the EC listed the kinds of U.S. laws it considered protectionist: California legislation requiring a minimum amount of recycled content in glass containers sold within that state, restrictions in fifteen states on corporate ownership of farm enterprises, restrictions in twenty-nine states on foreign ownership of land, labels that tell the customer where a car was built and assembled.

All the laws the EC criticizes were democratically enacted by communities to reduce pollution, create jobs, or retain a measure of influence over their own futures. All of these laws are threatened by misguided free-trade policies. In the nineteenth century, the U.S. Supreme Court used the interstate commerce clause of the U.S. Constitution to severely limit the authority of states and cities to enact rules that would protect their small farms and small businesses and neighborhoods. In the late twentieth century, international trade panels are doing the same.

Those who oppose and those who support new trade agreements agree on one thing: The world economy is broken and needs new rules. The debate is about what those rules should be. Those who favor strong communities do not accept that trade agreements should have as their only objective the elimination of all obstacles to the flow of resources.

Trade agreements should establish minimum, not maximum, global environmental and social standards, as the United States did in 1938. That year Congress enacted the Fair Labor Standards Act (FLSA) to discourage states from competing for business investment by lowering the quality of life of their residents. The FLSA created national minimum wage and maximum hour standards but allowed individual states to exceed these standards. In the 1970s and 1980s federal environmental legislation usually embraced the same principle by establishing minimum, not maximum, pollution standards.

Trade agreements should permit states and localities to impose the same environmental and social standards on imports as they do on domestic producers. Communities, businesses, and nations should compete on the basis of productivity and efficiency, not on the basis of wages and working conditions. Cities and states should be given great leeway to protect their neighborhoods, small business enterprises, and diversified locally owned economies, even when this may impede international trade.

"The Clinton administration has approached free trade from a national, not a community, perspective."

The Clinton administration has approached free-trade agreements from a national, not a community, perspective. That is understandable. After all, the president represents the nation. In international negotiations only nations and not communities are at the table. From now on, however, President Clinton must shoulder both responsibilities, to represent communities as well as the nation.

Perfecting Ends

It seems oxymoronic to argue that the federal government can promote self-reliant communities. Yet we are at an important crossroads in world history. People are clamoring for a more effective voice in government at the same time as corporations are moving farther and farther away from their workers and their communities. The federal government can play a key role in mediating between local demands and global realities.

In the 1990s the federal government will design new environmental rules that will alter the material foundations of economies. The federal government will also help write global trade agreements that may change the nature of citizenship and the reach of government. In creating these new rules, we need to clarify the direction and the ends of policy. As Albert Einstein once observed, "Perfection of means and confusion of ends seems to characterize our age." While the Clinton administration has offered a set of intricately worked-out means, it has been less precise about the ultimate goals of policy. Improving efficiency, reducing pollution, creating jobs, and building information highways are all beneficial objectives. But there needs to be an overarching goal, an organizing principle that informs all of these policies. That principle should be the development of strong territorial communities.

The arguments against self-conscious and powerful territorial communities come in many forms. Economists, for instance, fear that production units and markets will be fractured, breeding inefficiencies and higher costs. Yet, after a century of mass production, factories are getting smaller, not bigger. And new technologies like flexible manufacturing, just-in-time production, and rapid prototyping are moving us away from mass production and back to small-lot production. Small units working together can achieve the same economies of scale as a single large corporation relying on hundreds of production units.

Sociologists and political scientists worry about cultural insularity and isolation that could lead to Yugoslav-type ethnic violence. Delegating authority to communities, some argue, is an invitation to the oppression of minorities. This fear of balkanization is a more formidable concern and not as easily deflected. Cohesive, self-conscious communities will undoubtedly view themselves as different and perhaps superior to their neighbors. But this does not mean they will instigate violence or wars. History shows that most wars result from unsustainability, territorial ambitions, a lack of material resources, or a desire to conquer new markets.

Can semi-autonomous communities also view themselves as part of a larger community? Of course they can. The provinces of Canada have much more authority than do U.S. states. Indeed, Canada is a confederation, not a union like ours. But citizens of Manitoba and Ontario view themselves as part of a nation, not only a province.

Increasingly the environment also ties us together. We all share the same biosphere and thus our individual freedom of action must be constrained by the needs of the general welfare. If individual communities or nations maximize their fish catches, the fishing stocks will rapidly disappear for all communities. We are now designing the global rules that will allow autonomous communities to share equitably in the limited but bountiful resources of nature.

Coherent, self-conscious communities will tend to be exclusive, but that does not necessarily mean they will be parochial, isolationist, or inefficient. Singapore, Quebec, and the Mondragon cooperative in the Basque region of Spain are three examples of linguistic or culturally based communities. Each favors its primary ethnic group. Yet each has developed a vital, vibrant, innovative, cosmopolitan economy whose enterprises successfully compete with those in the rest of the world.

Authority, responsibility, capacity: the ARC of community. Without authority, democracy is meaningless. Without responsibility, chaos ensues. Without a productive capacity we are helpless to manage our affairs and determine our economic future. Federal policy should be evaluated on the basis of how it strengthens all three cornerstones of strong communities.

Restoring
Democratic Principles

RALPH NADER

While running for office, Bill Clinton said he had big plans for "fundamental change" in how our government and economy work. But after one year it is clear that the president, his Cabinet, and his allies in Congress all fail to understand that no significant change will occur, or endure, without an institutionalized shift of power from corporations and government into the hands of ordinary Americans. While politicians now make an art form of populist symbolism, virtually none has a serious agenda to truly empower individuals in their five basic roles as voters, taxpayers, consumers, workers, and shareholders.

Chiding corporate special interests, President Clinton has promised to enact far-reaching reforms in health care, environmental protection, and economic development, among other areas. But that agenda will inevitably be emasculated or thwarted unless he adopts a more fundamental priority: the rejuvenation of the democratic culture of this nation. After all, it has been primarily the supremacy of the corporate state and the overpowering of our "civic infrastructure," rather than fate or isolated mistakes, that has produced so many intractable national problems. If civic values received as much television airtime as Morris the Cat, the savings-and-loan scandal would have never occurred: outraged voters would have intervened long before it became a $500 billion debacle.

Each generation must reinvent and rediscover democracy for itself, Thomas Jefferson declared. This can never occur through mere exhortation. It cannot happen simply by celebrating the values of civic engagement, praising a thousand points of light, or hosting quadrennial candidate forums. Instead, democracy must be brought to life in arenas where people are already engaged and where they already have interests.

All sorts of latent energies are waiting to be tapped. What is needed is a new toolbox of empowerment to give some noble eighteenth-century constitutional principles a practical application in the twenty-first century. These tools are mechanisms of civic communication, political organization, government assistance, and legal rights that can advance the distinct interests of ordinary Americans.

But how to revive a vigorous democratic tradition in America? A new "fifth estate" of individual Americans needs to arise, independent of entrenched corporate and governmental power. Through new forms of joint action, this insurgent force in American life can reclaim our government from the oligarchy that has made it a caricature of the Jeffersonian vision.

Central to this redemption of democratic traditions are new structural and procedural reforms that can empower individuals. Such reforms are the only way that our society will ever deal with its pervasive sense of powerlessness, alienation, and fatalism in the face of rampant inequities and loss of control over the future. Here is the North Star that must guide political and economic governance: Reassert fundamental democratic principles and give them new and creative facilities and applications in everyday life.

Voter Initiatives

The 1992 campaigns dramatically illustrated the depth of voter disillusionment with politics as usual—as well as the deep yearning of ordinary Americans to participate in the democratic process. Unfortunately, except for a few media-driven vehicles such as call-in talk shows and candidate forums (which, significantly, were convened by candidates, not by voters), citizens have few opportunities to take the initiative in bringing issues to the public's attention.

One of the best tools for breaking this logjam is the voter initiative— the process by which citizens may enact or reject laws *directly* through the voting booth rather than through elected officials. The process is simple. Citizens gather signatures of a specified number of voters on petitions. An initiative appears on the ballot and is then enacted or rejected by popular vote. Through the initiative process citizens can propose new laws, state constitutional amendments, or city or county charter amendments. Through the referendum process, a law or amendment is

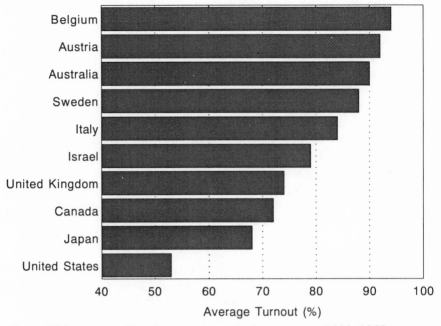

Figure 15.1   Average Voter Participation in Ten Democracies, 1980–1989

Source: Brookings Institution.

passed by elected officials and then submitted to the voters for approval or rejection.

Citizens groups turn to initiatives when state legislators or city officials refuse to respond to an issue, despite public opinion. Without initiatives, self-government all too often means only giving voters a choice of electing the lesser of two evils. With the initiative process, however, voters can control specific policies of government and even change its structure. Frequently, just filing an initiative petition will spur legislators into action and call attention to a citizen or community campaign. Government becomes more responsive. Political power cannot be so easily monopolized by a few influential officials. New and often crucial items can be put on the political agenda. And citizens are more likely to participate in civic life.

Any politician who is serious about rejuvenating our democratic traditions should promote the use of the initiative process. This should be pursued in states where initiatives are not yet possible, as well as at the national level. Congress, by a majority vote of both houses, could create a nonbinding national initiative process or mandate national referenda on any subject at any time. This act alone would send a powerful message to the American public that democratic principles are indeed valued, that citizen-driven participation is important in our public life, and that legislators are willing to be directly responsive to the public will.

Campaign Finance Reform

It is now a well-accepted fact that our system for financing presidential and congressional campaigns is fundamentally corrupt and pernicious. Over 4,000 political action committees (PACs) dominate campaign donations, and among individuals, "housewife" is the most frequently listed occupation of large donors. ("Housewives"—i.e., large donors hiding behind their spouses—contributed $14 million in 1990 alone.)[1]

The only way to ensure effective and honest representation by lawmakers is through basic campaign finance reform, with public funding of campaigns. Although candidate Bill Clinton promised far-reaching reform in this area, the proposal he introduced in his first year in office failed to eliminate the influence of special-interest money in elections.

In February, a coalition of 300 citizen organizations launched a massive "Clean Up Washington" campaign with its own 800 number (1-800-847-6611) to marshal citizen support. The object of the campaign is to promote public financing of elections and to achieve overall spending limits for congressional races, a reduction in the limits on PAC and individual contributions, a ban on "soft money" contributions (which are channeled through political parties), and the elimination of special tax breaks for lobbying. By loosening the grip of entrenched interests, these reforms promise to unleash new possibilities for the civic culture.

Term Limits

Few issues have so galvanized spontaneous citizen leadership as the idea of term limits. It is one of the healthier signs that the American people have not given up on self-governance. The chief value of term limits is its ability to liberate new energy for political elections. Not only can a fresh crop of candidates emerge—and win—but more citizens can become excited recruits to electoral campaigns. Since incumbents typically have a hammerlock on re-election, ordinary citizens who used to participate actively in campaigns have largely given up. They reasonably say, "Why bother? How could I possibly make a difference? There's no chance that my challenger-candidate could possibly unseat a lifetime politician."

Term limits change this equation. Suddenly congressional elections matter again. New blood enters the democratic process. Diversity of representation is enhanced. Legislators can be elected who have energy and

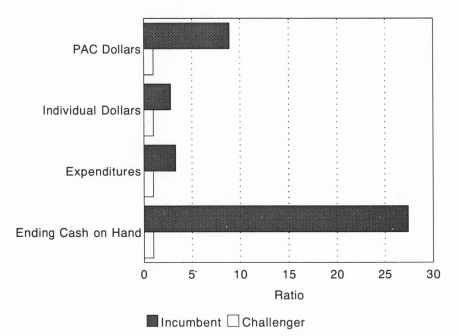

Figure 15.2   Incumbent vs. Challenger Fundraising, U.S. House of Representatives, 1992

Source: U.S. Public Interest Research Group.

determination, who are not burned out or bought out. Newcomers will generally be closer to their constituents than the career politicians of Washington. Their arrival can help end the reign of the ruling cliques, whose entrenched power is a potent barrier to progressive change.

Opponents of term limitations warn that inexperienced citizen legislators will be at the mercy of special-interest lobbyists and that the voters will lose the experience and wisdom of career lawmakers. But this argument is not convincing. There were a lot of amateurs in Philadelphia 200 years ago; they didn't do too badly. The more formidable argument may be constitutional. Some experts argue that only Congress itself— and not the states—can limit its terms by a constitutional amendment ratified by two-thirds of the states. This was the method used to limit presidential terms in 1951. At the very least, however, it is clear that the states can limit the terms of state officials. Many states already limit the number of terms that their governors may serve.

Obviously, members of Congress are not likely to limit their own terms. So attention must turn to ways to compel Congress to act. The twenty-two states with the initiative-referendum process—where voters have direct access to the ballot box—will have a head start in organizing term-limit campaigns. These states account for nearly half of the House of Representatives, and forty-four of the nation's 100 senators. A state-by-state drive of term-limitation initiatives will create national momentum to limit congressional terms, even in the twenty-eight noninitiative states. In those states, citizens must demand that their legislators vote for term limits or that the question be placed on the ballot for the public to make its voice heard.

Citizen Standing Rights

What can be done when government itself becomes lawless, flouting the very Constitution and congressional laws that it is duty-bound to uphold? This is one of the most important yet neglected problems of self-governance of our time.

Historically, one important tool for citizens and taxpayers has been a broad right of legal standing to gain access to the courts. Unfortunately, the U.S. Supreme Court over the past twenty years has reversed that former corpus of case law and developed a highly restrictive law of standing. This has made it easy for government agencies and officials to disregard the laws under which they operate, for the simple reason that no one would have standing to challenge government misconduct in court.

To empower citizens to curb government illegality, it is vital that Congress enact remedial legislation that gives taxpayers and citizens broad standing to sue government. Such a reform would not only cost virtually nothing, it would greatly improve the quality and responsiveness of government operations. It would also send a strong message that our nation is indeed governed by law and not by the arbitrary caprice of political officials or government bureaucrats.

The Supreme Court recognized the importance of broad taxpayer and citizen standing in a series of decisions in the 1960s and early 1970s. In *Flast v. Cohen* (1968), for example, the Court upheld the standing of taxpayers to challenge the expenditure of tax revenues in a way that was alleged to violate the Establishment Clause of the First Amendment. In *United States v. SCRAP* (1973), the Court upheld the standing of ordinary users of the environment to challenge the legality of environmentally harmful government regulations even though the interest of the particular plaintiffs was generalized and diffuse.

The Supreme Court first began to curtail the standing rights of taxpayers and citizens in the mid-1970s. The Court refused, for example, to grant standing to a taxpayer who wished to argue that secret CIA funding violated the Constitution's requirement of a public accounting of public expenditures.

What has emerged from the Rehnquist Court is a complex and convoluted body of standing law that is too arcane for ordinary citizens to understand. Using esoteric terms such as "injury in fact," "redressability," "logical nexus," and "zone of interests," the law of standing has been transformed into a smokescreen that masks and sanctions much governmental illegality. To make matters worse, the Supreme Court has frequently denied standing in a way that makes it clear that no plaintiff would have standing. This gives government officials license to violate the law whenever it is expedient for them to do so, because no one, except their attorney general, will ever be able to hold them accountable in court.

Obviously, this is no way to promote official compliance with law or citizen confidence in the operation of government. If public confidence in the legitimacy of government is to be restored, Congress must immediately enact new legislation to broaden standing rights for citizens.

Taxpayer Assets

On behalf of the American people, the U.S. government owns and manages a wide variety of taxpayer assets: national forests, grazing lands, mineral deposits, power projects, information resources, research and development rights, and broadcast frequencies, among others. The Reagan and Bush administrations boasted of their intention to run government "like a business"—before proceeding to host a massive fire sale of taxpayer assets to assorted corporate interests. Here, too, citizens and taxpayers must be empowered to stop the widespread abuses of government stewardship of publicly owned assets.

"Citizens and taxpayers must be empowered to stop the widespread abuses of government stewardship of publicly owned assets."

The federal government has historically funded about half of all U.S. expenditures on research and development (R&D)—some $74 billion in fiscal year 1992. Over the past twelve years, the allocation of property rights in these research projects has dramatically changed. Before the

Reagan-Bush era, the government generally sought to have research products enter the public domain, or to patent inventions or license them on a nonexclusive basis. Exclusive licenses were used but only sparingly and often for limited terms. After 1980, however, a series of statutes, rules, and policy memoranda sanctioned a broad use of exclusive licenses. In effect, taxpayers invest billions of dollars in R&D every year and then the returns on these investments are privatized.

One of the more egregious abuses of taxpayer assets involves azidothymidine (AZT), the AIDS treatment developed chiefly through government grants. Despite the government's development funding, Burroughs Wellcome later gained monopoly rights to the drug, charging more than $4,000 per year to AIDS patients, many of whom have no health insurance and must rely on Medicaid (that is, taxpayers).

This same pattern is replicated in the government's stewardship of federal information resources, much of it available through electronic means. The U.S. government is the largest publisher of information in the world. Yet the government has raised prices for these taxpayer-sponsored information resources; given them away to private vendors who sell the identical materials at inflated prices; and eliminated many publications altogether, effectively barring public access to government information and policy.

One partial solution that deserves immediate congressional action is pending legislation that would require the Government Printing Office to set up a one-stop-shopping program for online access to hundreds of federal databases. The service would be free to 1,400 federal depository libraries and would be available to everyone else through subscriptions priced at the "incremental cost of dissemination."

Another way to help taxpayers defend public assets against waste and abuse is to create a taxpayer watchdog group, in the form of a set-aside program, as a requirement for all uses of taxpayer assets. This money—say 1 or 2 percent of a given subsidy—would finance ongoing citizen oversight of private use of taxpayer assets. Like other accountability mechanisms, this expenditure could be one of the most cost-effective ways for the government to prevent waste and damage to public assets.

Already there seems to be greater receptivity to such ideas. Interior Secretary Bruce Babbitt has announced, for example, that the U.S. government will no longer charge nominal fees for grazing rights, mineral rights, and other private exploitation of federal lands. Instead, taxpayers will begin to receive about one-third of market rates. Standards will constrain these private users to treat these resources more responsibly. Whether President Clinton will be able to overcome the cattle, farming, and mining interests' power in Congress is, of course, another matter—which is precisely why the democratic reforms mentioned above are so vital.

Public Airwaves

The privatization of one of our most important taxpayer assets—the broadcast airwaves—has caused serious deformations of our politics and culture. The basic problem is that private broadcasters control what the public owns. They have been given licenses—for free—to use taxpayer property. But in return, broadcasters give us a steady stream of increasingly coarse, sensationalistic, and superficial programming that caters to the lowest common denominator of audience exploitation.

The most fundamental civic needs receive no air time. Ordinary citizens can speak to their neighbors, but they cannot speak to millions of their fellow Americans without paying a giant toll and obtaining the permission of large corporations. The grotesque paradox is that free-speech rights originally intended for individuals and the community have become the exclusive property of business entities, most of which have little interest in public forums.

To give the audience access to the airwaves that it already owns, the Clinton administration should support the establishment of a new broadcast vehicle, the Audience Network. This national, nonprofit, nonpartisan membership organization would be granted one hour of prime-time television and one hour of drive-time radio on every commercial channel each day. It would function as a separate licensee, airing diverse programming shaped by the membership. It would be open to all citizens over age sixteen for a nominal fee, such as $10 annually, and be democratically controlled. Finally, Audience Network would represent consumer interests before the Federal Communications Commission (FCC), Congress, and the courts. This would redress the long-standing disenfranchisement that millions of viewers and listeners have suffered under the current regulatory regime.

Audience Network and its professional staff would be managed by persons accountable to the membership through a direct elective process. Besides membership fees, the Network could lease some airtime back to stations or networks. This would help assure the Network's financial security and allow it to prohibit paid advertisements. During its time slot, the Audience Network could air a variety of cultural, political, entertainment, scientific, or other programs that it produced or obtained. Major abuses that are not publicized for years by the commercial media would receive more prompt attention free of the constraints of corporate advertisers.

Over time, Audience Network would gradually transform a powerless, voiceless audience, which has been conditioned to accept a debased regime of programming, into an active audience with the ability to initiate new, innovative, and consequential programming. Its open programming by diverse noncommercial groups would greatly invigorate the civic marketplace of ideas—a signal challenge for our times.

Shareholder Democracy

That corporate democracy has been an illusion for nearly 100 years has not deterred business executives and the New York Stock Exchange from annually proclaiming its viability. What is the scope of management power and what are the checks upon it? In nearly every large American business corporation, one person or a small coterie of executives have unquestioned operational control. In theory, this small group of managers is selected by the board of directors to run the corporation; in reality it is just the reverse. The chief executive or executive clique chooses the board, and, with its acquiescence, controls the corporation.

The legal basis for such a consolidation of power is the proxy election—what British law professor L.C.B. Gower calls "this solemn farce."[2] Given the nearly insuperable barriers faced by insurgents challenging management, however, it is no surprise that the board of directors has ceased to perform its statutory function of "managing the business and affairs of every corporation." Indeed, it is often hard to tell whether the boards of many corporations perform any independent function at all or whether they simply mirror managers' desires. "Directors," William O. Douglas complained as early as 1934, "do not direct."[3] Management control has overwhelmed the rule of law.

Such autocratic corporate governance entails serious economic and social costs—in terms of self-dealing, inefficiency, and illegality. Even *Business Week* now concludes, "So much of this trouble for America's corporate titans [General Motors, IBM, Westinghouse, American Express] might have been avoided had the same parochial perspectives not clouded the judgment of many outside directors. They simply failed in their duties."[4] Many institutional shareholders such as the California State Employees Pension Fund, newly aware of the long-term economic costs of unaccountable managements, have mounted campaigns to oust lackluster management teams. This is a step in the right direction, but the impulse needs to be taken much further.

A Corporate Democracy Act is needed to give all stakeholders in corporate decisionmaking a real voice in corporate governance. Redistributing rights and obligations among shareholders, boards of directors, and executives can make giant companies both more efficient and law-abiding. Critical to this task is the installation of a full-time outside board of directors selected by "cumulative voting" of shareholders elections funded entirely by the company. To discourage states from wastefully competing among themselves to woo corporate investment—by

---

*"A Corporate Democracy Act is needed to
give all stakeholders in corporate
decisionmaking a real voice in
corporate governance."*

---

sanctioning unfair labor practices, pollution, wasteful subsidies, and so forth—federal chartering of corporations with minimum national standards is essential. Finally, the victims of corporate malfeasance—workers, consumers, local communities, shareholders, and small business-people—should be accorded greater access to the court system to redress their complaints.

If all the societal costs of our baroque, ineffectual sham of corporate governance are tallied, it becomes clear that corporate autocracy is not conducive to a robust, productive economy, nor to socially benign corporate behavior. But this will not change unless shareholders are empowered to gain greater access to reliable corporate information, participate in fair elections for board seats, exercise meaningful oversight of management, and begin to abide by minimal national standards of business responsibility.

Citizens' Utility Boards

Mancur Olson, in his excellent book *The Logic of Collective Action*, asks, "Why is it that throughout history large numbers of people are preyed upon by small numbers of people? What is it about the victim class that makes it incapable of asserting itself?"[5]

One answer is that the "victim class" has great difficulty in ever bringing itself together, as a group, through a cheap and continuous communication system. It has no organizational means for asserting its collective will or developing a common identity and culture. This dynamic is played out in dozens of milieus in our political economy, as sellers, who are consummately capable of organizing themselves to protect their interests, develop myriad means to exploit buyers, who have preciously few means of organizing themselves. Those public-interest groups that do exist often cannot provide a consistent presence that is technically competent, financially stable, and directly accountable to consumers.

The 1980s saw the emergence of a promising solution to this classic problem. The Citizens' Utility Board, or CUB, is a model approach for bringing together diffuse consumers into a voluntary organization, which can then pursue a common citizen-consumer agenda in banking, insurance, housing, and dozens of other arenas. CUBs are the "silicon chip" for the citizen movement because the concept is so versatile and inexpensive to implement yet it is powerfully effective.

Typically, residential consumers do not have the organization, resources, or expertise to respond to utility arguments on such matters as ratesetting, safety, and other issues. A CUB offers an ingenious way to provide effective citizen representation. By authority of state legislatures, a CUB is given the right to enclose notices inside certain state mailings to invite the public to become voluntary members of the organization for a modest annual fee of $5 to $10. The CUB pays for this enclosure. This "piggybacking" of state mailings is a convenient, effective way for the CUB to organize a membership and to communicate with it. It also provides a basis for self-sufficiency and financial accountability. Since there is no reliance on tax monies or government bureaucracy, liberals and conservatives alike find the concept attractive.

All members of the CUB have the right to vote in the election of the CUB's board of directors. This process ensures that the leadership of the CUB reflects the interests of the ratepayers. The directors serve without pay and hire full-time staff such as accountants, attorneys, economists, organizers, and lobbyists. The staff can intervene, for example, in rate proceedings, advocate before the legislature, research issues of concern to consumers, survey public opinion on energy and telecommunications issues, provide analysis of utility complaint handling, and provide information and assistance to consumers interested in conserving energy.

Independent CUBs now exist in Wisconsin, Illinois, and other states, attracting tens of thousands of members and saving literally billions of dollars in gratuitous rate hikes. It would be easy to apply the CUB idea to organizations like insurance companies, banks, mutual funds, the U.S. Postal Service, and the Social Security Administration.

The beauty of the CUB concept is that, as a voluntary group, it costs taxpayers virtually nothing. It is anti-bureaucratic, because no new government personnel or procedures are needed. It enhances civic participation, because the CUB depends for its success on the energy and vision of its members. And it counters the massive inequities of power that afflict consumers in their dealings with government and business.

Victims' Rights

Another constituency of individuals that is increasingly powerless are the innocent victims of dangerous products, unsafe workplaces, toxic waste, and other hazards. In recent years, a massive campaign has been waged by insurance companies, manufacturers, and other corporate interests to roll back the legal rights of plaintiffs to obtain full compensation for their injuries through civil litigation. In one of the most unprincipled public relations scams in the history of American industry, this coalition has pursued a draconian package of changes that it deceptively calls "tort reform." In essence, the proposals seek, among other things, to place arbitrary caps on "pain and suffering" awards; eliminate punitive damage awards (often the only effective deterrent against intentionally unsafe products and practices); impose mandatory limits on plaintiff lawyers' contingency fees, without limitations on the fees of defense lawyers; and eliminate strict liability, one of the most effective deterrents against unsafe products and workplaces.

The coalition's fundamental message is that the jury system is out of control because both the common law and jury awards are unpredictable. Claiming a ruinous "litigation explosion," insurance companies and their corporate clients dislike the jury system because they cannot precisely budget it as a cost of doing business. This cost unpredictability is the very essence of deterrence—a function of the civil justice system equally important to compensating the victim, which, along with the system's other social utilities, cannot be quantified in dollars and cents.

A citizen empowerment agenda must deal frankly and forcefully with the structural problems of the insurance industry. Congress should repeal the industry's exemption from antitrust laws, federal regulation, and Federal Trade Commission scrutiny—all of which contribute to a cycle of surge-and-decline of cash flow, which in turn has precipitated the bogus "insurance crisis." Congress should also establish a federal office of insurance to monitor the industry and establish standards for state regulators to follow. Finally, to exert downward pressure on reinsurance rates and thus enable insurers to reduce their rates, Congress should establish a national industry-funded reinsurance program to compete with foreign reinsurers.

At the state level, insurance companies must be required to routinely disclose how much they take in on premiums and investment income, and how much they pay out in verdicts and settlements, plus reserves and other expenditures. State insurance departments need more authority and funding, and consumers need greater representation before insurance regulatory bodies. Insurers should be required to engage in greater loss-prevention efforts, and to disclose evidence of known defective products or hazardous conditions to appropriate law enforcement and regulatory authorities.

Society does not suffer when the rights of injured people are vindicated. It benefits by having victims fairly compensated and careless or unsafe behavior deterred. Eroding victims' basic rights will not stop premium-gouging and policy cancellations. Only effective insurance reforms will stop the cyclical insurance crisis that leads to the volcanic eruptions of premiums and contracted coverage.

Whistleblowing

Alfred North Whitehead wrote, "Duty arises from our potential control over the course of events." Since the early 1970s this insight has given rise to the ethics of whistleblowing—the lone individual of conscience within a corporate or governmental organization who sees wrong and tries to right it, often at great personal risk.

"Society has an acute interest in fostering a more muscular whistleblowing ethic."

Society has an acute interest in fostering a more muscular whistleblowing ethic. Corporate and government employees are among the first to know about industrial dumping of toxics into waterways, defectively designed automobiles, or the undisclosed adverse effects of prescription drugs and pesticides. They are the first to grasp the technical capabilities to prevent existing hazards. But they are very often the last to speak out.

There is a great need to develop this ethic further, so that it may be practically applied in many contexts, especially within corporate and governmental bureaucracies. This ethic will flourish, however, only if employees have the right to due process within their large organizations, and if they have at least some of the rights, such as the right to speak freely, that now protect them from state power. Each corporation should have a bill of rights for its employees and a system of internal appeals to guarantee these rights. Unions and professional societies should strengthen their ethical codes, and adopt such codes if they do not already have them. The courts, professional and citizen groups, the media, the Congress, and other sectors of society must work actively to prevent the trammeling of a fortified conscience within their midst.

If carefully defined and protected by law, whistleblowing can become another of those adaptive, self-implementing mechanisms that distinguish a free society from a closed one.

The tools for democracy have fairly common characteristics. They are universally accessible and can reduce corporate and government misbehavior, and they are voluntary to use or band together around. It matters not whether people are Republicans, Democrats, or Independents. It matters only that Americans desire to secure and use these facilities or tools.

Without this reconstruction of our democracy through such facilities for informed civic participation, as noted above, even the most well-intentioned president cannot deliver. Nor can our worries about poverty, discrimination, joblessness, the troubled conditions of education, environment, street and suite crime, budget deficits, costly and inadequate health care, and energy boondoggles, to list a few, be addressed constructively and enduringly. Developing these democratic tools to strengthen citizens in their distinct roles as voters, taxpayers, consumers, workers, and shareholders should be very high on the list of every citizen.

President Clinton and Vice-President Gore are quite aware of these proposals to build and strengthen our democracy. They have attended conferences and have spoken about many of these ideas. Over ten years ago I spoke to then-Governor Clinton at some length about CUB proposals and other direct democracy reforms. So have others. When he was a senator, Vice-President Gore received testimony about the Audience Network at a public Senate committee hearing and has heard other of the aforementioned proposals discussed in other meetings. Unlike Presidents Reagan and Bush, for whom such ideas would be alien to their structure of plutocratic values, the two men at the helm of our federal government understand the importance of shifting more power to enable citizens to act effectively and informatively.

Unfortunately, the frantic pace of the presidency, the crisis-by-crisis orientation, and the ritualistic grip that the past has on the presidential imagination does not encourage or provide for building democracy and getting to root causes of these crises, which are the gross imbalance of power, wealth, and information in the United States.

During his first year in office, President Clinton has shown no commitment or even any interest in building American democracy, except for modest campaign finance and motor-voter registration proposals. He has demonstrated much energy in soliciting the approval of the very power blocs in industry and commerce that are the obstacles to this democratic mission, while not redressing the overdue and shattered rights of labor and consumers. His palliative presidency has set the tone and direction for the remaining three years, unless, that is, a critical mass of citizens address these empowerment agendas in the White House and Congress with unmistakable determination and focus. The "business as usual" sign continues to drape the White House under the new president and the corporate government continues to reign.

Progressive Reform
and the "Clinton Moment"

HEATHER BOOTH, STANLEY GREENBERG,
SAUL LANDAU, JOEL ROGERS, AND ROGER WILKINS

It is a truism that good ideas, even the best of ideas, cannot by themselves alter the course of politics. In his first year in office, Bill Clinton has seen many of his good ideas—an economic stimulus program, an energy tax, the extension of civil rights to gays in the military—defeated or eviscerated, in large part, for want of an effective political strategy to ensure their adoption. Likewise, progressives have watched their hopes for a new national agenda challenged by conservative forces both inside and outside the Clinton administration.

In the interest of exploring the opportunities for progressive reform in the "Clinton moment" and the strategies required to translate progressive ideas into political reality, the Institute for Policy Studies brought together five leading political analysts to participate in the roundtable discussion below. Heather Booth, the former co-director of Citizen Action, is presently on the staff of the Democratic National Committee. Stanley Greenberg, president of Greenberg Research Inc., is pollster to President Clinton. Joel Rogers is professor of law, political science, and sociology at the University of Wisconsin–Madison and chair of the Interim Executive Council of the New Party. Saul Landau, who joined the second half of the discussion, is a fellow of the Institute for Policy Studies. And Roger Wilkins, who moderated this discussion, is Robinson professor of history at George Mason University.

WILKINS: We are going to talk today about the challenge of inserting progressive ideas into the U.S. policymaking process. I'd like to start by asking each of you what are the opportunities for progressive reform at the end of the Cold War and at the end of the Reagan-Bush era? And what are the prospects for progressive reform—in foreign policy, economic policy, health-care policy, etc.—under the Clinton administration?

BOOTH: There is opportunity now for progressive reform in all those areas because there is pent-up demand for reform. For most of the past twenty years progressive forces have been on the defensive, fighting largely to stop something bad from happening rather than promoting a vision of something good. We have had to concentrate on keeping bad justices off the Supreme Court rather than on expanding the notion of what justice is. We have had to focus on countering bad environmental regulations rather than develop the notion of an integrated, global, healthy environment. And we have had to resist growing inequality in the nation rather than conceptualize the kind of society that would bring healthy children into the world.

So there is now a new opening for change, but we have to learn or relearn how to engage a Democratic administration in order to achieve it. We need to engage this administration on the inside and mobilize on the outside to support and create the changes we hope to see.

WILKINS: Are we in fact beginning to see meaningful change?

"We've gone from a government that considered ketchup a vegetable to one that has made childhood immunization and Head Start top priorities."
—Heather Booth

BOOTH: We see directional change, movement forward instead of backward. We've gone from a government that considered ketchup a vegetable to one that has made childhood immunization, health care, and Head Start top priorities. We've gone from a president who skipped the Rio Earth Summit to one who signed the Rio Declaration, and from a vice-president who probably never read a book on the environment to one who wrote a book on the subject. We have a nominee for chairman of the National Labor Relations Board who has written about why unions are good, instead of a president who fires PATCO air-traffic controllers in an effort to bust unions. For the first time in a generation we have seen taxes shifted to the wealthy—over the enormous protests of Wall Street. We have family and medical leave, motor-voter registration, and repeal of the gag rule that inhibited the exercise of a woman's right to choose.

These are real changes in direction, but they are only first steps, not the final reform we need to win. Still, after more than a decade, the direction of change is definitely forward.

ROGERS: I see some of the opportunities Heather does, but not all. Maybe this is because we disagree about the nature of the Clinton administration, maybe because we disagree about what it will take to realize those opportunities.

For the past twelve years the White House has been occupied by people who were true social reactionaries in a deep and morally appalling sense. The Clinton people are clearly not that. They are going to be infinitely better on all sorts of social issues, and that's not trivial. But they are not going to contest corporate power in this country in any significant way, and unless you're prepared to do that then most of the great opportunities of this moment will be lost.

Maybe the term "progressive" is hanging us up here. As Heather pointed out, the left has been in opposition and on the defensive for a very long time. Looking for any allies it could find during this period, the left didn't feel much need to distinguish itself from corporate liberals—a term that I think better describes the Clintonians. Now there is that need.

WILKINS: I'd like to ask you to make that distinction between progressives and corporate liberals a little clearer.

ROGERS: I take a progressive to be someone who actually believes in democracy, including the belief that people of ordinary means and intelligence, if properly organized, can run the country themselves. I take a liberal to be someone who shares some of the same egalitarian democratic convictions that mark progressives but who has much less confidence in the capacities of ordinary people. Liberals basically aspire more to the "kinder, gentler" administration of such people than to their organized empowerment. They are generally not, for example, big fans of trade unions.

Because liberals don't encourage or rely on popular organization, and because such organization is the only counterweight to corporate power, liberals cannot do much heavy lifting against corporations. And that severely limits what they can deliver by way of public policy. I think that's especially true now, in this age of famously hard choices. Maybe thirty years ago—given the U.S. military position in the world, the strength of the U.S. economy, the character of popular expectations of racial and gender justice or about the environment—you could say that things would work out fine without limiting corporate power, at least for the bulk of the dwindling voting population. You can't say that anymore, though. How are you going to defend domestic living standards, reduce inequality, redress 400 years of racism, keep our inner cities from turning into charnel houses, or green our economy without putting some se-rious constraints on capital? You can't. But this is just what corporate lib-erals are unwilling and unable to do.

WILKINS: What sorts of measures are you referring to?

ROGERS: To give you an example, we need some sort of credible labor-market intervention to increase wage floors. As we all know there has been an effective internationalization of large portions of the U.S. econ-omy over the past twenty years, and that internationalization is trou-bling for wages and living standards here because the world is densely populated by firms paying a fraction of our wages. Unless you have some strategy for levelling up those wages or protecting our economy from them, then what you're buying into is downward pressure. Firms will continue to find it profitable simply to use sweat labor, and inequal-ity will increase.

We therefore need an international trading regime that does not, like the present one, punish countries for paying their workers a decent wage and providing safe conditions of work—a regime that integrates trade with developing nations in a way that changes trade flows from a race to the bottom on social protection to a race to the top. A social tariff regime that incorporates illegitimate producer cost advantages—like those derived from bashing labor or wrecking the environment—into consumer prices might be one way to do this.

To get a social base for these sorts of things, however, we need to give people the basic tools they require to practice democracy in the late twentieth century: organizing rights, access, information, means of communicating. Also critical is control over resources, starting with those they purportedly own—public lands, airways, pension funds. And we need to encourage a variety of on-the-ground organizations—again, those of a reinvented labor movement come immediately to mind—that can help manage and improve the economy and provide political ballast for egalitarian values.

All these moves I take to be pretty basic. But any of them would be vig-orously resisted by capital, as are their palest foreshadowings—in recent discussions of the investment stimulus, NAFTA, campaign-finance re-form, public-lands use, labor-law reform, and the minimum wage. And this is why Clinton won't do the right thing on them, even when he more or less occasionally would like to. He's got nothing on his left, so every time the right sneezes he's blown across the political spectrum.

WILKINS: How does that characterization of the problem strike you, Stan?

GREENBERG: I don't think we have the context right here—that is, I think we have to put the problem in the context of the political change that has taken place recently. Now, we may have different views of what hap-

*"Clinton's got nothing on his left, so
every time the right sneezes he's blown
across the political spectrum."*

—Joel Rogers

pened in 1992 but I think that virtually all of our prior political history
was shattered in '92. There was not a realignment; there was no new
Democratic majority or new progressive majority that emerged victori-
ous. What happened in '92 is that the traditional political coalitions and
visions that people have associated with the major parties were shattered.

There was a great Democratic era, basically a three-decade period
from the Great Depression to Lyndon Johnson, in which the Democrats
forged a notion of opportunity, an expanding governmental role, and a
bottom-up coalition—working to middle class. But that majority was essentially spent by 1964. The Great Society represented a failed attempt to
renew that Democratic vision and there really has been no dominant vision since. Voters, particularly middle-class voters, suburban voters,
who had to identify with that vision if it was going to have any durability,
walked away in the period after 1964. And Democrats until '92, and
maybe not even in '92, have not found a way of addressing those voters.

A similar fate befell the Republicans. You had a great Republican era
from 1896 until the Coolidge presidency and the Great Depression—
again, a three-decade period in which a business-led prosperity permitted a Republican ascendancy and a vision of a role for corporate America in assuring America's prosperity. Reagan represented a failed attempt
to renew that vision—to give America once again a notion of a business-
led prosperity. Maybe it had a couple of years of life to it but basically
from '86 onward it was collapsing and, in '92, it was rejected boldly.

We are living in a political moment, then, in which all the major party
alignments and major intellectual models have been repudiated. When
we think about the role for progressives, or the role for Clinton, therefore, we should think about it in that context. In other words, you can't
judge Clinton simply on his various specifics, on what he's done so far.
Progressives have got to decide whether there is a vision represented by
the Clinton presidency that they wish to shape or whether instead there
is some alternative vision they wish to create. And in my mind Clinton's
presidency represents a potentially new vision that centers around rais-

ing the living standards of middle class America, the expansion of personal freedom, and a larger, more credible role for government, particularly in the provision of health care but other social-welfare services as well.

Progressives have got to decide whether that is a vision they're comfortable with and, just as important, whether they can make it work for them. What is the meaning of a middle class–centered Democratic Party or Clinton coalition? Is it a bottom-up vision infused by work values? Does reinventing government mean cutting waste and inefficiency and creating greater choice, or does it include a more activist role for government that ensures that there are healthy children and universal health-care services?

ROGERS: After 1992 it's hard to tell many Democrats apart from Republicans. That's part of the problem. At their leadership level, both the Democratic and Republican parties are almost wholly business-dominated. Both worship, pretty mindlessly, the gods of growth, consumerism, and free trade without attending to the kind of economy we really want or the sorts of public goods and nonmaterial things, relevant to the general welfare, that are needed. Neither party is particularly concerned about inequality. Both are pretty aggressive in their view of the appropriate role of U.S. force abroad. Neither is committed to popular organization—again, look at how little either party is willing to do for unions.

There is this business of activism, of course, but I'm not overly impressed. As Reagan's activism of the 1980s should remind us, it's the direction of activism that counts. And here I would have to disagree with Heather; in my view most action under Clinton has been in retreat—caving in to Wall Street on his investment plan, to insurance companies on his health-care plan, to fat cats on campaign finance, and, shamelessly, to his own shadow on Guinier. To the extent that he remains positively "active," it's chiefly in promoting a restrictive fiscal policy and NAFTA. Should we be excited about that?

Look at the core of Clinton's vision of how to achieve middle-class prosperity. The Clinton economic plan was not intended to regulate labor markets or trade directly but instead to invest in physical infrastructure and human capital. The hope was that roving multinationals might then be attracted to our shores and give us some of their better jobs. Now, after the deficit cave-in to Wall Street, this vision lacks even its core premise of government investment in infrastructural renewal and massive training. Instead it relies almost entirely on the idea that global competitive pressures will somehow force generalized private investment in more productive labor and better-compensated labor. There is absolutely no evidence for this proposition and overwhelming evidence for its opposite.

If you want this economy to work again you've got to get it under stronger, not weaker, social control. And you can't do that without using the state to set some limits on what is economically permitted, and encouraging popular organization as a middle path between government and corporate administration of the economy.

BOOTH: You suggest a middle path between oppressive state bureaucracies, on the one hand, and untutored markets, on the other. But we have to break through these dichotomies—to find ways of putting people back in control of government. Unless this is done, people won't have confidence that government can work in their interests and serve as a tool to bring about change. And unless progressives engage themselves, reform won't succeed because the forces of opposition are so great. The Clinton administration can't do it on its own. Without pressure from the street, there will not be demand for change. And if there isn't responsive leadership, the change will never make its way into law.

Take health care. It is now on the national agenda primarily because of the actions people have taken around the country for four, five years and more *and* because President Clinton decided to engage this issue. It is now likely to be the single, boldest social policy introduced since the War on Poverty, if not since the New Deal. But it will only be won if we all participate in the struggle. And it is clear that there will and must be a struggle. This president received only a plurality, not a majority, of the vote, and while there is a nominal Democratic majority in Congress, on many of the issues that matter we do not have solid support.

> *"Our problem here is taking too seriously what's happening in the early moments of the administration."*
> —Stanley Greenberg

ROGERS: I agree that the Clinton people can't do it on their own. They need something on their left, independent of them but not determinedly unfriendly, to hold them accountable to some values they claim to share while providing critical support against the right. That's an appropriate role for progressives to play. At the moment, however, progressives are not doing that. They're so entranced by having a Democrat in the White House, and so worried about advantaging the right through any criticism of Clinton, that they're not doing that.

GREENBERG: Our problem here, in both analyses, is taking too seriously what's happening in the early moments of the administration. What's important is the political purpose of the administration because I think Bill Clinton is quite inventive and creative about achieving his goals. If you build a bottom-up coalition, in contrast to a suburban-elitist coalition, that broad coalition will have a political purpose, including rising living standards for middle-class America. You create a pressure within the administration, within Bill Clinton, to achieve those ends. The goals, in other words, become overriding. So we can analyze the specific policies of the administration's early moments in office; that's not uninteresting. But what's more interesting is how you create the pressures necessary to achieve policy goals over a four-year, eight-year, or longer period.

WILKINS: There are two things that are not in this conversation that make it very unreal to me. The first is money. Can the goals, as articulated by any of you, be achieved as long as American politics is funded the way that it is?

BOOTH: No. Bennett Johnston [D-LA], for example, now votes as if he were put in office by the oil companies, when in fact he was elected by working and poor people who were repelled by David Duke. Clinton is sensitive to this problem, and the administration has taken a bold step toward campaign-finance reform. The administration's original proposal called for limiting campaign spending, curbing special-interest funding, ensuring all candidates greater access to television, and giving some real authority to the Federal Elections Commission. The Democratic Party's support of these efforts, moreover, includes a willingness to sacrifice a third of its income, which comes from soft-money sources—contributions for so-called party-building activities that are exempt from the usual ceilings—to get the influence of big money out of the political process.

GREENBERG: This, by the way, is where the president has been very clear. He has said that we will not be able to achieve critical reforms—health-care reform, for instance—if the special interests can organize themselves to finance campaigns and prevent one or another initiative from being adopted by Congress. And I think that what the president has proposed goes to the limits of what can be done in the current context, though many of us might want to see the reforms go further.

ROGERS: I actually think he's gone nowhere near the limits of what might be done, if you're willing to get outside the Beltway. There is hunger out there for process reform, including campaign-finance reform, much more adventurous than what Clinton has produced. That's a big part of the attraction for Perot—big enough, indeed, that I was surprised Clinton didn't exploit the reform question more on tactical grounds even if he wasn't led to it by moral ones. A lot of people out there, especially but not only the Perot people, think government is really corrupt. A "clean up government" campaign could be very helpful to Clinton politically. Indeed, he could blame all his current misfortunes—not entirely inaccurately—on current corruptions.

GREENBERG: That could end up being counterproductive. If you persuade people that Washington is a fully corrupt set of institutions answerable only to special interests, you may mobilize support for throwing the rascals out. But you may also create such disdain for government that people lose faith in the capacity of these institutions to effect needed policy changes and in the utility of their own collective efforts. This is a delicate question, because meaningful change requires popular mobilization, and that mobilization is not possible unless you get the citizenry to the point where it believes that public institutions have the capacity to make life better.

BOOTH: You once used a figure, Stan, that I found very powerful: You said that only 23 percent of the population now believes that government will work in their interest most of the time, whereas when Kennedy was president, that figure was 75 percent.

ROGERS: I agree that lack of confidence in government is a huge obstacle to progressive reform. And I realize that in playing to popular concerns about government one has to be careful, but that's not a reason not to campaign for cleaning up Washington—as indeed you already do with all this reinventing government stuff. The more important point, I think, is this: Progressives are identified with the state, since they've so often looked to the state as against other governance mechanisms to solve problems. And now that people suspect the state, progressives are hurt by association.

We need to take the idea of reinventing government beyond privatizing garbage collection in Little Rock. We need to think about

---

"We need to take the idea of reinventing government beyond privatizing garbage collection in Little Rock."

—Joel Rogers

handing over more government functions to other sorts of democratic, popular organizations—for example, assigning more power to community organizations in housing and economic development, to labor and business organizations in training, and so on. At the same time, because lots of organic solidarities and associations no longer exist, we must nurture the associative supports needed for a working democracy.

GREENBERG: It's very hard to respond to your challenge. There are forces at work that have led to a decline of organizational life in this country, and that decline certainly needs to be reversed. But we face, this year, a situation where we have a president who has come from the center-left, who has taken over a government that is bankrupt financially and is also seen to be bankrupt in the sense that it's thought to be run by people who are crooks. In the midst of this, the administration is trying to introduce national health insurance, achieve a redistribution of wealth through a fairer tax system, impose fiscal order, and implement a range of other policies that are going to be fought, at least in their first round, in the next few months.

ROGERS: Stan, you were criticizing everyone earlier for focusing too much on the short term. Remember, you wanted us to engage the broader vision, not the early record of achievement. Now you're telling us to focus on yesterday's poll and the next three months. Which is it?

BOOTH: But that was in terms of making a final judgment.

GREENBERG: I'll take Heather's support on this. The question of when we draw our judgments as to the success of this administration or whether it's in fact progressive seems to me a different question from the one under discussion now. People are feeling extraordinary pressures because of a national health-care crisis and a jobs crisis. These are issues that progressives have sought to put on the agenda for decades and have failed to find a president to advance, from Roosevelt to Truman to Johnson. Now the opportunity presents itself and progressives have to figure out how to engage that debate, which is not to say that they should not also deal with the longer-term challenge to strengthen and build organizational life that can support this movement.

ROGERS: Fine. I think progressives need to forsake their factional differences, come together around a few key issues—the forgotten peace dividend, genuine democratic reform, progressive economic policies—and declare their independence of the administration even as they provide it with selective support against the right. At the moment I think progressives are all too compromised organizationally by the mere fact of a Democratic administration. They are not speaking up. And their values are going to get slaughtered if they don't. I believe, moreover, that it's possible to provide critical support in a way that will not advantage the right, if progressives unite behind programs of broad economic appeal to the poor and working class.

WILKINS: I said earlier that there were two things about this conversation that made it seem unreal to me. The first was money. The second is race. It's a factor in American politics. It's a profound factor in American culture. It's a factor in Bill Clinton's reformation of the Democratic Party. And even when it's not in everybody's political conversation, it's usually on everybody's minds. How does race figure in the Clinton moment? What does it mean for the goals we are talking about here?

GREENBERG: Let me speak to what I believe are the broad purposes of the Clinton political moment, which are also reflected in the administration. First, Clinton forged a multiracial coalition from the bottom-up in the primaries. He won 70 percent of the vote in the primaries, and obviously won overwhelmingly in the general election. He did it, not with specific appeals, but with a universal approach, which was to promote employment and income growth and social-welfare policies like health care that would be broadly available. The implicit argument was that the black community would be better served by a governing Democratic coalition that expanded services on a universal basis as opposed to a Democratic Party that's out of office and unable to deliver except in a symbolic way to its constituent groups.

Another thing: Clinton has been very conscious about the staffing of the administration as a diverse presidency. And against the tenor of criticism, which has been very sharp concerning the effect of diversity on achieving his other goals, I think Clinton has stuck with that goal in impressive ways. This explains, in part, the broad support he enjoys in the African-American community now. There is also very broad support for his health-care policies and other policies that are seen, correctly, to be of benefit to the minority community. And this approach, let me say again, is better than a politics that is dominated by civil rights discussion, where you are talking about specific remedies for targeted groups. It doesn't mean those remedies aren't applied, and aren't applied with vigor, but this is a different kind of discourse, which progressives need to address.

ROGERS: I'll let Stan try to handle, and defend, what Clinton has done on race and race symbols. If I might, though, I'd like to say something about how progressive multiracial politics has been complicated by what's happening inside the black community itself.

The previous generation of African-Americans saw major changes in its lives and in its lifetime in part because of progress made in civil rights. As a consequence you have a much more fractured African-American community today—fractured spatially, with blacks no longer living exclusively in racially defined areas; fractured in terms of class, because with new opportunities has come greater class stratification; and fractured by ethnic and cultural divisions within what white progressives casually lump together as undifferentiated "peoples of color." Under these conditions you get three very different impulses. One is a simple continuation of the civil rights strategy, but its very success tends to undermine its advance as a unifying theme and it doesn't get at the class issues. Another is a more or less nationalist, exclusivist politics. This has a much deeper cultural appeal but under current electoral rules and given class, spatial, and other fractioning, it's ultimately a dead end. A third is some sort of race-conscious class strategy directed toward broad economic benefit but insistent on the core prominence of racism in disabling the American working class from getting just that.

I think this last approach is structurally most promising in the long run and, given the decline in working class fortunes, actually increasingly possible. But at present it doesn't have anywhere near the organizational bases and leadership of the other two.

WILKINS: I would say you answered my question exactly upside down because you went immediately to what is going on in the black communities. I don't think that's the issue about race. I think it's what's in white people's heads. If you're talking about race and you don't talk about what's in white people's heads, you are not talking reality. The reason we've never had a successful lower-class, class-based politics is the racism of white people. I don't think that has changed. And therefore I don't see this oppositional force to a corporate-based politics going very far.

> *"If you're talking about race and you don't talk about what's in white people's heads, you are not talking reality."*
> *—Roger Wilkins*

BOOTH: But because circumstances have changed, so has the challenge. My involvement in politics began with the struggle for equal access in the early 1960s, when Woolworth wouldn't seat blacks at its lunch counters in the south. Since that time, with much sweat and even sacrifice of lives, the problem of equal access in many areas has opened up. Not in all, of course, such as banking practices, but in many. Now the problem is that a person can sit at the counter but cannot afford necessarily to eat; the problem is economic as well as racial. What makes the challenge so much more difficult is the fact that the previous administration gave a wink and a nod, and sometimes even overt encouragement, to efforts to sow racial division. Not surprisingly this has led to greater inequality.

We're now just at the beginning of a new experiment to overcome the long legacy of racial division and inequality. The cues from leadership do matter—as in a government that looks like America—as well as the substance, to bring us together and to encourage tolerance as well as equality. We now have an opportunity to promote policies that include investment in people as well as attempts to counter racial division.

LANDAU: When President Clinton nominated a woman who I think was the first person I've ever seen begin to address the race and the class question together from a legal framework—the Voting Rights Act—she was not only abandoned; she was stabbed in the back. Whereas when President Bush nominated a candidate to the Supreme Court who was black, he backed that candidate to the hilt. Not only did Clarence Thomas have hand-holders and P.R. flacks, but Bush did advance work with the Senate, issued threats if people voted against him, and so on to make sure that his candidate got on the Supreme Court.

I don't think it's accidental, given Lani Guinier's opinions—on democracy, representation, voting, and access to wealth and power and to the resources that historically have built this country—that she was the one they wouldn't go to bat for. She terrified the liberals. And the reason, fundamentally, is because the Democratic Party is not really a party; it's a money-laundering operation. Otherwise I don't see how it can contain segregationists and integrationists, tenants and landlords, bosses and workers, and polluters and environmentalists, all in the same thing called a political party.

"The Democratic Party is not really a party; it's a money-laundering operation."
—Saul Landau

GREENBERG: Are you saying the potential base of the Democratic Party is comfortable with the ideas of Lani Guinier? The reality is that if the Democratic coalition began with that assumption—and I recognize that we're dealing with perhaps a distorted notion of Lani Guinier's views but let's take the distortion of her views because it became the conventional wisdom—if that is the assumption behind progressive politics, then it does not understand the potential base for a governing coalition.

ROGERS: But Stan, part of what Saul is saying is exactly what you were saying and Heather was saying and I was saying. Among the points of agreement I thought we had earlier was that the Democratic Party as it is currently constituted is really not much of a party. It's just a campaign machine for candidates. It doesn't, as an organization, show much discipline of its elites, or linkage between them and its voting base. Without that internal discipline and connection to a base you're prepared to put in motion, it's hard to do much.

GREENBERG: What I'm saying is that Clinton was able to resolve the potential conflicts within a majority, bottom-up coalition by working from the presumption of support for civil rights, personal freedoms, and so forth and moving to a position that transcended these issues and sought to bring together diverse groups in a coalition that's trying to achieve rising living standards—social welfare policies that are broad-based in character—and not to center our politics around targeted benefits for specific groups. That I believe was what made it possible for Bill Clinton to win, and makes it possible to move to a broad, multiracial coalition. What Clinton was very clear about when he withdrew Guinier's nomination was that on some points, she was outside that presumption.

LANDAU: Well, I think you may be right, that she was outside that presumption, but what are you left with then? You get a party and now a government that works to eliminate discrimination in bank lending, which, don't get me wrong, is not a bad idea. But what it will mean is that a few percent of higher-income African-Americans will be able to get loans. The vast, vast majority of them, however, don't have a penny and couldn't get loans under any circumstances. If you want to pursue progressive politics, you have to pursue a politics that literally talks about the needs of the poor people, the working people, the lower middle class. If you want to include some environmentalists, some women who have defected from the Republican Party, that's fine, but basically you are talking about minority groups and blue-collar workers. That's the base of the Democratic Party.

GREENBERG: And you want to patronize them with the presumption that you can deliver anything out of this kind of politics?

LANDAU: I'm not going to patronize them at all. I'm suggesting that we say this is what the Democratic Party is about and should be about. And to hell with the Borens, the McCurdys, and the rest who stand around saying they're Democrats when in fact they're Republicans. I'm saying that if you want a progressive politics, you can't have a coalition with people who are Republicans and who are wearing the Democratic hat.

GREENBERG: I think the real test is whether the bargain that Clinton has talked about, which is a broad-based coalition and broad-based policies and initiatives, can deliver to the minority communities.

There is sort of a contract here. It says, we're not going to center our politics around targeted benefits; we're going to center it on the assumption that broad-based policies will lift all those in this coalition, from the bottom-up. And you've got an initial down payment on that if you look at the economic program, the budget program. You have the Earned Income Tax Credit, which provides for some redistribution within an overall package that is very redistributive. You have health-care initiatives, job-training initiatives, college loans—a whole range of policies—and the question is: Are these policies in fact broad-based? Are people in the position to take advantage of them? Will all those who are part of this coalition benefit? Joel will probably argue that given the world economic forces at work, it will be hard to deliver on that promise.

ROGERS: Although I think the programs as presently framed are wrongheaded, I agree that, at least in theory, policy could generate a rising tide that really did lift all boats. I also agree that some general measurable benefit—apart from the satisfaction of achieving racial justice—is probably necessary to win political support for targeted programs. But I don't think race and the effects of racism are reducible, analytically or practically, to class. And I don't think the Democratic Party, as presently constituted, is a natural vehicle for the race-conscious class politics necessary to realizing progressive ideals. The Democratic Party will need to be either fundamentally changed or replaced as the vehicle for such aspirations. Both tactics recommend formation of an electorally competitive new party. Even those who only want to reinvent the Democratic Party from within need a credible threat of exit from it. Otherwise they won't be listened to, no matter how polite they are.

GREENBERG: It's not a question of just reinventing something from within as if it were a closed system. The whole conception of building an inside-outside strategy—of external mobilization and leadership from above—is what's essential to moving from a period of retrenchment and reaction into a period that is a more progressive era.

BOOTH: Think about earlier eras of liberal reform, whether it was Kennedy or Johnson. Kennedy came to power with little consciousness of civil rights and human rights issues. It was bold movements from below that forced him to change. But he responded and he and Johnson moved the civil rights bill. The presidencies that were more troubled—Carter, Ford, and Bush—were the ones where popular mobilization and political leadership were disconnected. Health care provides the next great opportunity in which there must be popular mobilization to counter conservative forces.

"Health care provides the next great opportunity in which there must be popular mobilization to counter conservative forces."
—Heather Booth

WILKINS: Stan's analysis of the Clinton campaign I think is accurate as far as it goes, but there's a giant reality problem that it ignores. And the reality problem is that the UN survey of world development this year puts the United States at the top of its list if you just count living standards for American white people. If you factor in black people, we fall to sixth place. And if you look only at black people, we're at 31st place, down around Trinidad. So the whole idea of avoiding targeting leaves that third of black Americans who are damaged and distressed exactly where they are and growing in numbers because of these world forces we've been talking about.

The guys at Anacostia, here in D.C., cannot compete with children in sweatshops in Bangkok. So a larger and larger segment of the black population has become economically redundant—they are homeless or they're violent, and they're tearing the country apart and we have doubled our prison population in the last twenty years. This is not an attack on the president but when a large segment of what is passing for new politics says we have to abjure remedies that are targeted and that our civil rights policies, our racial policies, have to be conducted without divisiveness or conflict, we're talking about something that doesn't exist. We have never made progress in this country on race without conflict. We have never had remedies for black people that weren't controversial and that broad portions of white society didn't try to subvert, starting with the 13th Amendment and going to the Voting Rights Act.

GREENBERG: But there is a difference between "not targeted" and "not reached." If you look at the past data on when it is that incomes between blacks and whites narrow, it is essentially achieved during periods of fuller employment. So if we want to talk about effective policies to address the problems you're talking about, the most important thing we can do is to devise policies that move America toward full employment, complemented by broad-based training programs and health programs that make it possible for people to take advantage of those opportunities.

I don't know whether it's going to work. I'm not innocent about the context in which these policies are taking place. There are tremendous pressures here that are producing greater inequality in America and greater inequality between nations against which these policies must try to succeed. I don't know whether these policies will succeed but I suspect they have a better chance of succeeding than targeted policies that don't make economic change the first priority.

And I don't believe that any coalition that separates out African-Americans for targeted systems is going to be in power to achieve those policies. It must find a way of achieving common ground between groups that can form a majority coalition, which takes a five-year plan. I don't think we're going to drive the racism out of people's souls but we may make it less important to them relative to other things that they focus on. I do believe that a majority of black and white Americans find themselves hard-pressed financially, unable to keep up with some very basic things like health care and education, and therefore have a common reason for supporting a new Democratic coalition that offers the possibility of rising living standards. I think that's where you have to start.

Notes

INTRODUCTION

1. Bernard Sanders, "Clinton Must Go to the People," *The Nation*, June 21, 1993, p. 865.

2. Erik Eckholm, "The Uninsured: 37 Million and Growing," *New York Times*, July 11, 1993, p. E5.

3. Teresa Amott, "Eliminating Poverty," in this volume.

4. John E. Schwarz and Thomas J. Volgy, "Above the Poverty Line—But Poor," *The Nation*, February 15, 1993, p. 191.

5. Fox Butterfield, "U.S. Expands Its Lead in the Rate of Imprisonment," *New York Times*, February 11, 1992, p. A16.

6. Andrew L. Shapiro, *We're Number One!* (New York: Vintage, 1992), pp. 16–19.

7. United Nations Development Programme, *Human Development Report 1993* (New York: Oxford University Press, 1993), p. 18.

8. Shapiro (fn. 6), pp. 16 and 35.

9. Marcus Corbin, Center for Defense Information, Personal Communication, August 5, 1993.

10. Seymour Martin Lipset and Martin Schram, "Foreword: Interpreting the 1992 Election," in Will Marshall and Martin Schram, eds., *Mandate for Change* (New York: Berkley Books, 1992), p. xxii.

11. Joe Klein, "What's Wrong?" *Newsweek*, June 7, 1993, p. 16.

12. Amott (fn. 3).

13. Bob Herbert, "The 6.8% Illusion," *New York Times*, August 8, 1993, p. E15.

14. Amott (fn. 3).

15. Paul Davidson, "Putting Caution First," *The Nation*, March 1, 1993, p. 260.

16. Amott (fn. 3).

17. U.S. Department of Energy, "Budget Highlights—FY 1994," DOE-CR/0014, pp. 5–8.

18. Robert L. Borosage, "Meeting Real Defense Needs," in this volume.

19. "Defending America's Economic Interests," *Defense Monitor*, Vol. 22, No. 6 (1993), pp. 1 and 7.

20. National League of Cities, "Overview and Analysis of the President's FY 94 Budget," April 1993.

21. Robert Heilbroner, "The Case for Hope," *The Nation*, May 10, 1993, p. 619.

CHAPTER 1

1. These initiatives, of course, were not truly global but, rather, reflected political and economic condominiums among many of the world's major powers.

2. See Gaddis Smith, "What Role for America?" *Current History,* April 1993.

3. For instance, U.S. efforts to control domestic inflation through a tight money policy inhibited global economic growth in the 1980s. For an excellent discussion of the problems inherent in a dollar-denominated global economy, see Robert Kuttner, *The End of Laissez-Faire* (New York: Alfred A. Knopf, 1991).

4. Thomas L. Friedman, "U.S. Voicing Fears That Gorbachev Will Divide West," *New York Times,* September 16, 1989, p. 1.

5. "As Ethnic Wars Multiply, U.S. Strives for a Policy," *New York Times,* February 7, 1993, p. 1.

6. Paul Kennedy's term "imperial overstretch" has a decidedly military, as opposed to economic, meaning. He uses it to refer to the fact that "the sum total of the United States' global interests and obligations is nowadays far larger than the country's power to defend them all simultaneously." See *The Rise and Fall of the Great Powers* (New York: Vintage, 1987), p. 515.

7. Governor Bill Clinton and Senator Al Gore, *Putting People First* (New York: Times Books, 1992), p. 130.

8. "Time to Bury Keynes?" *The Economist,* July 3, 1993, p. 19.

9. Lester R. Brown, "A New Era Unfolds," *State of the World 1993* (New York: W. W. Norton, 1993), p. 5.

10. These figures come from Al Gore, *Earth in the Balance* (New York: Plume, 1993), p. 24.

11. Annual Report, "Unemployment: 8% ... 9% ...?" *Newsweek,* January 20, 1975, p. 54.

12. For the story of declining wages, see Bennett Harrison and Barry Bluestone, *The Great U-Turn* (New York: Basic, 1988), pp. 6, 114–117. For the story of declining leisure, see Juliet Schor, *The Overworked American* (New York: Basic, 1992), p. 29.

13. Peter Dreier and John Atlas, "Housing," in Mark Green, ed., *Changing America* (New York: Newmarket Press, 1992), p. 390.

14. Susan Faludi, *Backlash* (New York: Crown Publishers, 1991), pp. xvii, 364.

15. In 1974, in fact, a greater percentage of black high-school graduates went on to college than white graduates. See Thomas Byrne Edsall and Mary D. Edsall, *Chain Reaction* (New York: W. W. Norton, 1992), p. 116.

16. In 1974, the white unemployment rate was 5.0, the black rate 9.9, the ratio between the two 1.98. In 1990, the white unemployment rate stood at 4.1, the black rate at 11.3, and the ratio at 2.76—the highest it has been in at least twenty years. See Andrew Hacker, *Two Nations* (New York: Ballantine, 1992), pp. 102–103.

17. See Samuel Bowles, David Gordon, and Thomas Weisskopf, *After the Wasteland* (Armonk, NY: M. E. Sharpe, 1990), p. 149.

18. Martin and Susan Tolchin, *Selling Our Security* (New York: Alfred A. Knopf, 1992), p. 21.

19. Robert B. Reich, *The Work of Nations* (New York: Vintage, 1992), p. 197.

20. David Calleo, *The Bankrupting of America* (New York: Avon Books, 1992), p. 135.

21. Quoted in Edsall (fn. 15), p. 85.

22. William Greider, *Who Will Tell the People* (New York: Simon & Schuster, 1992), p. 199.

23. Christopher Jencks, *Rethinking Social Policy* (New York: Harperperennial, 1993), pp. 170–173.

24. Ibid., p. 76.

25. Quoted in Joel Bleifuss, "A Good Fight," *In These Times*, June 14, 1993, p. 13.

26. See, for example, Margaret Burnham, "The Supreme Court Appointment Process and the Politics of Race and Sex" in Toni Morrison, ed., *Race-ing Justice, En-gendering Power* (New York: Pantheon, 1992).

27. Cornel West, *Race Matters* (Boston: Beacon, 1993), pp. 23–32.

28. Katherine Newman, *Declining Fortunes* (New York: Basic, 1993), p. 39.

CHAPTER 2

1. United Nations Development Programme, *Human Development Report 1992* (New York: United Nations, 1992), p. 6.

2. See Richard J. Barnet and John Cavanagh, *Global Dreams: Imperial Corporations and the New World Order* (New York: Simon & Schuster, 1994).

3. Between 1982 and 1990, the sales of foreign affiliates of transnational corporations more than doubled to $5.5 billion, a figure that is the equivalent of one-quarter of the combined gross national products of the world. See United Nations Commission on Transnational Corporations, *Growth of Foreign Direct Investment in the 1980s: Trend or Bulge?* (New York: United Nations, 1993), p. 24.

4. Calculated from the World Bank, *World Debt Tables, 1992–93* (Washington, DC: World Bank, 1992).

5. Susan George, *The Debt Boomerang: How Third World Debt Affects Us All* (London: Pluto Press, 1992).

6. E. Lazlo et al., *Goals for Mankind: A Report to the Club of Rome* (New York: E. P. Dutton, 1977), p. 301.

7. By 1989, China was host to almost 16,000 foreign affiliates of global corporations, more than the United States or any other country. See United Nations Commission on Transnational Corporations, *The Universe of Transnational Corporations* (New York: United Nations, 1993), p. 5.

8. For an excellent account of this episode, see Michael Weisskopf, "Backbone of the New China Lobby: U.S. Firms," *Washington Post*, June 14, 1993.

9. Bob Davis, "A Language Barrier Is Erected in Place of a Trade Barrier," *Wall Street Journal*, July 19, 1993.

10. Alexander Cockburn, "Brazil's Poor Get Hungrier on Barebones IMF Menu," *Wall Street Journal*, March 23, 1989.

11. Robert S. Greenberger, "Administration Haggles Over $4 Million Amid Rise in Aversion to Foreign Aid," *Wall Street Journal*, June 28, 1993.

12. See also the 1993 statement of the Citizens' Commission for a New U.S. Policy Toward the Developing World, available from the Institute for Policy Studies.

13. David Korten, *Getting to the 21st Century: Voluntary Action and the Global Agenda* (West Hartford, CT: Kumarian Press, 1990), p. 67.

14. Walter Russell Mead, "Forget the World? Consider the Consequences," *New York Times*, August 2, 1992.

15. Burns Weston, *Toward Post Cold War Global Security*, Waging Peace Series, Booklet 32, Nuclear Age Peace Foundation, 1992.

16. This and the following two paragraphs are adapted from Robin Broad and John Cavanagh, "Beyond the Myths of Rio: A New American Agenda for the Environment," *World Policy Journal*, Vol. 10, No. 1 (Spring 1993).

17. The Development GAP, Bread for the World, the Sierra Club, et al., "The Development Cooperation Act of 1990: A Proposal for U.S. Support of Equitable and Sustainable Development." See also Stephen Hellinger, Douglas Hellinger, and Fred O'Regan, *Aid for Just Development: Report on the Future of Foreign Assistance* (Boulder: Lynne Reinner, 1988).

18. Lazlo (fn. 6), p. 308.

19. For a copy, contact the Alliance for Responsible Trade, 100 Maryland Ave., NE, Room 502, Washington, DC 20002.

20. See International Labor Rights Education and Research Fund, "Protecting Labor Rights in Connection with North American Trade," Washington, DC, 1993.

21. Richard Rothstein, "Setting the Standard: International Labor Rights and U.S. Trade Policy," *Economic Policy Institute Briefing Paper*, 1993, p. 12.

22. See March 1993 proposal on "Human Rights and Migration Under NAFTA," prepared by the Mexican Action Network on Free Trade.

CHAPTER 3

1. Douglas R. Sease, "World's Bond Buyers Gain Huge Influence over U.S. Fiscal Plans," *Wall Street Journal*, November 6, 1992, p. A1.

2. Ibid.

3. Robert Reich, "Curing America's Income Infection," *New Perspectives Quarterly*, Spring 1993, p. 8.

4. International Labour Organisation, "Multinational Enterprises and Employment," Working Paper No. 55, 1986, p. 5.

5. Jane Perlez, "Czechs Gear Up to Resume Weapons Exports," *New York Times*, July 4, 1993, p. A7.

6. U.S. Department of Labor, "Bureau of Labor Statistics Factsheet," February 26, 1993.

7. See, for example, a discussion of U.S. support of Zaire's Mobutu Sese Seko in Bill Berkeley, "Zaire: An African Horror Story," *The Atlantic*, August 1993, pp. 20–28.

8. Alan Riding, "Rights Forum Ends in Call for Greater Role by U.N.," *New York Times*, June 26, 1993, p. A2.

9. "Excerpts from Bush's Ukraine Speech: Working 'For the Good of Both of Us,'" *New York Times*, August 2, 1991, p. A8.

10. William Pfaff, "An Invitation to War," *Foreign Affairs*, Vol. 72, No. 3 (Summer 1993), p. 101.

11. Peter Passell, "Fast Money," *New York Times Magazine*, October 18, 1992, p. 42.

CHAPTER 4

1. Governor Bill Clinton and Senator Al Gore, *Putting People First* (New York: Times Books, 1992), pp. 75–76.

2. Calculation by Campaign for New Priorities.

3. Figures taken from the Office of Management and Budget's "A Vision of Change for America," February 17, 1993, passim.

4. See, for example, "Statement of Secretary of Defense Les Aspin Before the Senate Armed Services Committee," Department of Defense text, April 1, 1993, p. 5.

5. Quoted in Center for Defense Information, "President Clinton's First Military Budget," *Defense Monitor*, Vol. 22, No. 4 (1993), p. 2.

6. Laurence Jolidon, "Defense Cuts to Cost Nearly 2 Million Jobs," *USA Today*, April 13, 1993, p. 1.

7. Quoted from the radio broadcast, "Pentagon Paupers: Patrolling the High Tech Frontier," Australian Broadcasting Company, January 1993.

8. See, for example, *Americans Talk Security*, Survey #21, May 18, 1993.

9. Comparative defense figures taken from Steven Kosiak, "Analysis of the Fiscal Year 1994 Defense Budget Request" (Washington, DC: Defense Budget Project, April 14, 1993).

10. Comparisons drawn from *The Military Balance 1992–93* (London: International Institute for Strategic Studies, 1993), passim.

11. Quoted in John Lancaster, "Aspin Opts for Winning 2 Wars—Not 1 1/2—at Once," *Washington Post*, June 25, 1993, p. A6.

12. Secretary of Defense Dick Cheney, *Defense Strategy for the 1990s: The Regional Defense Strategy*, January 1993, p. 7.

13. Quoted in *Threat Assessment, Military Strategy and Defense Planning*, Hearings Before the Senate Armed Services Committee, January 22, 1992, p. 10.

14. Quoted in William Kaufmann, *Assessing the Base Force* (Washington, DC: The Brookings Institution, 1992), p. 52.

15. See Douglas L. Clarke, "Rusting Fleet Renews Debate on Navy's Mission," *Armies in Transition: Radio Free Europe Research Report*, June 18, 1993, p. 27.

16. Samuel Huntington, "The Clash of Civilizations?" *Foreign Affairs*, Vol. 72, No. 3 (Summer 1993).

17. Quoted in "President Clinton's First Military Budget," *Defense Monitor* (fn. 5), p. 3.

18. Joint Chiefs of Staff, *The National Military Strategy of the United States*, 1992, pp. 3–4.

19. *Threat Assessment, Military Strategy and Defense Planning* (fn. 13), pp. 480–481.

20. Testimony of CIA Director James Woolsey before House Permanent Select Committee on Intelligence, quoted in *Unclassified*, July 1993, p. 2.

21. Figures drawn from *The Military Balance 1992–93* (fn. 10).

22. For an extended analysis see Alan Tonelson, "Superpower Without a Sword," *Foreign Affairs*, Vol. 72, No. 3 (Summer 1993).

23. George Kennan, *Around the Cragged Hill* (New York: W. W. Norton, 1993), p. 225.

24. Quoted in Stephen Rosenfeld, "Gulf Giddiness," *Washington Post*, May 31, 1991, p. A19.

25. President Bill Clinton, "Remarks by the President to the 1993 National Education Association Representative Assembly," White House transcript, July 5, 1993, p. 3.

26. Quoted in Hobart Rowen, "Why Clinton Can't Close the Investment Deficit," *Washington Post*, July 18, 1993, p. H12.

27. See Defense Conversion Commission, "Adjusting to the Drawdown," Department of Defense, December 31, 1992, pp. 10–11.

28. See Stefan Halper, "Aspin Stuck in Hoax Over Funding," *Arizona Republic*, July 11, 1993, p. 3C.

CHAPTER 5

1. In a speech in Little Rock, Arkansas, on November 4, 1993, Clinton declared, "Today I want to reaffirm the essential continuity of American foreign policy and my desire to see bipartisan support for our role in the world."

2. The National Security Act of 1947, especially §1016, 50 USC §402 (1970), revised 1991. See also *Hearings before the Senate Select Committee to Study Governmental Operations with Respect to Intelligence Activities*, 94th Congress, First Session, 1975.

3. Note the Senate Intelligence Committee compilation in 1991 of several hundred pages that list current selected national security legislation and executive orders in its *Report of the Senate Intelligence Committee*, Report 2198 (1991).

4. For a discussion of the formulation of the National Security Act, see Strobe Talbott, *The Master of the Game* (New York: Alfred A. Knopf, 1988), pp. 54–59.

5. Quoted in ibid., pp. 55–56.

6. Note that this process preceded McCarthyism and actually began during President Truman's administration. Truman's Executive Order 9835 of March 1947—the loyalty oath order—sent the message to all Americans that the Cold War had begun. The humiliating defeat of former Vice-President Henry Wallace at the polls in November 1948 stimulated further the false loyalty craze, leading to paranoia and entrapment of citizens. See *Hearings on FBI Counterintelligence Programs before the Civil Rights and Constitutional Rights Subcommittee of the House Committee of the Judiciary*, 93rd Congress, Second Session, 1974.

7. Marcus Raskin, *Essays of a Citizen* (Armonk, NY: M. E. Sharpe, 1991), pp. 6–8, and H. Ginsberg, "Unemployment, Subemployment and Public Policy" (monograph), 1975.

8. Commission on Economic Conversion and Disarmament, *The New Economy: Report on Clinton Conversion Plans*, Vol. 4, No. 1 (Winter 1993). These budget figures are provisional pending completion of the Clinton administration's "bottom-up" review, which may add $20 billion to the defense budget. It is important to note that the defense budget is but a part of the total national security budget, which is estimated to be $350 billion.

9. See Tim Weiner, *Blank Check: The Pentagon's Black Budget* (New York: Warner Books, 1990).

10. *U.S. v Nicaragua,* opinion of the International Court of Justice. This was a nearly unanimous decision in favor of Nicaragua, with only the U.S. judge dissenting. See *ICJ Reports* (1986), p. 14.

CHAPTER 6

1. Michael Dee Oden, *A Military Dollar Really Is Different* (Lansing, MI: Employment Research Associates, 1987), pp. 20–35.

2. See the most recent study conducted by Data Resources, Inc. for the Congressional Research Service on behalf of the House Committee on Government Operations, "The Employment Effects of Shifting $3 Billion From Defense to State and Local Government-Related Activities," February 1, 1993. Also see an earlier study by Roger Bezdek, "The Economic Impact—Regional and Occupational—of Compensated Shifts in Defense Spending," *Journal of Regional Science,* Vol. 15, No. 2, 1975. Also see *Converting the American Economy: The Economic Effects of an Alternative Security Policy* (Lansing, MI: Employment Research Associates, 1991).

3. *Converting the American Economy* (fn. 2), pp. 26–28.

4. GDP forecasts taken from *The Economic and Budget Outlook: Fiscal Years 1994–98,* Congressional Budget Office, January 1993, Table 1.3. The baseline for nondefense infrastructure investment is taken from *Budget of the United States, Fiscal Year 1994,* April 1993, p. 72. The net additions (excluding investment tax credits) are calculated based on data presented in *A Vision for Change for America,* Table 5, pp. 135–139. Historical data on the relative investment rate in nonmilitary public investment as compared to GDP are taken from David Alan Aschauer, *Public Investment and Private Sector Growth* (Washington, DC: Economic Policy Institute, 1991), pp. 5–9.

5. Aschauer (fn. 4), pp. 16–17.

6. *The Competitive Strength of U.S. Industrial Science and Technology: Strategic Issues* (Washington, DC: National Science Board, 1992), p. 75.

7. *State of the World 1993* (New York: W. W. Norton, 1993), pp. 101–138, 180–200.

8. *Budget of the United States, Fiscal Year 1994* (fn. 4), p. 44.

9. Steven Fazzari, "Investment and U.S. Fiscal Policy in the 1990s," briefing paper, Economic Policy Institute, 1993.

10. See Congressional Budget Office, *Federal Debt and Interest Costs,* May 1993, chapter 6. Also see Congressional Budget Office, *The Economic Effects of Reduced Defense Spending,* Feburary 1992, pp. 12–20.

11. See, e.g., Jeff Faux and Max Swaicky, *Investing the Peace Dividend* (Washington, DC: Economic Policy Institute, 1991). An open letter to President Bush, Congress, and Federal Reserve Chairman Alan Greenspan by 100 of the nation's leading economists in March 1992 made the case for more economic stimulus and investment to solve both short-term and long-term economic problems facing the nation.

12. Economist Robert Eisner has advanced a sophisticated version of this argument in *How Real Is the Federal Deficit* (New York: Free Press, 1986). He argues that conventional measures of the deficit overstate its magnitude because they don't distinguish between capital investments and current expenditures. Ac-

cording to Eisner, a proper accounting for such investments would dramatically lower the estimates of the deficit. Yet critics have noted that not all government investments have discernable paybacks and therefore it might be difficult to treat all such fixed investments as capital outlays.

13. See M. Anderson, G. Bischak, and M. Oden, *Converting the American Economy* (Lansing, MI: Employment Research Associates, 1991), p. 26.

14. Herman E. Daly and John B. Cobb, Jr., *For the Common Good* (Boston: Beacon, 1989).

15. World Bank, *World Development Report 1992, Development and the Environment* (Oxford: Oxford University Press, 1992), pp. 174–178.

16. These estimates are higher than the $88 billion in savings usually reported in the press because the higher estimates compare the last budget actually enacted under the Bush administration—including a multiyear defense plan for 1993–1997—with the plan proposed by the Clinton administration. It does not consider the defense plan submitted by President Bush for 1994 because it will not be acted upon.

17. John Deutch, "Memorandum for Secretaries of the Military Departments Directors, Defense Agencies," May 20, 1993 on "Notice Requirements Upon Termination or Substantial Reduction in Defense Programs," Office of the Secretary of Defense, Washington, DC.

18. *Interim Report of the Federal Facilities Environmental Restorations Dialogue Committee* (Washington, DC: Environmental Protection Agency, 1993), p. 1.

19. Ann Markusen and Joel Yudken, *Dismantling the Cold War Economy* (New York: Basic Books, 1992).

20. William Kaufmann and John Steinbruner, *Decisions for Defense, Prospects for a New Order* (Washington, DC: Brookings Institution, 1991). Also Steinbruner's "Statement to the Senate Budget Committee," February 5, 1992.

21. Nathan Rosenberg, *Inside the Black Box: Technology and Economics* (Cambridge: Cambridge University Press, 1982), p. 236.

22. For a short history of this episode see Barry Commoner, *The Poverty of Power* (New York: Bantam Books, 1977), pp. 177–183.

23. Ibid., chapters 3 and 4.

CHAPTER 7

1. Bennett Harrison and Barry Bluestone, *The Great U-Turn* (New York: Basic Books, 1989).

2. Between 1980 and 1988, of 9.3 million new high-wage jobs, white men received 35 percent, white women 44 percent, black men 3 percent, Latinos 3 percent, black women 3 percent, and Latinas 3 percent. The remaining percentage of jobs went to members of other ethnic groups. U.S. Department of Commerce, Bureau of the Census; Current Population Survey, 1988; *Economic Report of the President, 1993*, Table B-32. White figures corrected for percentage of Latinos in labor force in Martin Carnoy, Hugh Daley, and Raul Hinojosa, *Latinos in a Changing U.S. Economy* (New York: The Inter-University Project, Puerto Rican Center, Hunger College, 1990).

3. U.S. Department of Commerce, Bureau of Census, *Statistical Abstract of the United States, 1992*, Table 658.

4. Governor Bill Clinton and Senator Al Gore, *Putting People First* (New York: Times Books, 1992), p. 3.

5. Quoted in Sidney Blumenthal, "A Beautiful Friendship," *The New Yorker*, July 5, 1993, p. 35.

6. See Bronwyn Hall, "R&D Tax Policy During the 1980s: Success or Failure?" National Bureau of Economic Research Working Paper 4240, Stanford, CA, December 1992.

7. Robert Reich, *The Work of Nations* (New York: Vintage, 1992).

8. See Donald Harris, "A Model of the Productivity Gap: Convergence or Divergence?" in Ross Thomson, ed., *Learning and Technological Change* (New York: Macmillan, 1992).

9. See, for example, *Youth Apprenticeship in America: Guidelines for Building an Effective System* (Washington, DC: The William T. Grant Foundation Commission on Work, Family and Citizenship, 1992).

10. Dieter Timmerman, "Costs and Financing Dual Training in Germany: Is There Any Lesson for Other Countries?" Paper presented at the International Symposium on the Economics of Education, Manchester, England, May 19–21, 1993.

11. Anthony Carnevale, "Return on Investment: Accounting for Training," *Training and Development Journal*, July 1990.

12. See Laura McClure, "Rush to Compromise," *The Progressive*, June 1993.

13. Claire Brown, Michael Reich, and David Stern, "Innovative Labor-Management Practices," Report to the Department of Labor, Center for Industrial Relations, University of California at Berkeley, 1992.

14. Derek Jones, "The Productivity Effects of Employee Participation in Control and in Economic Returns," presented at the ILO Conference on Industrial Restructuring, Moscow and St. Petersburg, October 1992.

15. Cory Rosen, *Employee Ownership and Corporate Performance* (Oakland, CA: National Center for Employee Ownership, 1992).

16. Between 1980 and 1988, low-wage jobs increased by 5 million. White males received 12 percent of these jobs, black men 12 percent, Latinos 20 percent, white women 32 percent, black women 10 percent, and Latinas 8 percent. The remaining percentage of jobs went to members of other ethnic groups. This pattern contrasts sharply with the 1960s and 1970s when people of color made their greatest employment gains in high- and middle-wage occupations. See citations for fn. 2.

17. David Card, "Do Minimum Wages Reduce Employment?" A Case Study of California, 1987–89," *Industrial and Labor Relations Review*, Vol. 46, No. 1 (October 1992), pp. 38–54.

18. Brown et al. (fn. 13).

CHAPTER 8

1. Committee on Ways and Means, U.S. House of Representatives, *Tax Progressivity and Income Distribution*, March 26, 1990, p. 1. See also the study by

the Tax Policy Research Project at the University of Missouri, reported on in *Washington Post*, April 8, 1992. This study was conducted by H&R Block.

2. Congressional Budget Office, *The Changing Distribution of Federal Taxes: 1975–1990*, October 1987, p. 47.

3. Arthur B. Kennickell and R. Louise Woodburn, "Estimation of Household Net Worth Using Model-Based and Design-Based Weights: Evidence from the 1989 Survey of Consumer Finances," unpublished paper, April 1992.

4. Donald L. Barlett and James B. Steele, *America: What Went Wrong* (Kansas City: Andrews and McMeel, 1992), p. 47.

5. *Economic Report of the President 1992*, p. 387.

6. Individuals can qualify for this credit if they own stock in foreign companies, but it primarily benefits corporations.

7. Barlett and Steele (fn. 4), p. 216.

8. *Statistical Abstract of the United States 1992*, Table 497 (Tax Expenditures, 1993 est.).

9. Ray Sommerfeld et al., *An Introduction to Taxation*, 1990 edition (San Diego: Harcourt Brace Jovanovich, 1989), pp. 1–30.

10. Gallup Poll, April 8, 1992.

CHAPTER 9

1. See Sec. 2 (Purpose) of the National Environmental Policy Act of 1969.

2. For a more detailed discussion of these and similar data on water pollution, see Barry Commoner, "Failure of the Environmental Effort," in *Environmental Law Reporter*, Vol. 18, No. 6 (June 1988), pp. 10195–10199.

3. See *Federal Register*, Vol. 54, No. 16 (January 1989), p. 3845.

4. These data are from a report by David M. White and Mehdi Maibodi, "Assessment of Technologies for Reducing Emissions of SO_2 and NO_x from Existing Coal-fired Utility Boilers" (Research Triangle Park, NC: EPA Office of Research & Development, September 1990).

5. For further discussion of the relationship between the ecosphere and the technosphere, see Barry Commoner, *Making Peace with the Planet* (New York: Pantheon, 1990).

6. Secretary Babbitt's role in the Clinton administration is discussed in Timothy Egan, "The (Bruised) Emperor of the Outdoors," *New York Times Magazine*, August 1, 1993, p. 20.

7. This statement is quoted in Peter Montague's informative account of the EPA's incinerator policies in *Rachel's Hazardous Waste News*, #338 (May 20, 1993).

8. See *Regulatory Program of the United States Government, April 1, 1986–March 31, 1987*, Executive Office of the President, Office of Management and Budget, 1987, p. xxi.

9. See Judge Aldrich's order in *Greenpeace et al. v Waste Technologies Industries et al.*, U.S. District Court, Northern District of Ohio, Eastern Div., p. 45 (March 5, 1993).

10. This statement is quoted from a letter from Robert M. Sussman, deputy administrator, EPA, to Ms. Terri Swearingen, Tri-State Environmental Council, dated July 16, 1993.

11. Timothy Noah, "EPA Seems to Alter Clinton Position on Incinerator," *Wall Street Journal*, February 2, 1993, p. A6.

12. Timothy Noah, "EPA Chief Carol Browner's First Months in Office Echo the Approach of Her Bush-Era Predecessor," *Wall Street Journal*, July 8, 1993, p. A14.

13. Commoner (fn. 5), p. 51.

14. International Joint Commission (IJC), 1992. Sixth Biennial Report on Great Lakes Water Quality (Ottawa, Ontario).

15. See "Technology for America's Economic Growth, A New Direction to Build Economic Strength," Office of the President, February 22, 1993.

16. For a detailed analysis of such an electric vehicle procurement program, see Mark Cohen and Barry Commoner, "How Government Purchase Programs Can Get Electric Vehicles on the Road" (Flushing, NY: CBNS at Queens College, June 1993).

17. The proposed photovoltaic procurement program is described in detail in Holger Eisl and Barry Commoner, "Photovoltaic Cells: Converting Government Purchasing Power into Solar Power" (Flushing, NY: CBNS at Queens College, July 1993).

18. See World Commission on Environment and Development, *Our Common Future* (New York: Oxford University Press, 1987).

CHAPTER 10

1. "Health Insurance Coverage: 1987–1990. Selected Data from the Survey of Income and Program Participation," U.S. Department of Commerce, Economics and Statistics Administration, Bureau of Census. Data is through 1990.

2. *New York Times*, August 3, 1993.

3. Gallup Poll, June 1991. Cited in Rosita M. Thomas, "Health Care in America: An Analysis of Public Opinion," Congressional Research Service Report, Oct. 26, 1992.

4. Peter Franks, Caroline Clancy, and Martha Gold, "Health Insurance and Mortality: Evidence from a National Cohort," *Journal of the American Medical Association*, Vol. 270, No. 6 (August 11, 1993), pp. 737–741.

5. "National Health Expenditures for 1991," *Health Care Financing Review*, Vol. 14, No. 2 (Winter 1992), p. 1.

6. "1994 Budget Perspective: Federal Spending for Social Welfare Programs," Congressional Research Service Report, May 1993. Based on Office of Management and Budget data.

7. "Economic Implications of Rising Health Care Costs," Congressional Budget Office, October 1992.

8. World Bank, *World Development Report 1992* (New York: Oxford University Press, 1992), p. 273.

9. *State of the World's Children, 1992* (New York: UNICEF, 1992).

10. United Nations Development Programme, *Human Development Report 1991* (New York: Oxford University Press, 1991).

11. Robert J. Blendon, Robert Leitman, Ian Morrison, and Karen Donelan, "Data Watch: Satisfaction with Health Systems in Ten Nations," *Health Affairs*, Summer 1990, p. 185.

12. Information from Citizens for Tax Justice.

13. Statement of Robert D. Reischauer, testimony before the Committee on the Budget, U.S. House of Representatives, February 17, 1993; "Single-Payer and All-Payer Health Insurance System Using Medicare's Payment Rate," Congressional Budget Office staff memorandum, April 1993; "Managed Competition and Its Potential to Reduce Health Spending," Congressional Budget Office, May 1993; "Estimates of Health Care Proposals from 102nd Congress," Congressional Budget Office, July 1993; "Canadian Health Insurance: Lessons for the United States," Committee on Government Operations, U.S. House of Representatives, General Accounting Office, June 1991.

14. "Estimates of Health Care Proposals from 102nd Congress," Congressional Budget Office, July 1993. The figure for the uninsured is projected for the year 2000.

CHAPTER 11

1. Maya Angelou, "On the Pulse of Morning," *New York Times*, January 21, 1993.

2. Poverty data from U.S. Bureau of the Census, Current Population Reports, Consumer Income, Series P-60, No. 181, *Poverty in the United States: 1991*. For a description of the poverty line and an alternative calculation that would raise the threshold by about 50 percent, see John E. Schwarz and Thomas J. Volgy, *The Forgotten Americans* (New York: W. W. Norton, 1992), Ch. 3.

3. Cited in Polly Callaghan and Heidi Hartmann, *Contingent Work: A Chart Book on Part-Time and Temporary Employment* (Washington, DC: Economic Policy Institute, 1991), p. 24.

4. There has been some controversy over the exact share of new jobs paying poverty-level wages. Bennett Harrison and Barry Bluestone found that over one-third of new workers employed between 1979 and 1986 earned less than $11,103 in 1986 constant dollars (Bennett Harrison and Barry Bluestone, *The Great U-Turn*, New York: Basic Books, 1988, pp. 124–125). Additional estimates can be found in Gary Burtless, ed., *A Future of Lousy Jobs* (Washington, DC: The Brookings Institution, 1990). The highest estimate was provided by the Democratic staff of the Senate Budget Committee, which found that between 1979 and 1987 more than half of the year-round full-time jobs created paid wages under $11,611 in constant 1987 dollars. "Study of New Jobs Since '79 Says Half Pay Poverty Wage," *New York Times*, September 26, 1988.

5. U.S. Bureau of the Census, Current Population Reports, Consumer Income, Series P-23, No. 47, *Workers with Low Earnings: 1964–1990*.

6. U.S. Bureau of the Census, Current Population Reports, Population Characteristics, Series P-20, No. 458, *Household and Family Characteristics: March 1991*.

7. Timothy Smeeding, "Why the U.S. Antipoverty System Doesn't Work Very Well," *Challenge*, January-February 1992, p. 33.

8. Karen Lightfoot and Paul Leonard, *Funding for Low-Income Programs in FY1993* (Washington, DC: Center on Budget and Policy Priorities, May 1993), pp. 3–4.

9. Ibid., p. 3.

10. Isaac Shapiro and Robert Greenstein, *Making Work Pay: The Unfinished Agenda* (Washington, DC: Center on Budget and Policy Priorities, 1993).

11. Smeeding (fn. 7), p. 33.

12. Shapiro and Greenstein (fn. 10), p. 8.

13. For a description of the federal poverty line and a discussion of its adequacy, see Patricia Ruggles, *Drawing the Line: Alternative Poverty Measures and Their Implications for Public Policy* (Washington, DC: The Urban Institute Press, 1990).

14. U.S. Bureau of the Census, *Poverty in the United States: 1991* (fn. 2).

15. "A Second Chance," remarks by Bill Clinton, Clayton County Office of Family and Children's Services, Jonesboro, Georgia, September 9, 1991.

16. Jason DeParle, "Clinton Aides See Problem with Vow to Limit Welfare," *New York Times*, June 21, 1993.

17. Steven Greenhouse, "New Support but Few Gains for Urban Enterprise Zones," *New York Times*, May 25, 1991. For a critical examination of enterprise zones, see Roy E. Green, ed., *Enterprise Zones: New Directions in Economic Development* (Newbury Park, CA: Sage Publications, 1991). Also see *Enterprise Zones: Lessons from the Maryland Experience* (Washington, DC: U.S. General Accounting Office, 1988).

18. Paul Davidson, "Clinton's Economic Plan: Putting Caution First," *The Nation*, March 1, 1993, p. 262.

19. Executive Office of the President, *A Vision of Change for America*, February 17, 1993.

20. Paul Leonard and Robert Greenstein, *The Congressional Budget Resolution, Fiscal Year 1994 Appropriations, and the Outlook for the Clinton Investment Package* (Washington, DC: Center on Budget and Policy Priorities, May 1993), p. 5.

21. Over 300 U.S. economists, including six Nobel Prize laureates, signed a statement calling for greater public investment in 1989. Their statement is available from the Economic Policy Institute in Washington, DC.

22. Welfare Reform Working Group, Administration for Children and Families, Department of Health and Human Services, August 1993.

23. Richard A. Cloward and Frances Fox Piven, "The Fraud of Workfare," *The Nation*, May 24, 1993, p. 694.

24. Ann Nichols-Casebolt and Marieka Klawitter, "Child Support Enforcement Reform: Can It Reduce the Welfare Dependency of Families of Never-Married Mothers?" *Journal of Sociology and Social Welfare*, Vol. 17, No. 3 (September 1990), pp. 23–52 (see table 2, p. 32). Child-support monies collected on behalf of AFDC recipients currently are retained by the state to offset AFDC spending; only $50 of child-support collection are "passed through" to the recipient.

25. James T. Patterson, *America's Struggle Against Poverty 1900–1980* (Cambridge, MA: Harvard University Press, 1981), pp. 206–207.

26. Mark Greenberg, "The Devil Is in the Details," unpublished manuscript, Center for Law and Social Policy.

27. Vee Burke, "Time Limited Welfare Proposals," *CRS Issue Brief,* Congressional Research Service, Library of Congress, April 9, 1993.

28. Cloward and Piven (fn. 23), pp. 693–695.

29. Teresa Amott, "Ending Poverty: Unconventional Wisdom," *Christianity and Crisis*, June 8, 1992, pp. 199–202.

30. Michael E. Stone, *One-Third of a Nation: A New Look at Housing Affordability in America* (Washington, DC: Economic Policy Institute, 1990).

31. Green (fn. 17), pp. 122–135.

32. Daniel Meyer et al., "The Costs and Effects of a National Child Support Assurance System," Institute for Research on Poverty, Discussion Paper No. 940-91, University of Wisconsin, Madison, WI. See also David P. Ellwood, "Child Support Enforcement and Insurance Proposal," in *Youth Policy*, December 1992, pp. 10–16.

CHAPTER 12

1. Andrew Hacker, *Two Nations* (New York: Ballantine, 1992), p. 46.

2. Andrew Hacker, "The Blacks and Clinton," *New York Review of Books*, January 28, 1993, p. 12.

3. Hacker (fn. 1), p. 203.

4. Salim Muwakkil, "Faith No More," *In These Times*, July 12, 1993, p. 14.

5. *The State of Black America 1993* (New York: National Urban League, 1993), p. 69.

6. Monte Piliawsky, "Blacks and Clinton: Taken for Granted Again," *Reconstruction*, Vol. 2, No. 2 (1993), pp. 42–43.

7. Jason DeParle, "Housing Secretary Carves Out Role as a Lonely Clarion Against Racism," *New York Times*, July 8, 1993, p. A16.

8. Al Kamen, "Administration Defends Hispanic Appointments," *Washington Post*, May 19, 1993, p. A17.

9. Clint Bolick, "Clinton's Quota Queens," *Wall Street Journal*, April 30, 1993, p. A12.

10. Peter Applebome, "Where Ideas That Hurt Guinier Thrive," *New York Times*, June 5, 1993, p. 9.

11. "The Last Frontier," *Wall Street Journal*, May 3, 1993, p. A16.

12. Randall Kennedy, "Still a Pigmentocracy," *New York Times*, July 21, 1993, p. A17.

13. Frank McCoy, "Will Clinton's Plan Work for Us," *Black Enterprise*, June 1993, p. 214.

14. Ibid.

15. Ibid., p. 210.

16. For example, 24.4 percent of black men and 18 percent of black women belong to unions, compared to 18.8 percent of white men and 11.7 percent of white women. See Hacker (fn. 1), p. 232.

17. Laura McClure, "Rush to Compromise," *The Progressive*, June 1993.

18. Governor Bill Clinton and Senator Al Gore, *Putting People First* (New York: Times Books, 1992), p. 56.

19. See Cathy Powell, "'Life' at Guantánamo: The Wrongful Detention of Haitian Refugees," *Reconstruction*, Vol. 2, No. 2 (1993), p. 58.

20. "Necklacing Haiti," *The Nation*, August 9/16, 1993, pp. 159–160.

21. Gayle Pollard Terry, "Randall Robinson: Keeping Africa on the Foreign-Policy Front Burner," *Los Angeles Times*, May 30, 1993, p. M3.

22. Summers maintains that the memo on dumping toxic waste in Africa was a joke. Even if this explanation is taken seriously, Summers's sense of humor is still quite revealing.

CHAPTER 13

1. Susan Faludi, *Backlash* (New York: Crown Publishers, 1991), p. 257.

2. Teresa Amott, *Caught in the Crisis: Women and the U.S. Economy Today* (New York: Monthly Review, 1993), p. 132.

3. Faludi (fn. 1), pp. 259–263.

4. Lawrence Mishel and Jared Bernstein, *The State of Working America 1982–1992* (Armonk, NY: M. E. Sharpe, 1993), p. 138.

5. Faludi (fn. 1), see Chapters 5, 7, 8, and 12.

6. *Women's Voices*, Ms. Foundation and Center for Policy Alternatives, September 1992.

7. Governor Bill Clinton and Senator Al Gore, *Putting People First* (New York: Times Books, 1992), p. 169.

8. U.S. Bureau of the Census, Current Population Reports, Series P-60, No. 174, *Money Income of Households, Families, and Persons in the United States, 1990* (Washington, DC: U.S. Government Printing Office, 1991).

9. Mishel and Bernstein (fn. 4), p. 41.

10. *Money Income of Households* (fn. 8), p. 120.

11. Brooke Grundfest Schopf, "Gender Relations and Development: Political Economy and Culture," in Ann Seidman and Frederick Anang, eds., *Twenty-First Century Africa: Toward a New Vision of Self-Sustainable Development* (Trenton, NJ: Africa World Press, 1992), p. 209.

CHAPTER 14

1. James Patterson and Peter Kim, *The Day America Told the Truth: What People Really Believe About Everything That Really Matters* (New York: Prentice-Hall, 1991).

2. Barbara Defoe Whitehead, "Dan Quayle Was Right," *The Atlantic*, Vol. 271, No. 4 (April 1993), p. 47.

3. Dave Beal, "A Piece of the Action," *St. Paul Pioneer Press*, June 14, 1993, p. D1.

4. Susan Chira, "Is Smaller Better? Educators Now Say Yes for High School," *New York Times*, July 14, 1993, p. A1.

5. Reuters, "Benefits of Big Mergers Said to Vanish Quickly," *American Banker*, December 11, 1991, p. 2.

6. Robert J. Samuelson, "Bigger Banks—But Better?" *Washington Post*, July 24, 1991, p. A19.

7. Karen Pennar, "Small Companies Are Still Afraid to Add Workers … ," *Business Week*, August 3, 1992, p. 16.

8. John Case, "A Company of Businesspeople," *Inc.*, April 1993, p. 79.

9. Tony Hiss, *The Experience of Place* (New York: Knopf, 1990).

10. Dan Morgan, "Think Locally, Win Globally," *Washington Post*, April 5, 1992, p. H1.

11. *School Choice: A Special Report* (Princeton, NJ: The Carnegie Foundation for the Advancement of Teaching, 1993).

12. In 1983, banks held 84 percent of the combined total of bank deposits and mutual fund assets. Today, their share is just over 50 percent. General Electric, General Motors, and Sears all have finance subsidiaries that rival the top ten bank holding firms in asset size. *National Journal*, July 24, 1993.

13. David Moberg, "Broadening the Battle Against Plant Closings," *In These Times*, January 24–30, 1990, p. 7.

14. Tom Peters, "'De-Massified' Workplace Looms on the Horizon," *Star Tribune*, March 2, 1993, p. 2D.

15. Gar Alperovitz, "Ameristroika Is the Answer," *Washington Post*, December 13, 1992, p. C3.

16. *Citizens and Politics: A View from Main Street* (Dayton, OH: Kettering Foundation, 1991).

17. "The War Against the Poor," *New York Times*, May 6, 1992, p. A28.

18. David Shribman, "More States, Taking a Leaf from Federal Book, Pass on Their Spending Programs to Localities," *Wall Street Journal*, September 3, 1991, p. A20.

19. Jane Jacobs, *The Death and Life of Great American Cities* (Harmondsworth, Middlesex: Penguin Books, 1961), p. 338.

20. In 1991, Congress did break open the highway trust fund. For the first time, the Intermodal Surface Transportation Efficiency Act (ISTEA) allows about half of all federal gas tax revenues to be diverted from roads. Passage of this bill has galvanized local and state citizen groups to become actively involved in transportation planning. The Clinton administration has to date taken no position on their efforts.

21. James MacKenzie, Roger Dower, and Donald D.T. Chen., *The Going Rate: What It Really Costs to Drive* (Washington, DC: World Resources Institute, June 1992).

22. Robert Wright, "The New Democrat from Cyberspace," *The New Republic*, May 24, 1993, p. 24.

23. See Brenda Platt and David Morris, *The Economic Benefits of Recycling* (Washington, DC: Institute for Local Self-Reliance, 1993).

24. David Morris and Irshad Ahmed, *The Carbohydrate Economy: Making Industrial Materials and Chemicals from Plant Matter* (Washington, DC: Institute for Local Self-Reliance, 1992).

25. Robert Kuttner, "The Corporation in America," *Dissent*, Winter 1993, p. 49.

26. See *Report on United States Trade and Investment Barriers* (Brussels: Services of the Commission of the European Communities, 1993).

CHAPTER 15

An earlier version of this chapter appeared in *Boston Review*, Vol. 18, No. 2 (March/April 1993).

1. Interview with John Bonaface, Center for Responsive Politics, Washington, DC, August 16, 1993.

2. *Big Business Reader on Corporate America*, ed. by Mark Green with an introduction by Ralph Nader (New York: Pilgrim Press, 1983).

3. "Directors Do Not Direct," *Harvard Law Review*, Vol. 47 (1934), p. 1305.

4. John A. Byrne, "Requiem for Yesterday's CEO," *Business Week*, February 15, 1993.

5. Mancur Olson, Jr., *The Logic of Collective Action: Public Good and the Theory of Groups* (Cambridge: Harvard University Press, 1971).

About the Book and Editors

State of the Union 1994 assesses the Clinton administration's first year in office and lays out progressive policy alternatives in the realms of foreign and domestic affairs. It charts the course of the nation in fourteen critical areas, giving readers a solid basis of information on which to compare trends historically and internationally and to make reasoned judgments about where the United States is and ought to be headed.

Original essays by well-known policy advisers and analysts focus on the theme of gauging the health of the nation. Each essay employs charts, graphs, figures, and tables to document America's standing. An introductory essay explores the themes, trends, and values underlying the volume, and a closing roundtable discussion reflects on the politics of setting agendas and achieving goals, especially those that run counter to conventional wisdom.

Sponsored by the prominent Washington think tank, the Institute for Policy Studies (IPS), *State of the Union 1994* seeks to enlarge the national public policy debate and to promote fresh policy directions in an effort to achieve "a more perfect union." It offers specific recommendations—such as a "global New Deal" for trade, a single-payer health-care system, a national jobs program, and a streamlined, reorganized national security establishment—in creating a valuable resource of policy ideas that work.

Richard Caplan is the New York director of the London-based Institute for War and Peace Reporting. He is former editor of *World Policy Journal* and has written for the *New York Times*, *The Nation*, *Harper's*, the *Los Angeles Times*, and the *Christian Science Monitor*, among other publications. **John Feffer** is the author of *Beyond Détente: Soviet Foreign Policy and U.S. Options* (1990) and *Shock Waves: Eastern Europe After the Revolutions* (1992). He is a former associate editor of *World Policy Journal*.

About the Contributors

TERESA AMOTT is associate professor of economics at Bucknell University and the author of *Caught in the Crisis: Women and the U.S. Economy Today* (Monthly Review, 1993).

RICHARD J. BARNET is co-founder and a fellow of the Institute for Policy Studies and the author of numerous books, including (with John Cavanagh) *Global Dreams: Imperial Corporations and the New World Order* (Simon & Schuster, 1994).

GREG BISCHAK is executive director of the National Commission for Economic Conversion and Disarmament.

HEATHER BOOTH is on the staff of the Democratic National Committee. She is the former co-director of Citizen Action.

ROBERT L. BOROSAGE is a fellow of the Institute for Policy Studies and director of the Campaign for New Priorities.

ROBIN BROAD is a professor at the School of International Service at The American University and the co-author (with John Cavanagh) of *Plundering Paradise: The Struggle for the Environment in the Philippines* (University of California Press, 1993).

RICHARD CAPLAN is New York director of the Institute for War and Peace Reporting.

MARTIN CARNOY is professor of education and economics at Stanford University.

JOHN CAVANAGH is a fellow of the Institute for Policy Studies and the co-author (with Richard J. Barnet) of *Global Dreams: Imperial Corporations and the New World Order* (Simon & Schuster, 1994).

BARRY COMMONER is director of the Center for the Biology of Natural Systems at Queens College, City University of New York, and the author of *Making Peace with the Planet* (Pantheon, 1990).

BARBARA EHRENREICH is an essayist and author of numerous books, including *Fear of Falling: The Inner Life of the Middle Class* (Pantheon), and most recently, *Kipper's Game* (Farrar, Straus & Giroux).

RALPH ESTES is professor of business at The American University and a visiting scholar at the Institute for Policy Studies.

JOHN FEFFER is the author of *Shock Waves: Eastern Europe After the Revolutions* (South End, 1992).

STANLEY GREENBERG is president of Greenberg Research, Inc., a national survey and polling firm, and pollster to President Bill Clinton.

GERALD HORNE is professor of history and Black studies at the University of California–Santa Barbara.

SAUL LANDAU is a fellow of the Institute for Policy Studies.

JULIANNE MALVEAUX is an economist and syndicated columnist based in San Francisco.

DAVID MORRIS is vice-president of the Institute for Local Self-Reliance, based in Washington, D.C., and Minneapolis.

RALPH NADER is a consumer advocate.

MARCUS RASKIN is co-founder and a fellow of the Institute for Policy Studies and the author of a forthcoming book about the "vision thing."

JOEL ROGERS is professor of law, political science, and sociology at the University of Wisconsin–Madison, and chair of the Interim Executive Council of the New Party.

ELLEN R. SHAFFER is health-policy adviser to Sen. Paul Wellstone.

MICHAEL H. SHUMAN is director of the Institute for Policy Studies and co-author (with Hal Harvey) of *Security Without War: A Post–Cold War Foreign Policy* (Westview, 1993).

PETER WEISS is former chair of the board of the Institute for Policy Studies and chair of the Working Group on Economic and Social Rights at the Center for Constitutional Rights.

PAUL D. WELLSTONE is a U.S. Senator (D-MN).

ROGER WILKINS is Robinson professor of history at George Mason University.

Index